THE MANAGEMENT
SKILLS GUIDE

Second Edition

THE STUDENT SKILLS GUIDE
Second Edition

SUE DREW

and

ROSIE BINGHAM

Learning and Teaching Institute

Sheffield Hallam University

Published by
Gower Publishing Limited
Gower House
Croft Road
Aldershot
Hampshire
GU11 3HR
England

Gower Publishing Company
131 Main Street
Burlington VT 05401-5600 USA

Some of the materials in this book were originally written with financial assistance
from what is now called the Department for Education and Skills. The views
expressed herein are those of the authors and not necessarily those of the
department.

Sue Drew and Rosie Bingham have asserted their right under the Copyright, Designs
and Patents Act 1988 to be identified as the authors of this work.

British Library Cataloguing in Publication Data
Drew, Sue
    The student skills guide. - 2nd ed.
    1. Study skills 2. Students - Great Britain - Life skills guides
    I. Title II. Bingham, Rosie
    378.1'7'0281

ISBN 0 566 08430 9

Typeset in England by Neil Straker Creative
and printed in Great Britain by MPG Books Ltd, Bodmin, Cornwall

CONTENTS

ABOUT THE AUTHORS

Sue Drew and **Rosie Bingham** are both Senior Lecturers in the Learning and Teaching Institute of Sheffield Hallam University, where they work with academic staff on curriculum development.

Sue Drew has worked at Sheffield Hallam University since 1975, before which she was in industry doing personnel work. She was a Careers Adviser until 1987, when with a colleague she initiated the Personal Skills and Qualities Project. Since then she has supported the integration of Key Skills into the University's curriculum. She has managed two Key Skills Projects, one in 1993 which led to the development of the materials in this book, and another 1998-2000 which focussed on an internet Key Skills support system.

Rosie Bingham has many years experience teaching in primary schools in Sheffield and in Teacher Training for the School of Education at Sheffield Hallam University. She supports staff across the University in course planning and in academic review and has authored staff support materials. She takes a lead within the University on the development of Progress Files.

1.1 How this book can help you, why it is important

There are two main reasons for the topics included in this book. They will help you to be successful

- **on your course**
- **in future employment.**

This book is a valuable aid to your learning, whether you have just started a new course, your existing course is demanding new skills from you, or you feel a need or desire to improve your performance.

1.1.1 Helping you be successful on your course

You will want to do as well as possible on your course. This book aims to help you improve your performance by focusing on areas which are relevant to the study of any subject and which will have a significant influence on your mark or grade. You are responsible for your own learning and development and there are skills you can use to improve your performance.

You may think of your course mainly in terms of its subject content, but your success will not only depend on your interest and ability in the subject and your knowledge of it, but will also be influenced by a range of other factors. For example:

- your notes need to be good enough to use later (eg *for revision*), and you need to organise and store them so you can find them again easily
- the quality of your assignments will depend on how effectively you allocate your time
- your performance in examinations will be influenced by your revision and exam techniques, and how you cope under pressure
- your ability to find and use information will influence how well you tackle your work.

In assessing work, lecturers and tutors mark or grade according to their view of what good work should be like. They are not only concerned with the content, but with a range of other factors, such as how well the work is presented, how you've selected what to cover, and how much work you've done. They might even be influenced by the general impression you make on the course – eg *whether you actively contribute to class sessions or whether you usually submit your work on time*. It might be worth putting yourself in their position, and asking yourself what would influence you.

Ideally, lecturers and tutors will tell students what they will be looking for and the factors, or criteria, against which their work will be assessed. In identifying assessment criteria some lecturers or tutors will explicitly refer to factors such as, for example, the presentation of a report or how well you've worked with others in a group. Often, though, such factors do not appear as explicit criteria, although there is evidence that lecturers and tutors are influenced by them when they mark or grade work. Such factors might include:

- how easy it is to read your work
- how much and what information you have included and how accurate it is
- how well you explain or present your case if giving a seminar paper or oral presentation
- how much time have you spent on your work, whether it looks rushed and whether you met the deadline
- how good you are at asking for help from tutors, librarians or friends.

If you are unsure of the criteria your lecturers use, it can be very helpful to ask them to explain them to you.

The time you spend at college or university is quite short, and you may find that you have to get up to speed in such areas very quickly before you are assessed.

1.1.2 Helping you with future employment

The second benefit is more long term. Most students hope to improve their job prospects by being successful on their courses. Some employers may be very interested in your subject knowledge, particularly for vocational courses like engineering or computing. Others may be more interested in the fact that you are educated and intelligent. For example, in 'Prospects Today', a vacancy sheet produced by the Higher Education Careers Services Unit, almost 50 per cent of the jobs advertised for graduates fall into this 'any discipline' category, including selling, marketing, accountancy, journalism, retail management, the Civil Service, health service management, personnel work etc.

All employers want something in addition to evidence that you know about your subject. For one job there may be several, sometimes many, candidates. If you all did similar courses, how do they decide between you?

Employers want to know that you will be able to **use** your knowledge or your intelligence at work. They are keen to recruit people who can write and talk effectively, who can work well with others, who can solve unforeseen problems and learn new things quickly. In other words they are seeking a range of skills which make an employee personally effective. Such skills are generally applicable to all areas of work, and are additional to the professional skills which are required by specific areas of work, such as design, laboratory or language skills.

Employers complain that students often leave their courses without many of the skills they are seeking. Recruiters look out for such skills when they read application forms and at interview. Some employers use 'selection or assessment centres', where applicants carry out simulations of work tasks, with the recruiters observing.

Many courses now ask you to carry out activities which simulate work situations, to give you practise in the skills employers want. This is why courses may include group work or report writing or oral presentations. They may present real case studies for you to practise solving problems, and some courses include project work with employers or work placements. All require you to communicate, use information, plan your time, deal with others and cope with pressure.

This book helps you to develop skills you will need not only on your course but also later at work. Using it will make you more aware of these skills and help you when completing application forms or attending interviews for jobs. Employers will want to hear examples of projects you've undertaken with others, how well you manage your time and so on. This book will begin to help you gather such evidence together.

1.2 How to use this book

1.2.1 The chapters in this book

This book consists of a series of chapters on different topics. You can use the chapters to help you carry out course activities, which might also include a work placement.

You will find using the chapters when you have a task to do is much more helpful than reading them without a particular situation or task in mind. Reading through the book from cover to cover is not the best approach, as the information will be most useful when it is immediately relevant to you – eg *using the chapters on 'Report Writing' when you need to produce a report on your course.*

Each chapter contains a mixture of suggestions and exercises to complete, which will help you think about your task and how you might approach it. **The book is intended to be written in and used over and over again**. For example, if you want to improve your revision techniques, you can use the relevant chapter for one set of exams, and then for your next exams refer back to your notes to see what you did last time, what worked and what didn't, and what you can do now to improve.

So, write in the book and keep your notes to help you in the future.

Some of the chapters are very clearly linked to tasks you are likely to meet on your course or on work placement.

For example:

Chapter	Possible uses include when...
Note Taking	you need to take notes in lectures; from films, videos or other visual material; from books or other written material.
Gathering and Using Information	you need to gather information for essays, reports, oral presentations, projects or any other purpose.
Essay Writing	you need to write an essay. It can also help in longer pieces of writing such as dissertations.
Report Writing	you are asked to write an individual or group project report; laboratory reports; placement reports; reports needed by an employer.
Oral Presentation	you need to make individual or group presentations; give a seminar paper; teach or train others; present information to clients at work.
Solving Problems	you need to carry out a problem based assignment or course task – eg *case studies, projects, workshop or laboratory activities*; you need to deal with problems at work.
Group Work	you need to carry out a group project; you have to work in a team.
Revising and Examination Techniques	you have exams coming up.
Seminars, Group Tutorials and Meetings	you need to operate in a seminar/tutorial; make minutes for a group project.
Visual Communication	you need to produce a presentation, or a poster.

Other chapters refer more to skills you are likely to need throughout your course as well as for specific tasks. Use them when a particular situation arises where they might be helpful.

For example:

Chapter	Possible uses include when...
Identifying Strengths and Improving Skills	you want to identify which other chapters you need to use; you have to 'sell yourself' when completing application forms or preparing for interviews; you have to present evidence of your abilities in a portfolio (see 1.2.3 below).
Organising Yourself and Your Time	you are given the schedule for assignments for the term or semester; there are bunched deadlines ahead; you need to revise; there are conflicting demands on your time.
Negotiating and Assertiveness	you want others to pull their weight in group work; others are difficult to deal with; you need help from a tutor or fellow students; you must agree with a tutor the work to be carried out (eg *for learning contracts or agreements, or for the topic of dissertations or projects*); you want to complain to a landlord or flatmates or agree something with them; you need to agree something with colleagues or have a problem on a work placement.
Coping with Pressure	exams are coming up; you have a heavy workload; there are difficulties with other people or at home; it is difficult to juggle all your activities.
Improving Your Learning	you need to work out how you can best learn.
Reflecting on Your Experience	you need to think about your performance and your development, in order to build on strengths and improve weaknesses, (this may also be linked to assessed work).
Action Planning	you are planning how to improve your performance.
Critical Analysis	you are looking at information/ideas, to make judgements about their worth.

1.2.2 Combining chapters

For any one course activity several chapters may be helpful. For example:

- if you have exams coming up you may want to look at 'Revising and Examination Techniques', 'Note Taking', 'Organising Yourself and Your Time' and 'Coping with Pressure'
- for a group project you might want to use 'Gathering and Using Information', 'Group Work', 'Negotiating and Assertiveness' and 'Report Writing'.

1.2.3 Assessing yourself; tutor assessment

On some courses you are asked to assess yourself for a piece of work either by writing an evaluation of what you have done or by completing a form which gives assessment criteria. This may involve assessing not only your work but how you went about it and the skills you used. Some tutors or lecturers may also ask you to collect together evidence of the skills you have used in a file or portfolio (a portfolio is a collection of evidence that demonstrates what you have achieved), which is then assessed. If this is so you should find some of the chapters helpful. You could, for example, photocopy a chapter, fill in the self-completion boxes as evidence of what you did, and include the completed chapter as part of portfolio evidence of the skills you have used or of how you have carried out course activities.

1.2.4 Confidentiality

In some of the chapters you may make notes on things you would prefer to keep confidential. If you do show your notes to others, either for assessment or just because you would find it helpful to discuss issues, remember that you can be selective about what you choose to tell them.

1.3 The structure of this book

1.3.1 The two parts of this book

There are two parts to this book.

- **Part I – Starter Level** – contains chapters at a level suitable for students with some, little or no existing expertise in the area. We suggest you start with this Part even if you feel you can already handle a topic, as the chapters may remind you of things you have forgotten or give you a new slant on the issues.

- **Part II – Development Level** – contains chapters on the same topics but at a more advanced level. This Part assumes that you have some existing expertise, and builds on the chapters in Part I. The chapters cover the same topics as Part I apart from 'Note Taking', 'Visual Communication', 'Seminars, Group Tutorials and Meetings' and 'Improving your Learning', which are at the first level only, and 'Critical Analysis', which is at the second level only.

Where there are topics which are only at Starter Level, we suggest which Development topics follow on naturally from them (see 1.3.3).

1.3.2 Differentiating the levels

Each chapter in each Part includes lists of what you should be able to do (the learning outcomes) after you have worked through that chapter. The differences between the starter and development levels are indicated by these lists. At the higher level you should be able to:

* **use more aspects or elements of that skill**
* **be able to use the skill in a wider range of situations**
* **have less need for guidance from lecturers, tutors and others.**

1.3.3 The progression of chapters

Chapters in Part I	Chapters in Part II which follow on from this starter topic
Identifying Strengths and Improving Skills	Identifying Strengths and Improving Skills
Organising Yourself and Your Time	Organising Yourself and Your Time
Note Taking	Gathering and Using Information
Gathering and Using Information	Gathering and Using Information Critical Analysis
Essay Writing	Essay Writing
Report Writing	Report Writing
Oral Presentation	Oral Presentation
Visual Communication	Oral Presentation
Solving Problems	Solving Problems
Group Work	Group Work
Seminars, Group Tutorials and Meetings	Negotiating and Assertiveness
Negotiating and Assertiveness	Negotiating and Assertiveness
Coping with Pressure	Coping with Pressure
Revising and Examination Techniques	Revising and Examination Techniques
Improving Your Learning	Reflecting on Your Experience Critical Analysis
Reflecting on Your Experience	Reflecting on Your Experience
Action Planning	Reflecting on Your Experience Action Planning The final action planning sections in all chapters

1.4 How this book was developed

The original material in the chapters was thoroughly trialled and evaluated with over 2000 students studying a wide range of subjects and in different years at Sheffield Hallam University. Additions to this edition have been trialled as an evaluation of *Key Skills Online* (Drew and Thorpe 2000). The students' views and comments on what they found useful and tutors' feedback were used in deciding both on the content of the material and on its format.

1.5 Who should use the different chapters

During the trial of the material, it was clear that such factors as age, gender and employment or educational background influenced which topics students thought were important, even on the same course where all students had to carry out the same tasks.

Your view of the importance of a topic may be partly influenced by your own experience, rather than by the actual needs of the course. **We would strongly suggest that you give serious consideration to all the topics**. Even if you think one isn't important or that you can do it already, it's worth looking at it to check out that your views are correct. For example, you may feel you already have a lot of experience of taking notes and need no further guidance. However, you may have to cover much more material than in the past, and your notes may need to be used for different purposes at college or university level than for lower-level courses.

You may be studying a course in which you do not come across some of the tasks covered by the chapters. However, most students will encounter assignments or activities requiring most of the topics at some time on their courses.

1.6 QCA Key Skills

You may be studying a Key Skills Qualification or a Key Skills Unit. The following only applies to you if this is the case.

If you are studying for such a qualification, you will need to provide evidence that you have skills at certain levels. The chapters in this book have been designed to meet relevant aspects of the Key Skill specifications so, for example, 'Report Writing' covers some of the written communication specifications for the Key Skill Communication, as does 'Essay Writing', while 'Oral Presentation' covers aspects of verbal communication.

The chapters in Part I are based on Key Skill specifications (QCA 2000) at level 3 and those in Part II at level 4. The learning outcomes given at the start of each chapter are based on the QCA Key Skills specifications. This does not mean that completing the relevant sections will automatically mean that you have Key Skills to that level, but it will help you collect evidence for them. The following shows which chapters relate to which key skills.

Key skill	Relevant worksheets
Improving Own Learning and Performance	Identifying Strengths and Improving Skills Organising Yourself and Your Time Revising and Examination Techniques Coping with Pressure Improving Your Learning Reflecting on Your Experience Action Planning
Communication	Essay Writing Report Writing Oral Presentation Visual Communication Gathering and Using Information Critical Analysis Note Taking
Dealing with Others	Group Work Seminars, Group Tutorials amd Meetings Negotiating and Assertiveness
Problem Solving	Solving Problems

This book does not cover the Key Skills of Information Technology and Application of Number. See Pettigrew and Elliot (1999) for help with IT skills.

1.7 Summary

This book should help you in a very practical way not only to improve your performance on your course, but also to develop skills which employers see as important. It will therefore support both your academic and professional life; some aspects of the book may even be helpful in your personal life.

PART I

STARTER LEVEL

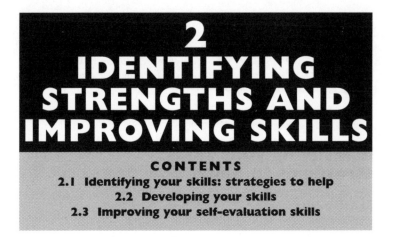

2
IDENTIFYING STRENGTHS AND IMPROVING SKILLS

CONTENTS
2.1 Identifying your skills: strategies to help
2.2 Developing your skills
2.3 Improving your self-evaluation skills

'I just want to get on with the course. Why bother thinking about myself?'

Taking stock, identifying what you are good at and what you need to improve should make you feel more confident about your strengths, help you work out how to do things better, and improve your learning and performance on the course.

'Leopards can't change their spots. Old dogs can't learn new tricks.'

This chapter is based on a different view – that people **can** and **do** change.

We suggest you use this chapter:

- to identify your current skill level
- to identify evidence of your abilities (important if you are asked to demonstrate that you have a skill for coursework assessment, or if you are applying for placements or jobs)
- to identify which other chapters might help you and which actions to take to improve your skills.

When you have completed it, you should be able to:

Agree targets
- identify and select possible strategies to self-evaluate
- identify your own strengths and areas to improve
- identify possible sources of evidence to illustrate strengths and areas to improve
- plan actions to build on strengths and improve skills, with targets, timescales and resources/support needed
- identify factors which might affect your plans.

Use your plan
- prioritise skills to focus on it
- carry out plans, monitoring and revising them as needed
- seek feedback on your own performance and use feedback and support to improve.

Review progress and achievements
- summarise your own skills and provide evidence for your strengths and areas to improve
- identify progress made in developing skills and what affected this
- identify ways of improving your skills in self-evaluation in the future.

(Based on QCA Key Skill specifications, QCA 2000)

Confidentiality

This chapter is designed for your use alone, although you can show it to others if you choose. You can keep it and extract information from it in the future (eg *if you need to provide evidence of your abilities on your course – students on some courses need to do so in portfolios, or for a placement or job application*).

2.1 Identifying your skills: strategies to help

2.1.1 Starting out

In identifying your skills, it helps to think of a particular situation. 'What are you good at' is more difficult to answer than 'What did working on that project/laboratory experiment/essay show that you were good at?'

What activities have you done on this course, or on a previous one (*eg projects, seminars, presentations, research, producing essays or reports etc*)? You could also use activities from any work situation.

Course activities

You could think about these situations/activities, as you complete the Skills Evaluation in Section 2.1.4. It is based on the titles of other chapters in this book, but feel free to add other skills which are important to you or your course.

2.1.2 Accurately assessing your skills

When thinking about your skills, are you inclined to:

✔

put yourself down?	
put your positive side forward?	
over-emphasise the positives or be over-confident?	
vary this according to the situation?	

It is important to judge or rate yourself accurately. You could:

- ensure you are clear about what makes a good or bad performance (the criteria)
- rate yourself and return to your rating after a few days, to amend it
- if you tend to put yourself down, rate yourself a point higher than you were first inclined to
- look for evidence. How would you 'prove' it to someone else?
- if you tend be over-confident, you could ask others for their view.

Try looking at your skills from a different perspective, such as a SWOT analysis (Strengths, Weaknesses, Opportunities and Threats).

For example: *a presentation*

- What **strengths** do you bring to it (eg *well organised*)?
- What are your **weaknesses** (eg *nerves*)?
- What **opportunities** does it offer you (eg *becoming more confident*)?
- What **threats**, or risks, are there (eg *forget what I want to say*)?

What strategies will be most helpful to you, as you evaluate your skills?

2.1.3 Seeking and using feedback

In completing the Skill Evaluation Sheet you may find it helpful to ask others for feedback about your skills, to help you identify how good you are at something. There are many different types of feedback (eg *written comments from your tutor/employer, informal feedback from friends and fellow students*). It helps to ask specific questions.

- *'How do you think I coped with the pressure of the exams?'* could elicit useful information (eg *'You seemed to leave things until the last minute and then got quite tense about it'*).

- *'Can I cope with stress?'* is a more general question which may lead to sweeping statements in reply. It invites judgemental comments which may be less helpful (eg *'Yes, very well'*, *'No, you go to pieces'*).

When seeking feedback it helps to:

- **listen without interrupting or defending**
- **check that you have understood** (eg *'Do you mean that ...?'*)
- **weigh up which aspects of the feedback you agree with and what to take note of (you may think the other person is wrong or has misunderstood the situation).**

For more information on asking for and using feedback, look at Chapter 17 on 'Reflecting on Your Experience' in Part I.

2.1.4 Evaluating your skills

On the following Skills Evaluation please estimate:

- **your current level of skill on a 4 point scale where 1 = 'very good' and 4 = 'in need of considerable improvement'**
- **your need for improvement on a 4 point scale where 1 = 'very important to improve' and 4 = 'not important to improve'**
  (eg *if your skill level is low in a certain area, you could consider it very important to improve it, or you could think that on your course it does not really matter*).

For example:

Skill	Your estimate of your current level of skill				Evidence and examples (why you have rated your current skill level as you have)	Priority for improvement			
	1 high	2	3	4 low		1 high	2	3	4 low
Organising Yourself and Your Time				4	***Producing an essay*** *Failed to meet deadlines, had to stay up all night to get work done.*	4			
Negotiating and Assertiveness		4			***Group project*** *Managed to get others to pull their weight most of the time (but not all).*			4	
Oral Presentation	4				***Presentation to course group*** *Received good feedback, especially on visual aids. Got high grade. Felt confident.*				4

Skills Evaluation ✔

Skill	Your estimate of your current level of skill				Evidence and examples (why you have rated your current skill level as you have)	Priority for improvement			
	1 high	2	3	4 low		1 high	2	3	4 low
Action Planning									
Coping with Pressure									
Critical Analysis									
Essay Writing									
Gathering and Using Information									
Group Work									
Improving Your Learning									

✔

Skill	Your estimate of your current level of skill				Evidence and examples (why you have rated your current skill level as you have)	Priority for improvement			
	1 high	2	3	4 low		1 high	2	3	4 low
Negotiating and Assertiveness									
Note Taking									
Oral Presentation									
Organising Yourself and Your Time									
Reflecting on Your Experience									
Report Writing									

✔

Skill	Your estimate of your current level of skill				Evidence and examples (why you have rated your current skill level as you have)	Priority for improvement			
	1 high	2	3	4 low		1 high	2	3	4 low
Revising and Examination Technique									
Seminars, Tutorials and Meetings									
Solving Problems									
Visual Communication									
Others (please specify)									

2.2 Developing your skills

2.2.1 Identifying where you need to improve

The skills you need to improve might be areas:

- where the evidence shows you could have carried out that skill better
- where you need to use that skill a lot on your course
- you have identified as 'threats' in a SWOT analysis (see 2.1.2 above)
- where feedback suggests you could do better
- where you feel under-confident
- which you identified as priorities in Section 2.1.4.

2.2.2 Possible sources of help

- **Chapters in this book.** There are chapters on most of the areas listed on the Skill Evalutation Sheets. See the contents list for details.
- **A learning centre/library.** There are materials on the skill areas listed – you may also find some under the general 'study skills' title.
- **Your lecturers.** They may be able to spend some time in class on a particular skill area.
- **Friends and other students.** Either from your year, or in later years (where they have gone through the stage you are at). What ideas do they have for improving the skill?
- **Specialists.** For example, learning centre/library staff, computing support staff.
- In addition, your university or college may offer:
     study skills courses
     counselling services
     careers services.

What else would help (eg *changing your attitudes, getting more practice, setting time aside, keeping a diary to monitor what your are doing*)?

2.2.3 Action planning to improve your skills

Be as specific as possible about what you need to improve. It helps to identify targets to aim for, with dates (eg *organising yourself – a target might be to meet deadlines, or meet a deadline two days early*). See Chapter 18 on 'Action Planning' in Part I.

How could you develop your skills?

- Sometimes identifying the problem makes the solution obvious (eg *if you felt stressed because you started exam revision too late, you can plan to begin earlier in future*).
- Sometimes you may need to seek advice. Using the example of exam revision, you may need advice from a tutor about prioritising what to revise.
- Sometimes you may need more help (eg *some people feel so nervous about exams that they may need to talk it over with a specialist who can help*).

What factors might affect your plans? Possibilities are:

- current demands on your time
- priorities. What skills will you need most on your course?
- what skills will you need to use soon?
- what will affect your marks/grades most?

We suggest that you complete the action plan below.

As you carry out your plans, it helps to keep a regular check on your progress, and revise your plans as needed (eg *circumstances change, you may have different ideas, timescales may lengthen, different priorities arise*). You could review it with somebody else (eg *a friend*) and ask them for feedback. Use the final column in the table to keep notes on your progress and what is affecting it (positively or negatively).

Skills I wish to focus on	Target – what I want to achieve	Resources/support needed	Deadline	Progress notes
Solving problems	*Think about the problem before launching into it. Try to identify the main issues first.*	*The chapter on 'Solving Problems'.* *Ask other students how they deal with similar problems.* *Look at relevant material etc*	*next week* *in 2 weeks* *in 3 weeks*	

2.3 Improving your self-evaluation skills

In order to do well on your course, you will need to use your skills to identify what you do well and what you could improve on. Improving your learning is your responsibility and identifying how to improve your self-evaluation skills is important. What have you used so far? How helpful was this? Why was this?

What strategies have you used?	How well did they work?	What influenced/affected this?
eg *feedback from others in my group*	eg *not all comments were helpful*	eg *I found it difficult to accept criticisms*

What else could you do to improve your self-evaluation skills?

What do you need to do to improve your self-evaluation skills?	Actions/resources needed	Deadline

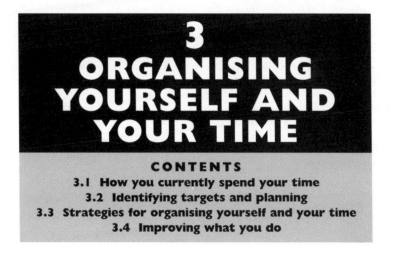

3
ORGANISING YOURSELF AND YOUR TIME

CONTENTS
3.1 How you currently spend your time
3.2 Identifying targets and planning
3.3 Strategies for organising yourself and your time
3.4 Improving what you do

This chapter aims to help you organise yourself to ensure you can meet the course requirements and to give yourself a good chance of performing well.

As a student at university or college, you are expected to do a lot of work outside class activities and the responsibility for success is placed in your hands. You are given assignments but it is up to you when and how you carry them out. You will be expected to read around your subject but how much you do will be up to you.

This may be very different from school, where teachers may exert pressure on you to work, or from employment, where managers may determine your workload.

Students need to balance different activities: social life; domestic commitments; work; the course. The evidence suggests that organised students do better than disorganised ones, and that students think this is a very important skill to develop.

We suggest you use this chapter:

- **to help you plan your work** (eg *for an actual task where you need to organise your self and your time*).

When you have completed it, you should be able to:

Agree targets
- review your current use of time
- identify what you want to achieve, ie aims/targets
- identify actions to meet aims, targets and deadlines, allowing for factors/possible difficulties which might affect your plans
- identify short and medium-term targets.

Use your plan
- prioritise actions
- estimate the time needed to carry out actions, carry out plans, monitoring and revising them as needed, to meet deadlines and deal with any difficulties
- identify and use feedback and support.

Review progress and achievements
- identify targets met and what affected whether or not they were met
- identify ways of improving in the future.

(Based on QCA Key Skill specifications, QCA 2000)

3.1 How you currently spend your time

Keeping a diary of your activities for a week helps you appreciate what you spend your time on. You could use the following either:

- to record your activities as you go, or
- at the end of each day or at the end of the week.

We suggest you select a 4 or 5 hour period in one day to record activities in more detail in 15 minute blocks.

Time	Mon	Tues	Wed	Thurs	Fri	Sat	Sun
7–8 am							
8–9 am							
9–10 am							
10–11 am							
11–12 am							
12–1 pm							
1–2 pm							
2–3 pm							
3–4 pm							
4-5 pm							

Time	Mon	Tues	Wed	Thurs	Fri	Sat	Sun
5-6 pm							
6-7 pm							
7-8 pm							
8-9 pm							
9-10 pm							
10-11 pm							
11-12 pm							
12-1 am							
1-2 am							
2-3 am							
3-4 am							
4-5 am							
5-6 am							
6-7 am							

✐

What does this tell you about how you use your time?

You might find it useful to discuss your diary and respond to these questions with others. Their feedback may be very helpful.

3.2 Identifying targets and planning

3.2.1 What are your targets?

An important first step is identifying what you have to do by when. What are your short and medium-term targets? This could include both work for your course and activities outside university or college.

Main target	Deadline	Estimated time to complete
Write an essay	Two months away	6 weeks
Complete lab experiment	4 weeks time	2 weeks
Prepare group presentation	6 weeks time	4 weeks
Apply for part-time work	1 week	3 hours

What are your main short and long-term targets?　　　　✐

Main target	Deadline	Estimated time to complete

What is involved in achieving a target? It can help to break it down into smaller tasks. How long will each sub-task take? For example:

Main target	Deadline	Estimated time to complete
Write an essay	*Two months away*	*6 weeks*
Sub-tasks		
Gather information	*1 month away*	*3 weeks*
Write first draft	*6 weeks away*	*1 week*
Final editing and final draft	*2 months away*	*3 days*

3.2.2 Make a plan

It helps to identify what each sub-task will involve, and to make a plan. For **one** of your targets, you could complete the box below, and give actual dates in the deadline column. You could look at Chapter 18 on 'Action Planning' in Part I.

Target			
What do you need to do to complete the task? (eg *number of books to read*)	**Time needed to complete**	**Resources/ support needed**	**When will you start?**

3.2.3 Allow for things going wrong

Have you allowed for problems, like everybody else wanting the same book, or everybody else wanting access to computers?

In your plan, allow for things going wrong:

* Allow for unforeseen circumstances in your work plan (eg *the bus is full, there is a long queue at the library, the computer crashes*) and build in leeway. Estimate the time you'll need and then add half on again.
* Work out in advance what difficulties there might be, and plan to avoid them
* Identify resources and people who might be able to help you
* Depending on the difficulty, you could refer to other chapters (eg *look at 'Solving Problems', 'Negotiating and Assertiveness', 'Group Work'*) – see contents.

What difficulties might you face with your current work?	How could you plan to deal with them?

You may need to revise your work plan and re-estimate the time needed.

3.2.4 Prioritise

You are likely to have several pieces of work to do together, many with similar deadlines. You may also have non-course commitments or interests to fit in. How will you ensure it all gets done? The following suggestions cover a range of strategies.

* **Prioritise using the following system.**
  1 Urgent and important – do it now.
  2 Urgent but not important – do it if you can.
  3 Important but not urgent – start it before it gets urgent.
  4 Not important and not urgent – don't do it.

* **Have three trays and a waste bin. One tray each for 1, 2, 3 above and 4 into the bin.**

* **Identify which are your strongest and which are your weakest subjects.**
  – Should you allocate equal time to both?
  – Should you give more time to the weaker one?
  – Is there a danger of neglecting areas you are good at?
  – Is the time you are spending on something equal to its importance?

3.2.5 Monitor and revise your work plan

- **Check your work plan regularly.** Ticking off what you've already done will make you feel better.
- **See if you are on target.** You may need to amend your plans to allow for changed circumstances, problems, further work, or different ways you've found of working.
- **If you make changes, ask yourself if they are really needed** – changes can make extra work, particularly if you are working with other people.
- **You may need to re-prioritise your actions and tasks.**

3.3 Strategies for organising yourself and your time

3.3.1 Organise your work ✔

	Yes	No

Are your notes
    in piles on the floor?
    on the floor, not in piles?
    filed systematically?		

Could you quickly find notes for a piece of work you did two months ago?		
Can you find equipment quickly (eg pens, calculator, files, paperclips)?		
Have you got a workspace/desk?		
Is there any space on your workspace/desk, or it is cluttered?		
Do you have a reminder system for what you need to do?		✓

Giving attention to your organisation can save you hours of wasted time. It is well worth spending half a day setting up systems which suit you and a couple of hours a week to maintain them/have a 'sort out'.

How could you improve your organisation, given any limits in where you live (at home, shared accommodation etc)? You could get feedback from friends about their views on how well (or not) you are organised. How do they do things?

3.3.2 Save time

- **Work out how to do something in advance, plan for it.** Trial and error takes up time.
- **If you have a big job to do, try something out on a small part of it first, to see if it works** (eg *create a filing system for some notes and if it works, use the system for all your notes*).
- **Looking at the same piece of paper over and over again wastes time.** Look at it once and then take action on it – be decisive.
- **Get all the information you need from material at the same time,** to avoid going back later (eg *the correct reference*).
- **Be well organised** (eg *make out a list with the most important things first, tick off items as they have been completed*).

3.3.3 Avoid time wasters

The following is a list of possible time wasters. You may wish to avoid some altogether. Others may be enjoyable but detract from time available for study and you may, reluctantly, need to limit them. You could add your own items to the list. ✔

Item	Possible ways of limiting	Can remove	Can limit
Phone calls Visitors dropping by Demands by members of the family	Ask people to call by phone or in person at specific times. Answer the phone but say you'll call back. Specify a time which is yours. Lock the door.		
TV	Limit it by type of programme, or time each day.		
Socialising	Only go out after 9pm, or only on set nights or days.		
Operating by trial and error	Plan ahead. Ask for advice from lecturers/friends.		
Not able to contact people	Leave messages. Write notes rather than make repeated calls. Say where you can be contacted.		
Locating resources	Ask – the lecturer, learning centre/library, computing support staff		
Putting things off	Use this chapter.		

3.3.4 Identify and use feedback and support

Ask for, and use, feedback from others to see of you are working effectively (eg *ask learning centre staff if the way you search for information is the most effective, ask others in the group if your scheduling of work is helping them, ask computing staff about computer issues*).

You could also refer to Section 17.7.3 on Using Feedback in Chapter 17 on 'Reflecting on Your Experience' in Part I.

3.3.5 Identify the way you work

Everyone has different ways of working which suit them best. You could build this into your plans.

What time of day do I study best?

How long can I concentrate before I need a break?

Where do I study best?

What circumstances help me study?

Do I work better under pressure?

Do I work better alone or with others?

3.3.6 Look after yourself

You can't work effectively if you are over-tired or stressed.

- **If you are losing concentration on a task, take a short break** (eg *for coffee, a walk around the block, watch the news*). Build breaks into your planning.
- **Look at Chapter 14 on 'Coping with Pressure' in Part I.**
- **Give yourself a reward for reaching a target** (eg *a treat*).

3.4 Improving what you do

How well have you met your targets?

What influenced what you did (helpful and less helpful)?

What could you have done about those which were less helpful?

What do you need to take action on? Which ideas in this chapter could you try? What help do you need? Sources of help include other chapters (see contents), friends (how do they do things?), keeping a diary to monitor what you are trying to change, guidance from lecturers.

Area in need of attention	Actions to take and help needed	By when?

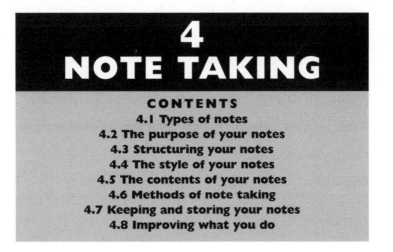

4
NOTE TAKING

'Notes' here means written work (including visuals, symbols, numbers) which helps you remember; records things; is not written in a full, polished way. You may need notes from lectures/seminars/tutorials; from written/computerised information; on visual images/video/film/art work; on research methods (eg *lab procedures/findings*).

This chapter covers:

* notes for your own use
* notes which may be seen by others (eg *for assessment*)
* minutes of meetings.

Why is it important to reconsider how you make notes? You may think you have been taking notes for years perfectly well. Why reconsider it?

* At university/college information may be complex, and you must look at it in more depth and more critically than, for example, at school. Your notes need to be different.
* You will be more reliant on effective notes than in the past. You will simply be handling much more information.
* It is easy to make notes, but difficult to make good notes: brief; accurate; summarising the essence of information; notes you can use and understand later.

We suggest you use this chapter:

* **at a point when you need to make notes**
* **to help you with the different sorts of notes you need to make**
* **together with Chapter 5 'Gathering and Using Information'.**

When you have completed it, you should be able to:

Plan work
* review your current use of notes and style of note taking
* identify the purpose of notes and how this influences the type of notes taken
* select appropriate types/format of notes to suit you, the purpose, the situation and the subject matter, including complex ones.

Use your plan
- use methods of note taking suitable for yourself, the purpose, the situation and the subject matter
- identify and record main points, including sources of inform-ation/ideas/images
- check your understanding, eg *unfamiliar words, concepts, abbreviations, acronyms*
- produce notes which are suitably structured and organised for retrieval
- check clarity of notes.

Review work
- evaluate the effectiveness of the process of making notes and the outcomes, identifying factors which influence both
- identify ways of improving your note taking skills.

(Based on QCA Key Skill specifications, QCA 2000)

4.1 Types of notes

You may need to make notes:

- for your own use (eg *for revision*)
- to help you produce work to be seen by others (eg *to produce an assignment*)
- which will be seen by others and may be assessed (eg *minutes of meetings, lab/research/interview notes*). In this case, check the format needed (eg *ask lecturers /tutors, look at examples*).

'**Minutes**' are the formal record of a meeting. You may need to give them as evidence for group work. All formal meetings have minutes and they are helpful for informal meetings – the person 'taking the minutes' is called the 'secretary' (not a secretary as in a clerical role, but a group member who makes notes in the meeting which are then turned into minutes). The main uses of minutes are:

- as record (eg *of decision and actions agreed*)
- as the basis for the next meeting (eg *to review what should have been done*).

Logs or diaries record your activities. They may be assessed (eg *record of what you did on placement, for a project*). You may need to:

- describe what you did
- describe how much work you did
- describe how well it went (see Chapters 17 and 31 'Reflecting on Your Experience').

Portfolios are used to present evidence of what you have done – they may be visual or written, and in either case they may include notes. You will need to ensure that:

- the person looking at your portfolio can understand your notes
- you label everything in the portfolio
- you make clear why you have included the items (what you want them to show)
- you organise it so somebody can find their way through it (eg *clear sections, contents list*).

Laboratory notes. There will probably be a set structure for these, depending on your subject, so check with your tutor.

4.2 The purpose of your notes

The reason for taking notes can determine the sort of notes you make. For example:

Is your purpose...	Implications for your notes	
for future revision?	*Must be understandable after a long time lapse, contain all main points, be easy to follow.*	
for an assignment?	*Must be accurate, may need to be detailed, able to be sorted to help structure the assignment. Not so important to understand them after a long time lapse (though you may need to use them again for other assignments).*	
for others to use (eg in group work)?	*Must be legible, use abbreviations and words others will understand.*	
to help you concentrate?	*If they are not going to be used later, all that matters is helping you focus now.*	
as a record (eg minutes, lab notes, interview notes)?	*Must be accurate, detailed.*	
Add in any other purposes...	*What do these notes need to be like?*	

4.3 Structuring your notes

You need to consider how you wish to use the notes in order to decide how to structure them. What would be most helpful for your purpose?

The following are common types of note taking.

4.3.1 Linear notes

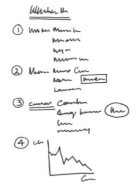

It helps to:

- use key words and phrases
- use headings; underlining; circles; boxes; diagrams; flowcharts; colours
- write on every other line, so you can add notes later
- use margins for your own ideas, questions, comments or criticisms (so you don't mix up your thoughts with those of the lecturer or author).

4.3.2 Patterns

Arrows/circles/lines connect key words/phrases, making a spreading pattern rather than words starting at the top and going down. It may look messy but it can be short, easy to read, and quick to re-draw later, to make it clearer. Some people with dyslexia find patterns helpful.

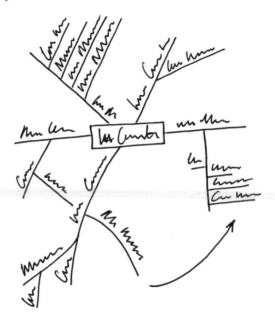

4.3.3 Visual information

It may be hard to record visual information in words. Possibilities include:

- freehand sketches
- taking copies (but check the copyright situation with a library/learning centre)
- taking down a good, accurate reference so you can find the visual again easily.

4.3.4 Combining types of notes

You could use linear and pattern styles in the same notes, using one piece of paper to draw patterns and another for factual information, lists etc.

You may find it helpful to add a short summary to any notes. If you are presenting a **portfolio** containing notes as evidence of your work (or visual images), it is very important to include a summary explaining the contents of the portfolio and what you want them to show.

4.3.5 Minutes

This is the usual format for the minutes of meetings.

* Title of organisation/department
* Name of group/committee
* Date of meeting
* Location of meeting
* List of those present (chairperson and secretary first, then in alphabetical order), and a list of those apologising for non-attendance.
* Notes in numbered paragraphs (with the same numbers as the agenda items, if there is one). For several points, sub-divide the numbers (eg *1.1,1.2*). This allows you to refer to items in future meetings. At the end of each point actions are noted. The last two items are usually 'Any other business' (AOB) (ie anything discussed not on the agenda) and the date/time/place of the next meeting.

Example (this is very brief, real minutes would be longer):

School of Engineering

Project Group 3

Meeting held on 11.4.01

Present

D Chan (chair)

N Black (secretary)

A Brown

R Li

Notes

1 Progress

1.1 R Li had collected information

*1.2 D Chan had been unable to locate information. **Action.** D Chan to ask for help from Learning Centre by 25.4.01*

2 Information found

2.1 The information on pistons showed that…

etc

5 AOB

Social event agreed for 20.4.01

6 Date, time, location of next meeting

24.4.01, 10am, Cutting Edge cafe.

4.4 The style of your notes

How will you use your notes and what will be best for this?

Long sentences take time to write and read back. All that may be needed to remember an idea are key words and phrases – but make sure you've got essential details. In notes for your own use you may miss out words like 'the' which won't affect your understanding, or use your own abbreviations (eg *'dev'* for *'development'*). If the notes are to be used by others this may not be OK – they need to understand them.

If you need to use the information in tables, graphs or charts, note it in that form.

For notes you need to make now or soon:

How will you use the notes?	What style do you need?

4.5 The contents of your notes

4.5.1 What are your current notes like?

Do the following apply to your notes?

Are your notes • selective (rather than trying to cover everything)? • easy to follow or understand later? Do your notes • highlight key points? • summarise main points? • clarify initial ideas? • give enough detail? • make the source of your notes clear (eg *so you can give references*)?	

It can help to compare your notes with someone else's (eg *somebody else's lecture or lab notes*). They may be different, even if you both were making notes on the same thing. Why? How? Looking at how others make notes can give you ideas for yours.

Remember that any individually assessed work must be your own, so do this exercise to get ideas on how to make notes, not to copy content (they may have got it wrong).

Questions to ask in comparing notes might be:

- in what ways are the notes different?
- how are the notes organised or structured?
- do you understand each other's notes (if they don't understand yours now, you may not understand them yourself in six months)?
- why did you include some things and not others?
- have they been rewritten, or added to later?

How could your notes be improved?

4.5.2 Selecting what to note

What do you need to make notes on and what can be missed out? You may be taking notes on complex areas (eg *information with many elements or with difficult ideas*).

If you don't think about this, you may end up with notes which are irrelevant, have bits missing or don't make sense. It is rarely necessary, for example, to write down everything a lecturer says.

It helps to go back to your purpose (see Section 4.2 above). What do you need for that purpose? What are the crucial aspects of the information?

It can help to think of three different types of information:

Type of information	When important	Examples of questions to ask
Underlying principles, concepts, theories, lines of argument.	At university/college this is very important. As you move into the final stages of a course it becomes crucial.	What are the ideas behind the detailed, factual information? What are the crucial principles? If you had to explain a theory to somebody who knew nothing about it, what would be essential? What are the steps in a line of argument?
Detailed, factual information (includes details of recommended reading or sources to follow up).	As evidence for an argument, concept, principle, theory.	What is the argument/concept/principle/theory which needs supporting? What evidence is needed to support it? Are there any essential steps (eg *in a mathematical calculation*) which must be included? What facts/details are really important? What is irrelevant/not needed?
Your own questions, criticisms, opinions of the information.	This becomes even more important as you move into the final stages of a course.	Why is the information like that? Who says? On what assumptions is it based? What alternative views might there be? Is it accurate/up to date? See Chapter 22 'Critical Analysis'.

You could complete the following for something you are working on now (eg *a lecture, a book, or a film*), to see how you could use this approach more generally.

Principles, concepts, theories, arguments

Relevant detailed factual information

My own questions, criticisms etc

✍

What is the source of your information? For the details needed for references, see Chapter 5 'Gathering and Using Information'

4.5.3 The content of minutes

You could use this to help you think about what to note in the minutes of a meeting.

✍

What is the meeting for? What is its aim or purpose?
Who will read the minutes and what do they need to know?
What was discussed which is relevant to the aim/purpose and readers?
What is important to note as a record of what has happened?
What is important to note as a record of what actions people need to take?

You may take more notes in the meeting than you include in the final minutes. It is good practice to:

- leave out repetition or detail which is not needed
- record the main points discussed
- avoid reporting which person said what (eg *not 'Jane said that it is important...' but 'It is important to...'*)
- note any papers which were 'tabled', ie brought to the meeting
- note decisions taken, actions agreed and who will do them by when.

4.6 Methods of note taking

4.6.1 Note taking in class

If you try to make notes of everything you may find it hard to keep up (see Section 4.5.2 above). To help, you could ask lecturers or tutors to:

- say at the start of a class what will be covered in what order. The first and last 10 minutes of a lecture often summarise the main points.
- say which aspects are really important
- allow you time to write notes, put in breaks to let you catch up
- explain what you don't understand (if you ask, you may find that others haven't understood either).

If you are given lecture or tutorial handouts, write additional notes during the class in the margin or add your own pages.

4.6.2 Sharing note taking

You can spend more time listening if you share note taking, but check that those you work with have similar aims for their notes and make understandable, legible notes.

If you share note taking with others, remember that any coursework or assignment which you submit as your own must be your own. If you hand in work which is so closely based on shared notes that it looks like the work of others, you may be accused of plagiarism or cheating. Your work needs to be clearly the result of your own individual effort, even if some of the preparation was done with others.

You could:

- sit in pairs in a lecture – one student makes notes on the first half, the other on the second half; discuss the notes after the lecture
- in group work, allocate a different person each week to write notes and photocopy them for the rest
- share looking at materials (eg *each person looks at different books, makes notes on relevant parts, comments on them, photocopies the notes for the others*).

4.6.3 Minutes

You need to take notes during the meeting to turn into minutes (see 4.3.5 above). Having an agenda helps, as items are discussed in a certain order. Minutes are a public record. All those attending, and possibly others, will see them. Those at the meeting may:

- not like what they said being reported inaccurately
- not want what they said to be noted (eg *conflict or criticisms*)
- have vested interests (eg *not want others who weren't present to know what was said*)
- want what they did or contributed to be acknowledged.

People may say what they want (eg *'Please can you not minute that'*) but they may not. To make sure you don't offend anybody you could:

- look at other minutes of similar groups to see how they were written
- find out about the group, to identify any vested interests or 'politics'
- ask the chairperson for advice
- ask other group members to check the minutes (at formal meetings the first point on the agenda is to 'agree the minutes', ie to check everybody thinks they are accurate).

You may find the following editing checklist useful.

In your minutes **have you avoided:**   ✔

reporting word for word what was said?	
using emotional language expressing negative feelings?	
statements attaching blame to individuals?	
humour (easily misinterpreted)?	
putting in things which were not actually said?	

4.7 Keeping and storing your notes

4.7.1 Retrieving notes

Can you find your notes again easily? How do you store them? Do you order notes by date, alphabetically, numerically, by topic or subject? For ideas, see Chapter 5 'Gathering and Using Information'.

You could store notes in the following ways.

Storage method	Possible advantages
Loose-leaf in files	Can introduce new divisions, add extra material
Concertina file/folders	Can introduce new divisions, add extra material
Computerised database	Easy to edit
Boxed card-file system	Good for an index or references, can be stored easily, eg *card box index - you write on a card a topic and where you have stored it.*
A notebook per topic	Keeps relevant material together

4.7.2 Finding information again

You may need to find again the original source you took your notes from.

Note where any information came from. If it is from text, include title; date; author; place of publishing; and publisher. You could also note chapter headings and page numbers (if you give a direct quote in your work you must give the page number). For help on referencing see Chapter 5 'Gathering and Using Information'.

It is helpful to date your notes and to number pages.

4.7.3 Reviewing and editing notes

Writing notes in your own words, rather than repeating the lecturer's or author's words, helps you to understand and to remember.

Go over notes soon after they have been made, while things are fresh in your mind, highlighting things you do not understand, making them clearer and perhaps adding a summary. Check acronyms (eg *SHU is Sheffield Hallam University*). For how to find out about things you don't understand, see Chapter 5 'Gathering and Using Information'.

Before you need to use your notes (eg *for revision*) sort them out, make them clear, check you understand them.

4.7.4 Minutes

Minutes should be sent as soon as possible (eg *within a week of the meeting*) to: all who attended the meeting; those who should have been there; anybody else the group wants to see them (eg *your tutor*). Attach a list showing to whom they have been sent.

If the minutes are confidential, make this clear by writing it on them.

File them with other papers for the group and take them to the next meeting, so you can refer to them.

4.8 Improving what you do

What do you think makes notes good – for you, your purpose, your subject?

How do your notes actually rate against your ideas on what makes notes good?

Think about the last piece of work you did. How could you have made and organised your notes better?

How do you think your notes affected the outcome of the work (eg *the grade/mark*)?

What influenced or affected how well you made and organised your notes?

How long does it take you to find notes? What would speed this up?

You can now identify actions you need to take to improve what you do.

Improvement needed	Action to take (including resources, support or help needed)	By (date)

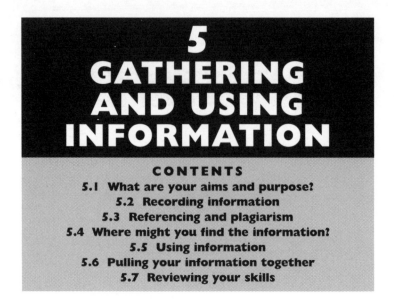

5
GATHERING
AND USING
INFORMATION

CONTENTS
5.1 What are your aims and purpose?
5.2 Recording information
5.3 Referencing and plagiarism
5.4 Where might you find the information?
5.5 Using information
5.6 Pulling your information together
5.7 Reviewing your skills

Course work requires you to find and effectively use good quality, relevant and up to date information. Your grades or marks will be strongly influenced by your skills in this area.

We live in an information society, and information skills are needed in most jobs and throughout life.

Information may be in different forms. In this chapter, 'information' refers to:

• written material
• numerical material
• electronic/computerised material (eg *Internet, CD-ROM*)
• audio-visual material (eg *videos, interactive videos, films, multi-media*)
• visual materials (eg *photographs, diagrams and graphs or works of art*).

We suggest you use this chapter:

• **when you need to gather information for a course activity or assignment, for example if you need to do a 'literature search'**
• **before you begin to gather any information**
• **then whilst gathering information.**

When you have completed it, you should be able to:

Plan an information search
• identify the purpose and aims of the information search, in relation to a complex subject
• find relevant sources using a range of types of information/data (eg *databases, extended documents, images*).

Implement an information search
• use appropriate strategies to cover material (eg *reading strategies such as skim, scan etc*)
• identify relevant information/data and key points
• compare information on a topic from different sources
• evaluate sources and information/data (eg *recognise opinion and bias*)
• bring together information in a coherent way for your purpose/aim/topic

- put information into a relevant format for your purpose/aim/topic
- accurately reference material using academic conventions and keep appropriate records.

Review work
- identify factors that influenced the outcomes
- identify how to improve.

(Based on QCA Key Skill specifications, QCA 2000)

5.1 What are your aims and purpose?

Being clear about your aims and purpose is vital so that the information you gather and use is relevant. Section 5.1.4 below contains a box for you to summarise your responses to Sections 5.1.1, 5.1.2 and 5.1.3. This chapter uses examples relating to transport.

5.1.1 Analysing the task

Any information seeking, even the most basic (eg *how to get from A to B*), starts with research questions (eg *what buses or trains go from A to B, when and at what cost?*). The more complex your subject (ie the more elements it has) the more it helps to clarify the main questions you need to answer – and most subjects at university/college will be complex.

A course task/assignment may not be phrased as a question, but it still helps to work out the questions you need to ask to complete it. If you are uncertain about what is needed, ask your lecturer/tutor – to avoid completing a task only to realise you misunderstood it.

Discuss the transport policy of the 'City of Sheffield'	Develop a database on transport 'in Sheffield'
Possible research questions	Possible research questions
• *What is the transport policy?*	• *Who would want to use the database?*
• *Why was it developed?*	• *How would they access the database?*
• *What are the costs and benefits?*	• *What information would they want to be in the database?*
• *What is right or wrong with it?*	

5.1.2 Why do you want the information? Who is it for?

Why you want the information and for whom, influences the amount and depth of information needed, as well as the focus. See the following examples.

Why discuss transport policy?	Who is the discussion for?
Possibilities are • *to persuade others that different transport is needed* • *to illustrate the main issues in developing transport policies* • *to give practice at discussing an issue from differing perspectives and argue a point*	Possibilities are • *your lecturer – to find out what you understand, see how you use information, assess your skills* • *your seminar group – to share information and understanding* • *the City Council – to help it make decisions*

Why develop a transport database?	Who is the database for?
Possibilities are • *to provide information about transport provision* • *to give practice in creating databases* • *to highlight the important issues in creating databases*	Possibilities are • *your lecturer – to find out what you understand, see how you use information, assess your skills* • *the public – to identify what transport they can use*

5.1.3 When do you need it by?

How much time you have influences how you collect information, and how much you collect (eg *if you only have a week you have no time to write for information; if you want a book or video which is out on loan, or which must obtained from another library, you may have to wait several days or a few weeks*).

This means planning ahead. See Chapter 3 'Organising Yourself and Your Time'.

5.1.4 Summary

We suggest you complete the following for an assignment/course activity you are working on now. 🖎

Why do you need the information? What is its purpose?	For whom?	By when? (deadline)

🖎

What questions do you need to answer?

5.1.5 Answering your research questions

You may not find information in exactly the right form for what you want. You will need to gather information from various sources and then make sense of it.

For example: *if you need to compare theories or authors or materials you may not find a text which does this – you will need to find the original materials and compare them for yourself.*

5.2 Recording information

5.2.1 Reasons for having good records

It helps to record information so that:

* you can find it and use it again in the future (eg *where it is in the library/learning centre, who gave it to you*)
* you will not have to return to the same source to check any details
* you know the details for referencing it and will not have to go back to find them (to see what is needed see Section 5.3.3 below)
* you can use it in an appropriate format (eg *if you will use it in a table – record it in a table; for word-processed work – word-process your records*)
* it suits your own way of working
* it saves you time.

5.2.2 Ways of recording information

For more help, see Chapter 4 'Note Taking'.

In the following box, tick the first column where you use a method and rate how useful it is in the next column 1–4, where 1= 'very useful' and 4 = 'not useful'.

✔

How do you record now?	If used	Rating 1–4
Notebook		
Writing on one side of paper to help in ordering your notes		
Loose-leaf folder with file dividers		
On cards		
In a portfolio of visual images		
On a computer database		
On a computer, using directories or folders or floppy discs		
In piles on the floor		
On scraps of paper		
Others (please specify)		

Your own classification system (ie putting your information under 'headings') helps you find information again easily.

✔

How do you classify information so you can find it again?	
by subject (eg *transport*)	
by topic (eg *trains*)	
by author (eg *Gunston, B.*)	

by cross referencing, ie you file alphabetically by topic and have index cards showing what other topics each file also contains. *In the example below, you could find information on engines in your buses file.*
 	
    Main file   **Cross reference index**
    Trains   *Chassis*
    Buses   *Engines*
    Lorries *Safety*	

In no particular way (just rifle through the piles)	
Other (please specify)	

You could use index cards to help you cross reference. This is what one might look like:

MAIN TOPIC/FILE	TRANSPORT
AUTHOR	GUNSTON B. **DATE** (1976)
TITLE	LORRIES, BUSES AND TRAINS
PUBLISHER	MACMILLAN
WHERE LOCATED	CITY CAMPUS LEARNING CENTRE
LIBRARY REFERENCE NO.	629.2GU

Other topics it contains
Roads
Railroads
Trucks
Buses

You could keep any notes you make on this book in a file called 'transport', but your other index card on 'roads' would tell you to also look in your 'transport' file. You could make 'author' your first line on the index card instead, and file your notes alphabetically by name of author.

5.3 Referencing and plagiarism

5.3.1 Plagiarism and the reasons for accurate referencing

Plagiarism is presenting somebody else's work as your own, without acknowledging it. It is very important to quote from or summarise published work which is correctly referenced, but if you don't reference it (see 5.3.3 below) assessors may think you are trying to pass off somebody else's work as your own.

You can:

- summarise in your own words what somebody else has written, if you reference it
- repeat a small section of what somebody else has written, if you put it in quotation marks and reference it, or reproduce a visual such as a diagram if you reference it.

You must not:

- use somebody else's work (including anything from electronic sources eg *the Internet*) and put it into your work without referencing it.

'Cheating' is copying another student's words or ideas when the assignment should be your own individual work.

Examples. These examples are based on the work of Jude Carroll (2000).

Example	Comments
Example 1 'There is the view that the world and its economy is changing rapidly, and that a nation's success is dependent on individuals who are flexible, able to continue to learn and have skills which are transferable between situations.' (Drew, 1998, p15) **Example 2** Drew (1998) suggests that an assumption behind the Key Skills movement is that, in a rapidly changing world, a nation's economy depends on the skills of individuals.	This is **acceptable and good practice**. These are examples of how you should refer to somebody else's work in your text.
Example 1 There is the view that the world and its economy is changing rapidly, and that a nation's success is dependent on individuals who are flexible, able to continue to learn and have skills which are transferable between situations. **Example 2** An assumption behind the Key Skills movement is that, in a rapidly changing world, a nation's economy depends on the skills of individuals.	This is **not acceptable and is bad practice**. This is **plagiarism**. Example 1 uses somebody else's exact words without giving a reference or using inverted commas. Example 2 uses somebody else's ideas, even though the words have been changed, without referencing those ideas. In both cases, the writer makes it look as if somebody else's ideas or words are their own.
There are various reasons why Key Skills have been seen as important by governments. There is a view that the world and its economy is changing rapidly, and that a nation's success depends on flexible people with skills which transfer between situations. HE is expensive and should justify that expense by developing individuals' skills (Drew, 1998).	This is **borderline**. It is not a bad case of plagiarism, but it is not good practice. The original author is mentioned, but it is not clear which part of the text is based on what the author said. The reader might think that only the last sentence refers to what Drew said, but the whole paragraph is based on Drew.

5.3.2 Copyright

There are legal restrictions on what you can photocopy (to protect the rights and incomes of authors). Ask for advice from library/learning centre staff.

5.3.3 Referencing

You should always acknowledge any thoughts, ideas and information which are not your own and use a standard form of referencing, to give the information needed should anyone else wish to look up the work.

This means you need to keep accurate records of references during your information gathering to avoid having to go back to check them again.

Referring to an item in your text is known as citing. You then need a list of references at the end of your work to indicate where that citation can be found – see below.

Citations

There are two universally accepted methods. You can use either, but stick to the same one in one piece of work. This book uses the Harvard System.

Harvard system

Give the author's name and the date of publication in brackets.

eg *Gibbs (1992) believes students should be active.*

Direct quotations should be in inverted commas and also include the page number.

eg *Gibbs (1992, p11) states that 'students need to be active ...'*

Numeric system

You number your references as they appear in the text and then use the same number each time you refer to it.

eg *In a recent report (26) it was stated that 'students need to be active...'*

Referencing

At the end of an assignment, all works referred to should be listed. If using the Harvard system, list them alphabetically by the author's last name (family name or surname), if using the numeric system, list them by number. In either case you need the following information.

Book
- name of author/editor, with initials of their first names
- date of publication, in brackets
- full book title, either underlined or in italics
- the publisher's name
- some lecturers may want you to give the place of publication

eg *Gibbs, G. (1992) Improving the Quality of Student Learning, Technical and Educational Services, Bristol.*

Media (eg *video*)
- name of author, with initials of first names
- date of publication
- full title, either underlined or in italics
- the publisher's name
- format and length
- any accompanying material

eg *Main, A. (1987) Study patterns: introductory programme plus units 1–4, 3rd edn, Audio Visual Services, University of Strathclyde: Guild Sound and Vision, VHS video cassette – 3 hrs and booklet.*

Article
- name of author(s), with initials of first names
- date of publication, in brackets
- title of article in single inverted commas
- name of journal, either underlined or in italics
- volume, number and page numbers of the article

eg *Rainer, R. and Reimann, P. (1989) 'The bipolarity of personal constructs', International Journal of Personal Construct Theory, vol. 3 (2), pp149–165.*

5.4 Where might you find the information?

5.4.1 What location?

Start with a library/learning centre catalogue. Libraries/learning centres have staff to give advice and guidance.

Where might you also try? Who might have an interest in the topic and have information on this area? Look back at Section 5.1.4 above for clues.

eg *Transport – transport providers (rail, bus companies etc), environmentalist groups, trade unions.*

How else might you get ideas? Talk to other students, friends, contacts, work colleagues; ask specialists (eg *lecturers*); look at the media (eg *TV, newspapers*). How might you contact organisations? Libraries/learning centres have directories listing them.

5.4.2 How might the information be organised?

Being aware of how information is organised helps in finding it. Libraries give each item a number. The items are then organised in numerical order based on decisions the librarian makes (eg *about what subject it belongs to*). Possible ways of organising information include:

by author	by publication type (eg *journal*)
by title	by language
by subject	by date
by key word, eg *in the example 'Transport policies in Sheffield' - transport might be a key word or Sheffield might be.*	etc

In an online catalogue you can 'search' for an item by using any of these starting points and will then find the number showing where the item is stored.

5.4.3 Electronic information

A large amount of information is produced electronically – it both repeats what is in print and also adds to it (eg *dictionaries, encyclopaedias, textbooks, journal articles*).

Check that you can do the following. If you can't handle electronic information you will miss out on a huge resource. See IT support materials (eg *Pettigrew and Elliott 1999*) or ask for help from library/learning centre staff.

How would you rate yourself on the following scale, where 1 = 'very good' and 4 = 'needs considerable improvement'?

✔

	1	2	3	4
Are you confident using computerised systems; the library catalogue; databases; the Internet? There is a range: bibliographic (eg *references to journal articles*); full text (eg *a newspaper on a CD-ROM*); data (eg *financial data about a company*).				
Can you carry out precise database searches, eg *searching on dates, or authors, or subjects*?				
Can you link terms, eg *searching by author and subject and date*?				
Do you understand the difference between word searching (gives everything where the word appears, whether or not it is the main topic) or subject searching (focuses on the topic, usually more specific)?				
Can you create and store data on a floppy disc?				
Other aspects of using computers needed to find information. Please list.				

5.4.4 At what point do you stop looking for information?

Which of the following are you more likely to do

✔

Give up after a quick search (*if so you may miss important information*).	
Follow up every clue until you have the last scrap of information (*are you going too far; do you really need it all; how much difference will it make to your work/grade?*).	

If you tend to give up quickly, you may need to persevere. Finding information is not like using a 'one-stop shop'. You need to be a detective following up clues: eg *a database may give references to printed articles; you need to find the articles; one article may refer to further articles.*

If you tend to search for too long and get overwhelmed by information, it helps to be clear about your research questions and to set realistic deadlines. Being critical and evaluative is important. Continually ask if you really need this information.

The following checklist may help in knowing when you have enough information.

✔

Has the information started repeating itself?	
Have you covered the core material (you may need guidance from the lecturer)?	
Have you answered your research questions?	
Is all the information relevant (eg *to your research questions and the topic*)?	
Does the information offer anything new?	
Can you digest (take in) any more information?	
Do you have time to look at more information?	

5.5 Using information

5.5.1 Covering all the information

How will you cover all the information you must consider? Try using three stages. The first can identify what you need to look at in the second; the second identifies what to look at in the third.

✔   ✔

Stage	Strategy	What I currently do	What I could try
Superficial	Skimming/Scanning. Don't read every word, or look at every detail, instead look at – titles – contents pages – headings – overall image (for visual items).		
Refined	Read introductions. Read first and last lines of paragraphs. Look at charts/diagrams. Look for key words.		
Detailed/ in depth	Careful, thoughtful reading or observation to understand all aspects.		

5.5.2 Understanding terminology and the topic

The topic may be new to you, and there may be words/aspects specific to your subject or professional area which you don't understand. It helps to use:

- general dictionaries and a thesaurus (gives words with the same or similar meaning)
- specialist dictionaries (eg *accounting, business, medical dictionaries*)
- glossaries in books
- encyclopaedias
- a general textbook
- reference books and electronic sources of information (eg *databases*) – they often have guides explaining how to use them.

Ask:

- your lecturer/tutor
- library/learning centre staff.

5.5.3 Making sense of and analysing the information

You can make notes here about your information for a current task/assignment.

What are the most important (key) points?
Are there any issues which arise over and over again?
Are there any connections between aspects of the information? What are they?
How does the information from different sources compare? What is the same/ different? Do they agree with/contradict each other? What do most sources say? Is there a minority view?
Is the information accurate?
Is the information up to date?
Does the source omit any information you need?
Did the person producing the information have a vested interest or bias? What is it? How does this affect the information?
Does the information include opinions (eg *as opposed to facts or statements supported by evidence*)?

5.5.4 Keep returning to your research questions and purpose

Keep looking back at Section 5.1.4 above. Is the information you are gathering appropriate?

5.5.5 Evidence

If you make a claim or give a view, you need to give evidence for it. This is very important in academic work (assessors will ask 'How do they know that, what's the proof?'). Your evidence may be from your information search (eg *a quotation from somebody else's work or some factual information; statistical data*). Remember to reference whatever you use from somebody else's work (see 5.3.3 above)

5.6 Pulling your information together

Once you've got your information you need to bring it together in the format you are using (eg *report, essay, presentation, poster etc*).

Whatever the format you need to have a clear 'argument'. This means putting the points you are making in a logical order which will make sense to the reader/viewer/listener and help them understand, and which will meet your aims and purpose (see 5.1.4 above).

You also need to consider how to present aspects of the information most clearly. For an assignment/task you are currently working on, you could note below how the aspects of your information might be best presented. Remember Sections 5.3.2 and 5.3.3 above (on copyright and referencing).

Written text	
Tables or spreadsheets	
Graphs, diagrams	
Plans, maps	

Images (eg *slides, sketches, video, photographs*)	
In an appendix	
Other (please specify)	

See the other chapters for guidance on formats in which to present work (eg *in written work such as essays*).

5.7 Reviewing your skills

What influenced how well you gathered and used information for your task? Identifying this can help you see what to do in future. Use this box to note what affected what you did – good and bad. It could be your skills (eg *in using computers*), how you went about it (eg *the time you allowed*), or factors outside you (eg *resource availability*).

What affected what I did?	What could I do next time?

Thanks to Aileen D. Wade of the Learning Centre at Sheffield Hallam University for her contributions to a version of this in Key Skills Online.

Based on an original Pack by Sue Drew/Rosie Bingham/Andrew Walker/Aileen Wade.

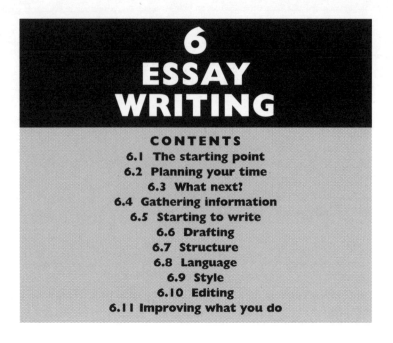

6
ESSAY WRITING

CONTENTS

The essay is the traditional form of assessment in Higher Education. Essays are used to a great extent in some subjects; in others you may be asked to write one only occasionally, to give you practice at this type of writing. They are often used in exams, where you may be required to write short essays about a topic (eg *a 2 hour exam with three questions*). A thesis or dissertation may be in the form of an extended essay (check with your tutor).

Essays are mainly used in the academic world. You write about a topic in a way which is well reasoned and moves logically from beginning to end. It allows a writer to explore a topic and write about it in the way they think is appropriate, with the structure being largely up to them. This 'freedom' can make it hard for a writer to see what to include and how.

How is this different from a report? Reports are widely used in employment, professional areas, government etc. A report has a specific structure, with clear numbered sections. It is concise, and gives the results of an investigation to somebody who needs it, usually to help them take action.

You may know your topic well, but how you write your essay will determine your mark or grade.

We suggest you use this chapter:

- **when you have an essay to write**
- **to help you improve your essay writing skills in general.**

There are margins for your notes and boxes asking specific questions to help you.

When you have completed it, you should be able to:

Plan work
- identify the features of an essay
- identify the purpose and audience for the essay, and how this influences it
- identify an appropriate/accepted structure and style for your purpose, audience, situation and the subject matter, including complex subjects
- plan the processes needed
- identify time, resource and information needs.

Use your plan
- use the essay format appropriately for the purpose, subject and audience
- organise and present information/ideas/images to make meaning and argument clear
- use style and language to make meaning and argument clear
- edit/redraft to ensure coherence and clarity, following standard conventions of grammar, spelling and punctuation
- pull together and include information/evidence which is accurate, identifying any opinion and bias
- use academic conventions (eg *referencing*).

Review work
- evaluate the essay's effectiveness for its purpose, subject and audience
- identify ways of improving the essay.

(Based on QCA Key Skill specifications, QCA 2000)

6.1 The starting point

You need to start by making sure you know exactly what is wanted. A **very** common reason for a low mark/poor grade for an essay is that it is not directed sufficiently to the question or topic and does not meet the requirements. This often happens in exams, when people can be nervous and in a hurry, and do not stop to think about what is needed.

In any writing you should start by identifying the reader and what s/he will expect. This is a vital step in being able to communicate your ideas well to the reader and is possibly **the** most important aspect to consider.

You also need to interpret what your topic or question means – it may sound straightforward, but it is not always easy to identify the purpose.

6.1.1 Requirements

Your reader is likely to be your tutor. What will s/he expect and judge to be a good essay? Making notes on the following will help you before you begin work. To find out about the following you could:

- look at any handouts you have been given ('brief') about this essay/assignment
- look at your course/unit handbook to find out about general expectations
- look at the assessment criteria for your assignment
- ask friends in your subject area if you could see their previous essays; try to work out why they got the grade they did
- ask your tutor – s/he may give you examples of good/poor essays.

What you need to know	Your notes
What 'requirements', if any, are there? eg *number of words, word-processed, can you include images?*	
What will get a good mark or grade? What are the assessment criteria? Is there any weighting, ie what are the things which will most improve your mark/grade?	
What is 'the norm' for essays in your subject area? eg *you might be expected to write in the passive voice (ie 'it has been found that...', or in the first person (ie 'I found that...') eg some subjects do not allow sub-headings, others do.*	
Please add other useful information (eg *any peer/self-assessment*)	

6.1.2 Your topic/questions – the purpose and focus

Before you begin working, it is important to know exactly what your topic or question means. You need to identify the words in your topic/question which will most tell you the purpose and focus. For example:

*<u>Discuss</u> the issues facing students **new** to university.*

The word we have underlined, '*<u>Discuss</u>*', is the 'instruction word', which tells you what to do, ie to write about the issues from various angles or points of view. It also implies that you need to identify the issues in order to write about them. In any topic/question you need to look for what is implied, as well as for what is actually asked for.

The word we have put in bold is '**new**'. The tutor wants you to focus on the issues facing new students. This implies that the tutor expects the issues to be different from those facing students who have been at university/college for some time. The tutor will want to hear about only those issues facing new students. This gives you the focus for the essay.

This was a straightforward example. The following is more complex:

The dramatic increase in student numbers in Higher Education has meant that teachers have had to change their teaching methods and develop new ones. Consider the implications of this for students.

Where is the instruction word, which gives you the purpose? '*<u>Consider</u>*'. This means something different from '*<u>discuss</u>*', as used in the first example – you need to weigh things up and make a judgement about them.

What are the words/phrases which give the focus? '*Implications of this for students*'. You are expected to write about the effect the changed and new methods have had on students.

What is implied? To write about this topic, you will need to identify what the changed and new methods are.

What else will you need to write about? You would need to give information about the increase in student numbers. What might be implied here? You could write about why the increase in student numbers has meant changes in teaching approaches. You might also want to identify the new teaching methods which seem to work best for students, or to identify methods you think would work.

So, if we underline the instruction word and put in bold the words showing the focus the topic might look like this.

*The dramatic increase in student numbers in Higher Education has meant that teachers have had to change their teaching methods and to develop new ones. <u>Consider</u> the **implications** of this **for students**.*

You can make notes in the box below about your own topic/question. If you are unsure about the meaning of any words in your topic/question, check in a dictionary (this can be very helpful with instruction words such as 'consider', 'discuss', 'describe' etc, even if you know what the word **usually** means).

What is your topic or question?
What is/are the instruction word/s? What do they suggest about the purpose of the essay and what you need to do?
What is/are the word/s giving the focus?
What is implied?
What else will you need to write about?

If you are uncertain, ask your tutor for help before you go any further. Other students may be unsure too.

6.1.3 Complex topics

The more complex your topic (ie with more elements), the more important it will be to analyse it in the above way – and the harder it will be to do so. The first example in 6.1.2 above was easier to analyse than the second one.

It may be that with a complex topic/question there is more than one way of interpreting it. Some students will identify certain words and phrases as being those giving the focus, others will think different words/phrases do so. Different students may see different issues implied by their topic and there may be no one correct interpretation. Indeed, the tutor may want to know how **you** interpret the topic or question.

It will help to think about your topic/question in the way suggested in Section 6.1.2, and to have good reasons for what you think are the instruction words, the focus words, what is implied, and to check this out with your tutor.

6.2 Planning your time

You will have a deadline by when to hand in your essay. To meet the deadline you need to identify what you have to do and how long it will take, then work back from your deadline to see when you need to start what. A good general rule is to:

- allow equal amounts of time for gathering and using information and for actual writing (people underestimate how long it will take to actually write)
- estimate how long each task will take and add at least half on again. It always takes longer than you think.

You will need to allow time for the other course work you have.

For example:

Deadline 12th December

Task	How long it will take	When to start
Clarifying the topic	*2 hours*	*1st Nov*
Identifying information sources	*1 day*	*2nd Nov*
Reading information and making notes on it	*3 days*	*5th Nov*
Starting to write	*up to one day*	*15th Nov*
Drafting	*2 days*	*17th Nov*
Editing, presenting final essay	*1 day*	*1st Dec*

The rest of this chapter will help you see what work you need to do to produce your essay and how long it might take. For more help see Chapters 3 and 20 on 'Organising Yourself and Your Time' and Chapters 18 and 32 on 'Action Planning'.

6.3 What next?

You will need to gather information for your essay. You also need to get started with the actual writing of it. There is no right order in which to do this and different people have different approaches. However, we suggest you look next at Section 6.4 'Gathering information' or Section 6.5 'Starting to write', moving back and forth between them as your ideas develop.

If you are unsure where to start, it might help to begin by gathering the main information you need, then to start writing, because the information will determine what you write about. Once you begin writing you may find you need to look for more information.

6.4 Gathering information

6.4.1 What information do you need?

Look at the box you completed in Section 6.1.2. This will tell you what you need to find out about.

What questions do you need to ask about your essay topic/question? Where might you find that information?

There is no right way. Two different students might identify different questions. One thing that makes some essays better than others is how good you are at identifying what to find out about – your 'research' questions.

What makes your 'research' questions useful or good? They are likely to:

- get to the heart of the matter, identify the key issues
- cover most of the important aspects of the topic
- look at different angles to the topic (though in your topic, you may need to look at something in depth from one angle only)
- be perceptive or imaginative.

Example. *The dramatic increase in student numbers in Higher Education has meant that teachers have had to change their teaching methods and to develop new ones. Consider the implications of this for students.*

Questions I need to answer	Possible sources of information
How did student numbers increase? What are the statistics? When did they increase?	• *Department for Education and Employment(DfEE) publications* • *Government papers* • *DfEE or government web sites* • *Journal articles/books on changes in Higher Education*
What are the implications of those increases for HE lecturers?	• *Journal articles/books on changes in Higher Education* • *Lecturers*
What were teaching methods like before the numbers increased?	• *Journal articles/books on changes in Higher Education* • *Lecturers*
How have teaching methods changed? What are the new ones?	• *Journal articles/books on changes in Higher Education* • *Journal articles/books on teaching in Higher Education* • *Journal articles/books on using IT to help learning* • *Lecturers*
What was good/poor about the old methods?	• *As above* • *Ex-students*
What is good/poor about the new methods?	• *As above* • *Current students*

You could complete the following box for your essay topic/question. Look at your notes in 6.1.2 to help you identify the questions. If you are unsure about sources of information, look at Chapters 5 and 21 on 'Gathering and Using Information' or ask at a library/learning centre. You could particularly look for guidance on the following:

- finding all the information you need
- efficient (quick but thorough) ways of gathering and using the information.

Questions I need to answer	Possible sources of information

6.4.2 Using information

When selecting useful information try to stay focused on your notes in Section 6.1.2 above and the questions you identified in Section 6.4.1 above.

In Higher Education, it will not be enough to only provide relevant and accurate information – you are also expected to identify any opinions and possible bias in the material you use.

Opinion. This is an idea for which there is no supporting evidence, someone's view.

Bias. This means selective, prejudiced or unbalanced (eg *only some information/ ideas/sources are chosen to present a particular view, with ideas/information deliberately missed out; incorrect/inaccurate interpretations/statistics*).

You will need to analyse the material you have selected (eg *making sure it is up to date, accurate, reliable, from a reputable source etc*). It may help to look at Chapters 5 and 21 on 'Gathering and Using Information'. You could particularly look for guidance on the following:

- finding all the information you need
- efficient (quick but thorough) ways of gathering and using the information
- critically analysing the information.

6.4.3 Referencing information

Plagiarism is seen as a 'very bad thing' in the academic world. It means using somebody else's ideas/work in your own work without acknowledging where it came from.

To avoid being accused of plagiarism you must give a 'reference' for everything you include in your essay which others produced (eg *from published work, the Web*). This means:

- in your text you show where you have included something from somebody else's work
- at the end of your text you give a list of all the works you have referred to.

For example, **in your text:**

In their book on student skills, Drew and Bingham (1997) give guidance on a range of topics which are relevant to student work in Higher Education.

Here the (1997) indicates a reference. It is the date of publication of the work.

At the end of your text:

References
Drew, S. and Bingham, R. (1997) The Student Skills Guide, Gower

It is very important that you look at advice on plagiarism and referencing. You could:

- check with your tutor – there may be specific requirements in your subject area
- look in your course/unit handbooks
- look at Chapter 5 on 'Gathering and Using Information'.

6.4.4 Making notes about your information

See Chapter 4 on 'Note Taking' for guidance on taking and organising notes on any information you use. For example *noting, at the time, all the information you need for the reference will avoid you having to find the item again to give the referencing details in your essay.*

6.5 Starting to write

Not knowing where to start when writing an essay is a common problem for students.

There is no one right way. You may hear advice that you should always start by making a plan, but this does not work for everyone. You should find a way which suits you. Each of the authors of this chapter, for example, has a different method of working:

- one gathers information, then writes the whole essay straight off the top of her head, and then goes back and re-drafts and revises it
- the other reads around the topic and gathers some initial information, then creates a rough plan and then produces a draft.

Try different ways of working until you find what is best for you, rather than just doing what you have always done. Something else may work better! Here are some different ways of starting to write. They are in no particular order.

6.5.1 Generating ideas

Brainstorming

The 'rules' are:

- give yourself a time limit (eg *10 minutes*)
- on a big piece of paper, write down all the ideas you can think of about your topic (or speak into a tape recorder)
- do not make any judgements about your ideas, just get them all out, no matter how daft or rude
- think of ideas which 'piggy back' (ie link to or come from) the ideas you've already had.

Then go back over your ideas. Remove those which do look daft or irrelevant (your notes in 6.1.2 and 6.4.1 will help you identify relevance). See which of the other ideas seem appropriate. You could then:

- group ideas together where they seem to be about a similar aspect
- put your grouped ideas into an order which seems to make sense (see Section 6.7 below).

Thinking and clarifying by discussion

Talking about your essay topic to somebody else can help your understanding and get it clear in your mind. If you do this with another student who has the same essay topic, remember that any individual work you hand in must be your own work. You can share ideas and discuss it, but if your work looks too similar to that of somebody else, you may be accused of cheating.

You could even talk to yourself about it, using a tape recorder. Listening to yourself speak on a topic can help you see where it sounds clear and where it seems confused, especially if you leave it for a couple of days before listening.

Creating a flow diagram/mind map

This is similar to brainstorming, but here you put your ideas into a diagram. You link your ideas together with lines or arrows to show relationships between them. Your 'map' may start as a 'doodle', which you refine as your ideas develop.

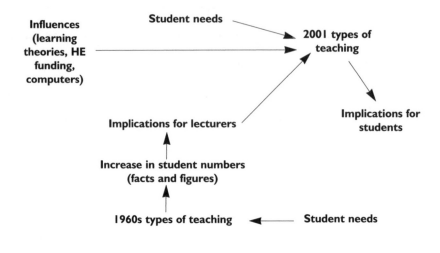

People who are better visually than with words may find this helpful.

Making a plan

You could begin by writing a plan, or create one after brainstorming/drawing a mind map. Writing one at some point may help you identify specific information you need to gather and keep you focused on the topic.

Your notes in 6.1.2 above are the beginnings of such a plan. You would show what you are going to include and in what order. See Section 6.7 below on 'structure' to help you make your plan. How you do a plan will vary with your subject and what works for you. An example is given below.

Example. *The dramatic increase in student numbers in Higher Education has meant that teachers have had to change their teaching methods and to develop new ones. Consider the implications of this for students.*

Plan

Introduction	*Essay will consider implications of recent changes in HE teaching methods*
Para 1	*Reasons for need to change teaching in HE* *Increase in student numbers from 1960–2000*
Para 2	*Increase in funding of HE number of lecturers not proportionate to increase in student numbers* *Reasons for need to change teaching methods* *– students having different learning experiences* *– new understanding of how people learn (eg by doing)* *– increasing use of technology*
Para 3	*What teaching was like up to 1960s*
Para 4	*How teaching approaches have changed*
Para 5	*How new approaches better for students*
Para 6	*How new approaches worse for students*
Conclusions	*Summary of main changes and whether on whole better or worse*

Plunging straight in

Some people start to write a draft straight off, as quickly as possible. They then revise and redraft it – or even re-write it completely.

Word-processing your essay is a great help, as you can cut and paste to move sections of your text, and can save different versions of the essay, in case you decide your early draft of a section was the best.

Which methods for starting to write your current essay will you use?

6.6 Drafting

At some point you must draft your essay. All good writers, no matter what methods they use, produce a draft which they revise and edit to produce a final version.

If you word-process your work you can quite easily make several different drafts, or keep reworking one draft.

If you handwrite your work, you could write your first draft on every other line and leave wide margins. You can use the empty lines to rephrase sections and the margins to show (eg *by lines or arrows*) where to move sections to. You can then handwrite your final version. If possible, have a break of a few days before reviewing your draft, so you come to it with fresh eyes.

If you have 'writers' block' and just cannot put pen to paper or type a word, you could try the following. This suggestion allows you to start writing without worrying about what you write:

- If handwriting, have two sheets of paper with a sheet of carbon paper between them. Write on the top paper using something with a sharp point, but not a pen or pencil. You will not be able to see what you write, but you will be copying it onto the sheet below through the carbon paper. You can look later at what you have written and amend it.

- If word-processing, switch on the computer, type on the keyboard but have your monitor switched off. You will not be able to see what you are typing but you can save it and amend it later.

6.7 Structure

You may have had feedback about the 'structure' of your essays, or tutors may tell you the importance of 'structuring the essay'.

This means how you organise the information/ideas/images in your essay, to make your argument flow or to emphasise your point of view. There are two main reasons why an essay may be difficult to understand – using English incorrectly (eg *poor punctuation*) or a confused structure. Poor use of English will reduce your mark/grade. Your structure can either reduce or increase it.

Essays have a beginning (introduction), a middle (main body), and an end (conclusion) and are divided into paragraphs. The following sections cover these areas.

6.7.1 Introduction

Your essay must have a clear introduction, which explains what you are going to focus on in your essay. It may explain to the reader your approach and how you have interpreted the essay topic or question (in your own words – you should not just repeat the topic word for word). It may say what your main message will be. If you have to prove a statement or hypothesis, it may say what that is.

The introduction should be clear and prepare the reader for what comes next.

Some people write their introduction last, after they have written the main body of the work, by when they are very clear about what they want the introduction to say.

6.7.2 Paragraphs

Paragraphs are the building blocks of an essay. (A paragraph is a number of sentences, grouped together, on an aspect of the topic.) If you are word-processing, it is divided from other paragraphs by an extra line space. If you are handwriting it can be divided by a line space or by indenting the first word, ie moving the first word in a few spaces.

This is a new paragraph. Paragraphs are made up of sentences. All the sentences in a paragraph must follow on from one another and be about the same aspect of the topic. A common fault is to confuse a reader by putting sentences about different things in the same paragraph. What confuses the reader even more is to have a sentence about something different in a paragraph, then several paragraphs later have another sentence about it.

If an aspect of the essay is too big for one paragraph (about a third of a page is the maximum length for a paragraph) break down the aspect into smaller parts and have several paragraphs which follow each other about the aspect.

6.7.3 Putting your paragraphs into an order

Look back at your notes in Section 6.1.2 above. What was your purpose or aim? In what order could you put your ideas and information to best meet your aim? For example:

If you want to show that new teaching methods are better than old ones, you could put a paragraph about the disadvantages of the old methods before one about the advantages of the new ones. This order might make the contrast stand out.

If you want to show that the old teaching methods are better, you might do the reverse.

You may want to show how teaching methods have developed. In this case a chronological order might be best – what happened first comes first.

There is no 'right order'. It depends what message you want to get over.

You could put items in the second box below in the order in which you think of them – then put a number next to each point to show what order might be best for them.

✐

What is the main message you want to get over?

What information or ideas will help you explain that message?

6.7.4 Reviewing your order

Once you have a draft, you can review it to see if the order you have used is best for your 'message'.

The following activity will be more effective if you use your own written work, preferably your current draft essay, or a completed earlier essay.

On a piece of paper write either one word or a few words to show the focus of each paragraph in your draft (or old essay).

You should now have a list of key words describing all your paragraphs. You can now consider the following questions.

Questions about each paragraph
- Are all the sentences in each paragraph about the key word/phrase you have used to describe that paragraph?

- If not, which other paragraph should that sentence be in?

Questions about the order of the paragraphs
- Is there a link between one paragraph and the next? If so what is it? Links might include eg *'We have seen that..., now we can consider...'*, or *'However,...'*, or *'A main idea, therefore,...'*, or *'Another major point is...'*

- If there is no link, does the paragraph comes naturally after the one before it?
  For example in Section 6.6 above there is a paragraph beginning
  'If you handwrite your work...'
  The next paragraph begins
  'If you have 'writers' block...'
  There are no linking words, but the second paragraph does follow on from the first.

- Do you need to change the order of your paragraphs or to add in linking words?

6.7.5 Examples

Clear	To be avoided
Example of a paragraph where all sentences are about the same aspect.	Example of a paragraph which includes sentences about different aspects.
Increasing student numbers, with no increase in funding or number of lecturers, has meant that new ways of teaching have had to be found. This has coincided with the advent of a new type of resource – the computer. A main concern in HE has been to see how the computer can help in teaching, both to make the most of this valuable resource and also to reduce pressure on teaching staff.	*Increasing student numbers, with no increase in funding or number of lecturers, has meant that new ways of teaching have had to be found. There are often problems in using computers for teaching, logging on time, for example. Types of room affect what sort of teaching can be done in them.*
Paragraphs in an order where they follow on from each other. NB these are short paragraphs to make the point quickly.	**Paragraphs not in an order where they follow on from each other. NB these are very short paragraphs to make the point quickly.**
A main concern in HE has been to see how the computer can help in teaching, both to make the most of this valuable resource and also to reduce pressure on teaching staff. *Using computers as a teaching aid does itself require time and effort from teaching staff. Many have found that adapting teaching materials for the computer takes as much time, if not more, than traditional teaching methods.* *However, the benefits of using the computer both to produce work and to find information far outweigh the costs in time in developing teaching approaches using them.*	*There are often problems in using computers for teaching, logging on time, for example. Students can become frustrated by network systems which do not work well.* *Types of room affect what sort of teaching can be done in them. There are limited teaching activities you can do in a tiered lecture theatre.* *Libraries are changing in nature. Many are being renamed 'Learning Centre' and the librarian's job is changing too.*
	Paragraphs which do not follow on from each other and where not all the sentences in one paragraph are related to one aspect. This is the most confusing (and also quite common).

Clear	Confusing
	There are often problems in using computers for teaching, logging on time, for example. Types of room affect what sort of teaching can be done in them.
	Libraries are changing in nature. Many are being renamed 'Learning Centre' and the librarian's job is changing too. Students can become frustrated by network systems which do not work well.
	There are limited teaching activities you can do in a tiered lecture theatre.

6.7.6 Conclusion

Your last paragraph should not include new ideas or information not covered earlier in your essay. It should round off the essay and draw it to a close. There are various ways of doing this. Which of the following would suit your essay? There may be more than one.

✔

Summarise the main points you have made	
State what you think are the main features of the topic	
Make a judgement about or evaluate aspects of your topic	
Make recommendation about what you think should happen	
Highlight any further areas you think need investigating or further issues to be explored	
Restate a hypotheses you set out to prove	
Other ideas	

6.8 Language

6.8.1 Academic language

You need to use language in a way which makes your meaning clear and which meets 'academic' expectations. Whatever your subject area your tutors will want you to use appropriate, and often, formal academic language in your essay. This is different from spoken English.

For example:

'We could of done that, no problem.'

Although this is fine in speech, it is unacceptable in an essay. It is not grammatically correct (it should be *'We could **have** done that'*) and it uses a slang phrase (*'no problem'*).

To convey the same meaning you would need to write, depending on whether you use the personal or passive voice in your subject area, either eg:

'We would have been able to do that without difficulty'
or
'It would have been possible to do that without difficult'.

Some slang phrases are so common they may seem acceptable to you. Until you get used to what is acceptable and what isn't (in an essay that would have to be 'is not'), ask somebody else to read what you have written and to point out any slang or parts which look like spoken English.

6.8.2 Correct use of English

Incorrect use of English may reduce your marks or grades. Tutors see this as important because it helps them understand your work, and also because any employers in the future will expect you to use good written English.

Areas to look out for include:

- **spelling correctly** – use a spell checker or a dictionary; ask somebody else to look at your work. If you are dyslexic word-processing your work can be a great help, because of the spell checker.

- **punctuation** – punctuating something wrongly may alter. The whole meaning of a sentence. Sorry, we meant 'Punctuating something wrongly may alter the whole meaning of a sentence'. Check your punctuation. Get somebody to read your draft and to point out mistakes you commonly make, to help you avoid them in the future. Use a book on grammar or punctuation (see the references for this chapter for suggestions).

- **grammar** – this can also make the difference between understanding and not understanding your work. Again, ask somebody to read your draft and to point out your common mistakes. Use a book on grammar (see the references for this chapter for suggestions).

6.9 Style

6.9.1 Choice of words

You need to use a style which helps your reader understand your meaning and argument. Style is partly about the words you use. Check what is acceptable in your subject area. Are certain technical terms common? If so, you can use them without explaining. If not, you may need to explain them or use other words.

You can create an impression by the type of words you use (eg *technical/non-technical, long/short*). What sort of impression do you want to create and what sort of words will do so?

Generally, it is better to use simple words the reader will understand. Using long or unusual words the reader has difficulty in understanding is not good practice (but some subjects do expect you to use quite sophisticated language). Look at other sorts of items written in your subject area (eg *journal article*s) and check with your tutor what is expected.

6.9.2 Length of sentences

Short sentences can be easy to understand, but if you only use short sentences, your essay may look simplistic and become tedious to read. Long sentences are more 'sophisticated', but too many following each other can be hard to read after a while. Very long sentences can be confusing.

A mix is probably best, but again, think what impression you want to create and what sort of mix would best create this.

6.9.3 Layout

How you present your work will help the reader follow it, but check what is expected in your subject area. In some subjects you can include sub-headings and visual images such as diagrams, but not in others.

Whatever the conventions in your subject, make sure the reader can easily read and find their way through your essay (eg *page numbers, 'white space', ie with no text, to break it up, neat*).

If there are requirements for the layout and length (see Section 6.1.2 above), follow them. Make sure you have a correct list of references.

What do you need to keep in mind for your subject and topic? (eg words, sentences, layout)

6.10 Editing

Once you have your final draft you need to edit it to make sure it will get the mark/grade you want. The following checklist may help.

✔

Does it meet the requirements you identified in Section 6.1.2 above?	
Does it answer the questions you identified in Section 6.4.1 above?	
Does it have a beginning, a middle and an end?	
Are all the sentences in a paragraph about one aspect?	
Do the paragraphs follow on from each other?	
Are the paragraphs in the best order to get your message across?	
Is your spelling correct?	
Is your punctuation correct?	
Is your grammar correct?	
Have you used formal academic language?	
Have you used appropriate words for your subject area?	
Have you used an appropriate mix of long and short sentences?	
Have you referenced others' work correctly?	
Does your layout help the reader and make the work look attractive?	

6.11 Improving what you do

You can evaluate how good your essay is by:

- using the editing checklist given in Section 6.10 above
- reviewing it against the assessment criteria (see Section 6.1).

You can then ask yourself what you most need to improve in producing essays and how to do so, eg you could:

- *work through this chapter again*
- *use the books suggested in the references for this chapter*
- *talk to friends or your tutor.*

What I need to improve	Sources of help	By (date)

Thanks to the following for their ideas, which have contributed to this version: Phil Bannister, Peter Hartley, Teresa Lillis, Noel Williams.

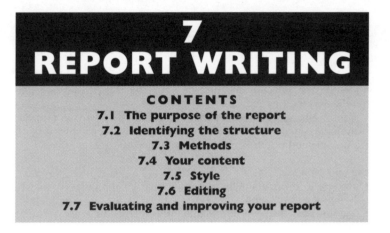

7
REPORT WRITING

CONTENTS

This chapter aims to improve your report writing skills. The way you write a report for an assignment will have a major influence on your grade.

What is the difference between a report and an essay?

Essays are mainly used in education. They use information to explore ideas and arguments, and their main purpose is to practise these skills and demonstrate your abilities to lecturers. They are usually more discursive.

'A report is a communication of information or advice from a person who has collected and studied the facts, to a person who has asked for the report because they need it for a specific purpose.' (Stanton 1990, p243)

Reports are the most usual way of communicating the results of projects or investigations – for employers, charities, government, political organisations. They should be concise and have a specific structure.

People who need reports are busy. A good report is one you don't need to re-read to get the point.

Courses require report writing to give you practise at producing information in a relevant way for employment.

We suggest you use this chapter:

- **in relation to a particular report you are writing**
- **before you begin any work, to see what is required, and while you are gathering your information**
- **to help you write and edit the report.**

When you have completed it, you should be able to:

Plan work
- identify the features of a report and when reports are used
- identify the purpose and audience for the report, and how this influences it
- identify an appropriate/accepted structure and style for your purpose, audience, situation and the subject matter, including complex subjects
- plan time and resource and information needs.

Use your plan
- produce a report in an appropriate format for the purpose, subject, audience and situation
- organise and present information/ideas/images to make meaning clear
- use style and language to make meaning clear
- edit/redraft to ensure coherence and clarity, following standard conventions of grammar, spelling and punctuation
- pull together and include information which is accurate, identifying any opinion and bias
- use academic conventions (eg *referencing*).

Review work
- evaluate the report's effectiveness for its purpose, subject, audience and situation
- identify ways of improving the report.

(Based on QCA Key Skill specifications, QCA 2000)

7.1 The purpose of the report

It is important to make sure your report fits the purpose and meets its aims.

- **Your audience.** Who is your report for? What are the readers' needs and characteristics? What will they know about the topic? (eg *if your topic is technical but your readers are not technical people, you need to explain things in non-technical language*).

- **Your aims.** What end result do you want – to inform, persuade, recommend? Will it lead to decisions, or policies (eg *a report to property developers wanting to decide on the use of a building would need to indicate the options, costs and profits*)?

  If your report is assessed do you know what will get a pass grade (the assessemnt criteria)? Your report will need to meet these criteria.

- **Your topic and focus.** What is the main subject area and which particular aspect/issues will you cover (eg *a report for estate agents might cover Sheffield, and the housing needs of a particular area within it*)?

If in doubt, ask your lecturer.

Your topic and focus	Your aims	Reader characteristics

What will these mean for your report?

Implications for the report

7.2 Identifying the structure

An appropriate and clear structure is essential, to help your reader understand and follow your meaning.

There is no one correct format for a report and it helps to ask your lecturers what they expect (eg *there may be an accepted way of producing a lab report on your course*).

A general rule which is applicable in most situations is:

- tell them what you are going to tell them
- tell them
- tell them what you have told them.

The following gives examples of possible formats. Example 1 may be more appropriate for formal, large reports (eg *Government reports*) rather than for a short report to colleagues. Examples 2, 3 and 4 may be more usual in our courses.

1	2	3
(The preliminaries) Title page Terms of reference Contents List of tables/figures Foreword Acknowledgements Abstracts/synopsis **(The main part)** Introduction Findings Conclusions **(Supplementary)** References/bibliography Appendices Index *From Stanton 1990*	Title page Aims/objectives Methodology (eg *for gathering information*) Findings Conclusions Recommendations References/ Bibliography Appendices	**(A possible format for a lab report)** Aims Methods Results Conclusions

		4
		Title page Summary Table of contents Body of report (introductions, findings, conclusions) Appendices Index *From Peel 1990*

The following clarifies the terms given in the above examples.

NB: Not all the following elements are needed in all reports (eg *an index is only needed for long reports where readers need to locate items; not all reports have terms of reference; a list of abbreviations/terminology might help if the readers are unfamiliar with them, but not otherwise*).

Title	Full title of the report – must give a clear idea about its focus
Author	Names of all those producing the report
Date	Date of publication (or handing-in date)
Summary	Gives the key points. It can be used at the start so those with no time to read the report can grasp the main points, or at the end to draw things together. It should only contain information covered in the main part, and it should be short.
Abstract/synopsis	A short paragraph at the beginning of a report which says what is in it and allows readers to see if it is relevant to them
Acknowledgements	Thanks to people or organisations who have helped
Terms of reference/remit	Specification by those commissioning a report of what they want. Indicates the scope of the report (eg *if the report is to consider chemical pollution in Yorkshire rivers, it would be outside its terms of reference to consider air pollution, or pollution in Devon*)
Foreword	Sets the scene (eg *why the report is needed, why it is important*)
Aims	The overall purpose of the report (eg *to investigate chemical pollution in Yorkshire rivers*)
Objectives	More specifically what you want to achieve (eg *to identify the causes of chemical pollution, to identify solutions*)
Introduction	Outlines what the report is about. May include background to the report, aims, objectives
Method	How you gathered information, where from, and how much (eg *if you used a survey – who was surveyed, how did you decide on the target group, how many were surveyed, how were they surveyed – by interview or questionnaire?*)
Findings/results	Statement of what you found out (eg *results of an experiment or survey or project*) with the interpretation and analysis
Conclusions	Drawing together your findings
Recommendations	What you think should happen
References/ bibliography	References are items referred to in the report. A bibliography is of additional material not specifically referred to, but which readers may want to follow up.
Appendices	Detailed information which is important but may distract from the flow of the report can be included.
Index	Alphabetical list of topics covered, with page or section numbers where they can be found

You need to use those sections which:

* will most suit your audience and topic
* help you achieve your aims
* suit your situation (eg *year/stage of your course, resources you can get, other commitments*).

You could:

* check with your assignment information
* look at examples in your subject area
* ask your tutor
* ask people working in the professional area/colleagues.

7.3 Methods

7.3.1 Planning your time

To meet your deadline it helps to break what you need to do into smaller tasks and make a plan, identifying how long each task will take. On average drafting, editing and presenting the report will take as long as gathering the information – it is common to underestimate this. In identifying your tasks, refer back to your aims (Section 7.1).

In the resources/support column, identify what and who might be useful (eg *specialists for advice on information or designing methods; materials to help you use a particular IT package*).

Tasks	Resources/ support needed	Time needed to complete	Deadline

You might find Chapters 3 and 20 on 'Organising Yourself and Your Time' and Chapters 18 and 32 on 'Action Planning' helpful.

7.3.2 Gathering information

This chapter focuses on writing the report rather than on gathering information for it. Chapter 5 on 'Gathering and Using Information' in Part I will help you here.

Your information may be gathered from:

- your own research/investigations
- published material
- unpublished work by others.

The following are particularly important to keep in mind.

- Identifying your purpose will help you see what information you need.
- The reader should be able to trace your information. This means you need a good recording system when you gather it, with all the details needed for when you produce the report. For further help on referencing, see Chapter 5 on 'Gathering and Using Information' in Part I or ask learning centre/library staff for advice.
- You need to give evidence for any arguments, views or conclusions. You need to identify any information based on opinion or biased in any way – see Chapter 22 on 'Critical Analysis' in Part II.

If you have collected the evidence yourself (eg *from an experiment or a survey*) you need to include how you gathered it, as well as what the evidence is. Again, this means having a good recording system.

- You may need permission to use the material (eg *from an author, employer or other source of the information*).

7.4 Your content

On university/college courses, you may need to manage complex information/ideas, where you must identify underlying aspects and make links between different ideas. These will need to be presented in a logical and clear manner.

7.4.1 Main points

You should identify the key points to include in your report. Look back at your audience and aims (Section 7.1).

Main points

Which points should have the most emphasis?

What is the best sequence for your main points? The content of the report should be ordered logically to fit the purpose. Possibilities are chronologically (what happened first goes first), by themes or following a line of argument (eg *if you want to persuade it may be good to start with a punchy key point*). Refer back to your aims identified in Section 7.1. You could look at your list of points and number them, in an order to help make your meaning clear.

7.4.2 The quality of your information

You need to identify any opinion or bias in the information you use. Further guidance is given in Chapter 22 on 'Critical Analysis' in Part II.

An **opinion** is an idea for which there is no evidence. At university it is bad practice to give an opinion without evidence and without stating that it is only an opinion.

Bias is where the information/evidence may be distorted or viewed from a particular standpoint, without acknowledging other interpretations/information.

You could identify:
- any possible reasons for bias in yourself (eg *based on your values or political views*). Ask
  – am I presenting this objectively?
  – how would somebody with opposing views present this information?
- others' assumptions. Might the sources of your information be biased?
- distorted information. Information might be distorted on purpose or by accident. Can you identify distortion and the reasons for it?

Information	Evidence	Possible bias

When you have collected and evaluated your information, use the checklist below.

✔

Is the information	
relevant to your aims?	
relevant to your readers?	
up to date?	
accurate?	
correctly referenced?	
covering your main points?	
supported by evidence?	
necessary?	
evaluated for opinion or bias?	

7.5 Style

7.5.1 Appropriate language

You can change the impression created by the language you use. The language needs to make your meaning clear, reflect the aims of the report and help the reader understand it.

- It helps to be precise (eg *'The victims may have been hit with a blunt instrument'* – were they or weren't they?). A thesaurus or *Gower's Plain Words* (see references at the end of book) can help in identifying words to use.
- Reports need to be concise. Can you 'tighten' up your writing?

  eg *'Salaries which are paid to teachers make up 65% of the school budget.'*
  'Teachers' salaries make up 65% of the school budget.'

  eg *'The committee took into consideration the adoption of the proposal.'*
  'The committee considered adopting the proposal.'

- Explain words/terms your reader may not understand.
- Abbreviations should be written in full first with the abbreviation in brackets, after which the abbreviation can be used (eg *Personal and Professional Development (PPD)*, *after which you would use PPD*).
  You need to be consistent – use the same abbreviation throughout (eg *always PPD*, *not sometimes Ppd or PpD*). To avoid confusion, be consistent in your punctuation, underlining, capital letters and 'bullets'.
- Use short sentences.
- A good dictionary is important and if using a word processor, a 'spell check' is invaluable.

Look at examples of reports for your subject. What sort of language do they use? To make it more formal:

- use the third person (eg *'it was felt that...'*, *rather than 'I felt tha...'*)
- avoid emotive words (ie feelings)
- avoid humour (beware, people's senses of humour vary).

Where do you need to improve your writing?

Improvements needed in my writing

7.5.2 Presentation

Presentation can make a report clearer.

Layout

- **Overall impact** – typed or word-processed reports are preferable, or at least use very neat writing. Big blocks of text are off-putting, so short paragraphs help. Also consider cost. Is it worth spending a lot of time and money on the presentation, or will something simple but clear be adequate?

- **Headings** – if you look at this chapter you will see there are three styles of headings - one for main sections, one for sub-sections, one for further sub-sections.

- **Numbering** – numbering your sections makes things clearer. An increasingly common system is to number a main section (eg *1*), then for sub-sections to place a dot after the main section number and begin to number again (eg *1.1*). You can continue to a further level (eg *1.1.1*).

It can help to number each paragraph. It is easier to refer the reader to 'item 4.5.2' than to 'about half way down page 6'. The following example gives possible headings and section numbers for a report on public transport in Sheffield.

Appendices often use Roman numerals, eg *Appendix (iii)*.

Example

1   INTRODUCTION
1.1   Background
1.2   Aims
1.3   Objectives

2   METHODS
2.1   The questionnaire
2.2   The sample group

3   FINDINGS
3.1   Response rate
3.2   Findings
      3.2.1 Who are the transport users
      3.2.2 Transport routes
      3.2.3 Users' opinions of transport provision

4   CONCLUSIONS

5   RECOMMENDATIONS
5.1   Public Transport
5.2   Private Transport

6   REFERENCES

7   APPENDICES
      (i)   The questionnaire
      (ii) Summary tables

Use of images/visuals
Images/visuals are best used:

- to make something clearer (eg *tables or graphs*) rather than to 'pretty things up'
- when something is difficult to describe in words/visual in nature (eg *photographs, maps*)
- to show how something works (eg *diagrams, flow charts or algorithms*).

For example, *in car driving...*

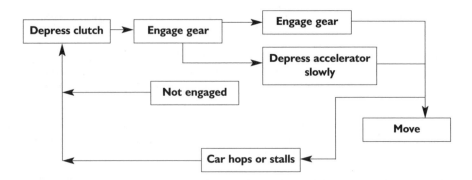

Some words of caution

Will readers be familiar with your images eg *accountants may use '+' on a balance sheet for outgoings and '–' for income (for most of us the reverse seems more logical)*?

Are your visuals misleading? A short book, referred to in the reference section, by Huff (1973), indicates how statistics can 'lie'.

Images to be included

7.6 Editing

You will need at least one draft before your final version. It can help to put it on one side for a few days before re-reading. You will be more distanced from it and able to spot shortcomings. Word processing makes it easier to amend a report. The following checklist should help.

The purpose

Have you clarified your purpose?	
Have you identified your readers' needs/characteristics?	

Information

Have you included the main points?	
Are points supported by evidence?	
Is the information relevant to the purpose?	

Accuracy

(Readers often delight in spotting what seem like tiny errors, which can then put the accuracy of the report into question.) ✔

Are there spelling mistakes?	
Is the grammar/punctuation correct?	
Do figures add up?	
Are the references correct, in the text and at the end?	
Are all sources of information listed in the 'references' section?	
Are abbreviations consistent?	

Format ✔

Is there a balance between sections? Do the most important items take up the most space?	
Is the report easy to follow?	
Is it easy to find information in the report?	
Are headings and numbering clear?	
Are the arguments followed through?	
Is it logical/easy to follow?	

Language ✔

Is it clear, direct, easy to read?	
Will the readers understand it?	
Will its tone help you achieve the purpose?	
Can unnecessary words/phrases be deleted?	
Is there any repetition?	

Presentation ✔

Is the layout appealing?	
Does it highlight important points?	
Are images clear?	

Finally...

...it's a good idea to keep a copy of your report and background notes – just in case the reader loses it, you need to revise it, you need to produce a further report, somebody wants to check your data.

7.7 Evaluating and improving your report

To help you judge how effective your report was, you could:

* look at any assessment criteria, to see how far it meets them
* look at your aims (see Section 7.1), to see if you've met them
* use feedback (eg *from tutors, other students, employers*).

Positive aspects of my report	Weaker aspects of my report

What could you do to improve your report, to get the best possible mark/grade? Who or what would be helpful (eg *sections in this chapter, friends, colleagues*)?

Actions	Resources/support needed	Deadline

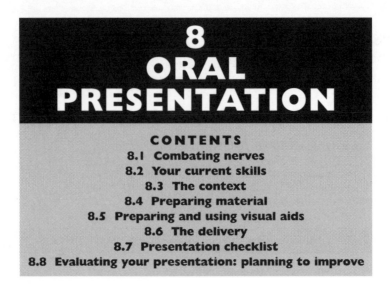

8
ORAL
PRESENTATION

CONTENTS

On many courses students give seminar papers, or make individual or group presentations about their work. Some students have better verbal than written skills. Presentations provide an alternative way for students to demonstrate their abilities.

Employers want to recruit graduates or higher diplomates with good verbal skills. Some jobs require you to make oral presentations, others may not but they do require the same verbal communication skills used when making presentations – presenting information, arguing a case, persuading, negotiating, explaining. Students are required to give presentations as part of courses to help them practise these skills

This chapter aims to help you make better presentations, and to combat the nervousness most of us feel.

We suggest you use this chapter:

- **to help you prepare for a particular presentation, either individual or group.**

When you have completed it, you should be able to:

Prepare a presentation
- review your current skills in giving presentations on various topics, including a complex one
- identify the aim, purpose, audience, topic, context
- suit the aim, purpose, audience, topic, context (eg *location*)
- produce appropriate materials, using relevant information (eg *speaker's notes, handouts, visual/audio aids*)
- structure the presentation to aid understanding
- plan to handle nerves.

Deliver a presentation
- in an appropriate way for the aim, purpose, audience, topic, context (eg *dress, style, manner, voice, use of visual/audio aids/handouts*)
- use techniques to engage the audience (eg *visual aids, examples, relate to the audience's experience, vary tone of voice*)
- deal with questions.

Evaluate your presentation
- identify how effective the presentation was and factors affecting this
- identify how to improve in the future.

(Based on QCA Key Skill specifications, QCA 2000)

8.1 Combating nerves

Being prepared and organised can be the biggest help in combating nerves. Avoid doing things at the last minute. You could also:

- rehearse in advance
- remind yourself that everybody feels nervous. Audiences often don't notice nerves, and if they do will make allowances.
- ask what is the worst thing that could happen and prepare for it (eg *Drying up? Have good speaker's notes. Awkward questions? Work out in advance what they might be*)
- try to relax. Relaxation techniques include deep breathing, tensing and then relaxing muscles, visualising a pleasant scene. 'Last minuting' will increase tension.
- have a glass of water ready
- use visual aids (the audience looks at them, not at you)
- have effective speakers' notes.

What do you usually do when you are nervous? What could you do about it? Who or what might help? You may find Chapter 14 on 'Coping with Pressure' in Part I helpful.

My symptoms of nerves are	Actions I could take

8.2 Your current skills

8.2.1 Identifying effective presentations

You might find it helpful to think about a presentation you enjoyed (by a teacher, lecturer, other students, salesperson, politician), and compare it with one you thought boring and uninteresting. What were the main differences? Try to identify what makes presentations good or bad. Does the situation in which the presentation takes place influence what is appropriate?

Presenter	What they do

8.2.2 Identifying your current skills

The following is similar to the assessment sheets tutors use to judge presentations. You can use it to help you identify what you feel you can do very well and where you need to give attention. It uses a scale where 1 is 'very well' and 4 is 'needs considerable improvement'.

✔

Aims for the presentation	1	2	3	4
Ceing clear about your aims				
Making them clear to the audience				

Material	1	2	3	4
Researching				
Arguing/explaining it				
Making it relevant to the topic/audience				

The delivery	1	2	3	4
Keeping to time				
Having a varied mix of inputs/visual aids				
Having relevant visual aids				
Having clear visual aids		.		
Making it appropriate for the topic/audience/aims				
Getting audience involvement/interest				
Being confident				
Projecting voice/self/content				
Dealing with questions				

This chapter deals with all the above issues.

8.3 The context

8.3.1 Aims and purpose

What do you want to achieve? Is the presentation to inform, train, persuade, entertain, sell, demonstrate? Being clear about this helps identify what to cover or omit, and what approach to use. For example:

- if to **inform** or **explain** – it helps to have a logical order, use examples, analogies (eg *'It's a bit like…'*)
- if to **persuade** – it helps to be convincing, use evidence, and show enthusiasm.

It can help to ask yourself increasingly focused questions.

- What is the **subject** (eg *'access for the disabled to buildings'*)?
- What is the **theme** (eg *'how to improve this access'*)?
- What is the **main point** or **'angle'** (eg *'current access is really poor'*)?
- What are the **objectives**/what do you want to achieve (eg *'to encourage better access'*)?

Subject	Theme	Point/angle	Objectives

8.3.2 The audience

Thinking about the audience is essential to pitch a presentation correctly.

Who will your audience be? What will they expect or need? How many will there be? One lecturer, other students, a mix?

What are the characteristics of your particular audience (eg *age, gender mix, interests, level of knowledge and experience with the topic*)?

What do these factors mean for your presentation (eg *type of language, degree of formality, your dress*)?

Audience characteristics	Implications for your presentation

8.3.3 Time

How long will your presentation be? The time may be specified by the tutor, but if you can decide for yourself you will find that 20 minutes is probably the maximum time. More than that can be tedious for the audience.

If you have longer than 20 minutes to fill, you could try to break your presentation up with different sorts of activities (see later sections for suggestions). Allow time at the beginning for people to settle. Will you allow time for questions? If it is a group presentation how will you divide the time between the presenters?

8.3.4 The room

The location and seating arrangement can influence what you do. It helps to look at the room in advance.

Presenter	Presenter	Presenter
Enables discussion, but visual aids hard to see for many.	Enables discussion, visual aids hard to see for some.	Better for a talk. Limits discussion. Can see visual aids well.

What equipment will be available (eg *overhead projector (OHP)*, *whiteboard*, *flip chart*, *computer*)?

8.4 Preparing material

On university/college courses, you may need to manage complex information/ideas, where you must identify underlying aspects and make links between different ideas. These will need to be presented in a logical and clear manner.

Preparing your material in good time will reduce anxiety. Knowing your topic well increases confidence. If preparing for a group presentation, you need to agree clearly who is preparing what material. Putting it in writing can avoid confusion.

8.4.1 Selecting material

Chapter 5 on 'Gathering and Using Information' in Part I will help you get information together. You then need to consider how to select material bearing in mind your topic, aims, audience, time allowed, and the room. The following questions may help.

Is all your material relevant to your aims and audience?

What key messages do you want to get over?

How long will it take to deliver the material (a rehearsal, possibly in front of a friend, may help you find out)?

What could you omit if you run out of time?

What are the absolute essentials (audiences tend to be able to take in less than you think)?

What could be added if you have time to spare?

8.4.2 Structuring the material

Structure helps your audience understand your presentation. How could the material be ordered? You could write it up, get an overview and then decide on an order, or write the main points on cards and shuffle them until the best order emerges.

A general rule is to:

- tell them what you are going to tell them (the beginning)
- tell them (the middle)
- tell them what you told them (the end).

Tell them what you are going to tell them (the beginning)

Making the format clear to the audience at the start means they know what to expect (eg *'Please could you leave questions till the end'*, *'Please ask questions as we go through'*).

Outline the content you will cover (eg *'I am going to talk about the poor provision for disabled people'*).

You need to set the tone and grab attention. Do something you feel comfortable with. Beginnings can include:

- a question
- a visual aid
- a true story
- a provocative statement
- a quotation
- a surprise (eg *a surprising statistic*)
- a joke (but if not funny, can embarrass).

Tell them (the middle)

Putting material into 'chunks' rather than flitting from one point to another helps the audience follow what you are saying. You need to decide on the best order for your 'chunks' (eg *for the topic of disability you could 'chunk' by type of disability or by problems faced*). The following questions may help:

- Are you explaining something where one step follows from another?
- Is date or time order important?
- Do you need to give one side of an argument, then the next?

Without structure audiences can become confused or bored. The following are ways of creating structure:

- verbal clues (eg *'We've looked at the access problems for disabled people, now we'll look at possible solutions'*)
- visual aids (eg *a new OHP slide can signal a change of topic or new point*)
- having varied activities (eg *asking for questions, asking if the audience have understood before moving on*)
- for group presentations, using different presenters (eg *'Now Jane will look at...'*).

Tell them what you told them (the end)

Possible endings include:

- briefly repeat the main points and draw them together
- emphasise the main point or 'angle'
- some of the 'beginnings' can be useful here too – a visual aid, an anecdote
- if discussion was involved, review the main points or future implications (eg *'It looks like we need to focus on... in the future'*)
- thank the audience.

8.4.3 Speakers' notes

Speakers' notes are important, especially if you are nervous, but a speaker reading a script can be boring and uninteresting. There are various ways of making notes, and it depends what works for you.

- Cards. Put each main point with notes on a card, and number the cards.
- Use OHP slides to remind you of the points.
- Notes on sheets of paper under bold headings. Margins can be used to show how long each section should take (and in group presentations, who is covering it).
- Write difficult sections in full, but rehearse and use notes to reassure, not to read from. Use marker pens to highlight key points.
- Mind maps, eg

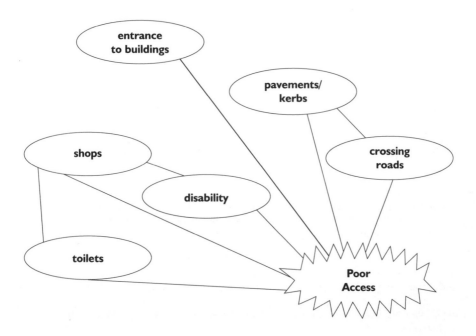

8.4.4 Preparing a group presentation

Many courses require you to give a presentation with others. How will the group prepare for it? You could:

- allocate tasks, so the workload is even
- allocate tasks according to group members strengths (eg *one may have expert computer presentation skills*)
- met regularly for progress checks
- agree deadlines and stick to them.

Further guidance is given in Chapter 11 on 'Group Work' in Part I.

8.5 Preparing and using visual aids

8.5.1 Preparation

> Visual aids grab attention, help the audience understand, make the presentation look professional, and help you if you are nervous (the audience will look at the visual aid – not at you).

Visual aids need to be clear, usable, visible (bold, big, avoid pastel colours) (eg *it is best to have few words on an OHP*). What would make more impact – using the above paragraph as an OHP slide or the format below?

Visual aids

- get attention

- aid understanding

- look professional

- help nerves

Different visual aids suit different purposes (see the following chart).

8.5.2 Usage

Simple is good, and complex can go wrong. An audience cannot focus on too many things at once. Try not to use too many visual aids (think of watching friends' holiday slides). A rough guide is one OHP for a two minute input.

It is important to make good use of them as the audience will be confused if you don't refer to them, and it is important to practise using them in advance. When using visual aids look at the audience, not at the aid or at the projected image behind you.

The following chart gives an overview of different visual aids, with their strengths and weaknesses.

Visual Aid	Good for	Cautions
Black/white board	Spontaneous use, simple messages, permanent background information.	Have spare pen, chalk, duster, rubber. Use quickly, can interrupt flow.
Flip chart	Background information, revealing successive bits of 'story', can record ideas from discussions and keep for future reference.	Cumbersome to use, needs to be bold, leaving it up can distract.
Overhead projector (OHP)	Prepared slides or write on acetate during presentation, can have complex 'overlays' of slides.	Turn off when not using, cover words not referring to as can distract, get slides in right order (paper between each one helps), check right way up and that all slide appears on the screen. Learn to focus in advance.
Slide projector	Real photos, makes an impact.	Use preloaded magazine, check slides right way up, learn to focus in advance, can leave slides on too long/short a time, can inhibit discussion.
Video	Real/live input. Entertaining.	Load, rewind, check sound/picture in advance. Select sections to use.
Film	Real/live input. Entertaining.	Have a projectionist, preview the material, have a contingency plan in case the film breaks.
Objects (models experiments, products)	Demonstrates, makes an impact, explains a process, makes a dry subject interesting.	Model/experiment – ensure it will work. Big enough to see. Allow time to pass item round the audience, can distract.

(Left axis, top to bottom: Cheap/simple → More complex/expensive)

8.5.3 Handouts

Handouts can be very useful in your presentation:

- to give more detailed information
- to give information which is too long for OHP slides
- to give the audience instructions (eg *if you want them to do something in the presentation*)
- to give further information the audience can follow up (eg *references*).

Handouts should:

* help the audience
* reflect what's important in your presentation
* be well laid out
* be correctly spelt and accurate
* be as short as possible
* not be too many as to confuse the audience
* be cheap to produce (photocopies are expensive)
* be sufficient in number (how many people will be there?).

8.6 The delivery

8.6.1 Dress

What clothes would be most appropriate for this audience?
What will make you feel comfortable and confident?

8.6.2 Organisation

Being well organised helps.

Try, within the room's limits, to organise seating in advance or just before the presentation starts.

Arriving at the last minute means you can be thrown if all is not as expected (eg *OHP not working, seating in the wrong arrangement*).

Have your notes and visual aids handy and ordered – not being able to find something can fluster you. Where will you put them during the presentation?

8.6.3 Timekeeping

Put your watch where you can see it easily, or for group presentations give each other warnings (eg *'You've got 2 minutes left'*). Running over time means other speakers have less time, can throw the organisation of the event, and can bore the audience.

A rehearsal will help.

8.6.4 Your voice and manner

If you think your voice might be monotonous break things up: use visual aids; ask questions of the audience; change pace; use pauses.

A speaker's mannerisms can be distracting (eg *swaying, playing with your hair, covering your mouth, fidgeting*). Getting feedback about this from others can help, as can videoing presentations to help you see your mannerisms. What could you do about them (eg *give your hands something to do, like hold prompt cards*)?

In group presentations the behaviour of those not currently speaking can distract (eg *chatting, passing notes, looking uninterested*).

8.6.5 Relating to your audience

Relating to your audience is very important and you need to create a 'rapport' with them (eg *by making eye contact try not to stare at one individual, but to 'scan' the group*). Can the audience see and hear you? If unsure, ask them. If you speak quietly, practise projecting your voice. Speak to the person at the back of the room, not the front.

Don't turn your back on the audience or look at the OHP screen. You might not be heard and you could lose the 'rapport'. Use a pointer (like a pen). Ensure everyone can see your model/screen/experiment, and if you are writing on a white/blackboard or flip chart, write quickly and use large lettering.

You need to get your audience to understand your points, so, when illustrating and emphasising your ideas/information, use examples which are relevant to your audience and which might relate to their experience.

When is the best time to give out your handouts? Don't irritate your audience by letting them take notes, only to be told at the end that you have a handout with all the information. If you hand them out at the beginning, your audience may look at them rather than listen to you, so allow time for them to read.

8.6.6 Dealing with questions

Will you ask the audience for questions? It can be important to reinforce your message and show your audience you thoroughly understand the material.

Dealing with questions should not be hard if you are well prepared and identify possible questions in advance:

- check that you understand the question
- waffling is obvious, it is better to admit ignorance
- you could pass the question back to the questioner or to others (eg *'What do you think?'*). This can generate discussion (but it may not be appropriate if the questioner is assessing you (eg *your tutor*).
- in a group presentation it helps to have somebody chairing questions. This means questioners address that person, she or he checks what the question means and then asks somebody in the group to reply. The 'chair' decides how many questions to take, and when to end the questionning session (eg *'Thank you. We will need to move on/end now'*).

8.6.7 Delivering a group presentation

How will the group organise the delivery? Possibilities are:

- each person presents the topic/area they have covered
- one person acts as 'narrator' and others contribute as needed
- each person has a specific task/responsibility (eg *for showing visual aids, dealing with questions, reporting findings*).

The group should practise the presentation together, rather than each person preparing their section and then putting it together on the day. You need to:

- check your timing
- ensure the presentation 'flows' and that links between sections are logical
- practise using visual aids
- ensure the behaviour of those currently not speaking will not distract the audience.

You may find it helpful to look at Chapter 11 on 'Group Work' in Part I.

8.6.8 Techniques which would help me

You could make a note of the techniques mentioned in 8.6.1–8.6.7, which might be helpful.

✍

Delivery techniques which would particularly help me

8.7 Presentation checklist

Are you prepared? The following checklist can act as a reminder: ✔

Identify aims	
Identify audience characteristics	
Identify time allowance for the presentation	
Check out the room	
Get material together	
Decide on a format and structure	
For group presentations, divide up roles and tasks for preparation and on the day	
Speakers' notes	
Prepare visual aids and handouts	
Be organised on the day	
The delivery • the beginning • the middle • the end	
Relating to your audience	
Dealing with questions	
Coping with nerves	

Watching others' presentations (there may be videos available in libraries) and getting feedback on your presentations can be very helpful.

8.8 Evaluating your presentation: planning to improve

Was your presentation effective? What influenced what you did (eg *audience response, time you allocated for questions*)? What affect did that have?

Reviewing what you did to prepare and deliver it will help you improve next time.

Preparing the presentation	
Main strengths	Main areas to improve

Delivering the presentation	
Main strengths	Main areas to improve

What will you do to improve for the next time you give a presentation?

Action needed	Resources/support needed	Deadline

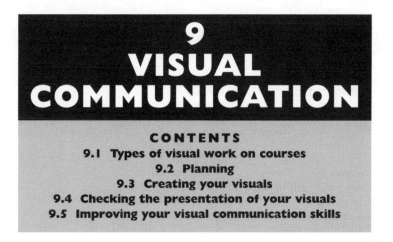

9
VISUAL
COMMUNICATION

CONTENTS
9.1 Types of visual work on courses
9.2 Planning
9.3 Creating your visuals
9.4 Checking the presentation of your visuals
9.5 Improving your visual communication skills

We live in a world where visuals are increasingly important – a world of TV, film, video, posters. We are used to seeing high quality visual images wherever we go. This means that people have high expectations for the quality of visuals – they have to be good.

Using visual images is important for many reasons, some include:

- to make things clearer and help others understand – some things can only be understood visually (eg *a map*)
- to make an impact
- to make the appearance more attractive.

On all courses you need to present information in visual ways (eg *a word-processed essay is enhanced by an attractive layout*).

This is a huge area, worthy of a book in its own right. All we aim to do here is to suggest some principles which apply for any visuals, and to consider some of the main ways in which visual information is presented on courses. It is at starter level only.

We suggest you use this chapter:

- **when you need to use specific visual images (eg *tables, graphs, photos, visual aids, works of art etc*)**
- **generally, to help you think about the visual presentation of your work**
- **if you need to produce visuals for course work (eg *for assessed work*)**
- **if you need to present visuals to others (eg *employers, clients*).**

This chapter focuses on the general visual skills all students need, rather than on specialised visual skills (eg *of artists and designers – although they too should find it useful, to see how to present their art or design work to others*).

When you have completed it, you should be able to:

Plan work
- identify information needed to produce your images and reference it correctly using academic conventions
- select an appropriate format for presenting visual information which will suit the purpose, context, subject and audience
- select an appropriate style for the purpose, context, subject and audience.

Use your plan
- use images which will engage the audience
- use images which will help the audience understand the materials and clearly illustrate complex points
- check presentation of images for clarity (editing).

Review work
- evaluate the effectiveness of the image(s), for the purpose, subject, audience and context
- identify ways of improving the presentation of the image(s).

(Based on QCA Key Skill specifications, QCA 2000)

Visually impaired students

If your sight is impaired, visual work on courses may be difficult – depending on the degree of impairment. Your college/university may have specialist advisers to help and special equipment you can use.

You should also talk to your tutors/lecturers and explain exactly what you can and cannot do and how they may help you. Perhaps you could work with other students (you need to check with tutors, in case work is supposed to be done individually), or perhaps there is a technician who could help, or tutors may be able to explain the assessment criteria.

9.1 Types of visual work on courses

What sort of visual work may you need to present on courses (or to others, eg *to clients*)? Some main types include:

- **presenting and laying out written work**
- **visual aids for presentations**
- **posters**
- **presenting numerical work (eg *in tables or graphs*)**
- **presenting evidence of your visual work (eg *in a portfolio*).**

Which of the above do you need to do now or in the near future on your course? What else may you need to do? You may need to use specialist visual skills which your course will teach (eg *technical drawing, map making*), and these are not covered by this chapter, although some of the guidance may still apply.

You can make notes here on the sort of visual work you need to do.

9.2 Planning

9.2.1 Identifying what is needed

To communicate anything well you need to first identify who you are communicating with, why and in what situation.

For assessed work, you may have been given a 'brief', ie instructions for the work. If so look at the requirements, or look at the assessment criteria.

You could complete the following box, for work needing visual presentation which you need to do now or in the near future (either assessed or not).

What is the subject or topic?		
Who will see your work? What will they need (eg *how much do they know already*)? What will they want to see?	Why will they want to see your work (eg *to assess it, to inform them etc*)? What is the purpose of the work?	What is the situation? What format will you present your work in (eg *poster, portfolio, presentation, report*)?

9.2.2 What does this suggest about what you need to do?

Your subject/topic, those who will see your work, its purpose, and the situation will all have implications for what you do. Here are some examples of possible implications, as an idea starter.

Issue	Implications
About your subject/topic...	
Numerical subject	Visuals must be accurate
Design topic	Visuals should follow conventions used by designers
About people...	
Those seeing your work have knowledge about your subject	You can use technical/subject specific terms in labelling your visuals
Those seeing your work have no knowledge about your subject	It might be best not to use technical/subject specific terms in labelling your visuals
Those seeing your work are non-native English speakers	Visual needs to be understood without using any words
About your purpose...	
Your purpose is to get a good grade	You need to find out what will get a good grade (ie the assessment criteria)
Your purpose is to explain something	Visuals need to be very clear and understandable
Your purpose is to make an impact	Visuals should immediately look good – bold
About the situation...	
Giving a presentation in a lecture theatre	People will need to be able to see your visual aids from a distance
Producing a handout for 100 people	Needs to be cheap to make

9.2.3 What will be most appropriate?

Sections 9.1, 9.2.1 and 9.2.2 above should help you think about the sort of visual presentation which would be best for your subject/topic, for people who will see the work, for the purpose and the situation.

This includes thinking about 'style'. Style is very important in visual presentation. Think of two very different poster adverts which you see around now. What is different about the impact they make? What causes this difference (eg *the colours used; just visual images or words too; type of words; jokey or serious*)? This is the 'style'.

What sort of visual presentation do I need to produce?	What will this have to be like: for the subject or topic; for those seeing it, the purpose and the situation?

It might help to work through the rest of this chapter and then return to this section, to amend it once you have more ideas or suggestions.

9.2.4 The information on which your visuals will be based

Before you can create your visuals, you may need to collect information (eg *statistics to use in tables, charts or graphs; knowledge about a process for flow diagrams*). Chapters 5 and 21 'Gathering and Using Information' will help you.

 If you gather information from somewhere else (eg *published work*) you must provide a reference for it (ie *information helping the user find the original*). The same academic conventions apply to giving references to visual images as apply to written work. Chapter 5 has guidance on how to reference material.

If you want to reproduce a visual from published work (eg *a diagram, photo, work of art*), check with your library/learning centre on the copyright. There are rules about what you can reproduce and how you can use it.

It is always worth checking that the information on which your visuals are based is accurate. Visual presentation really highlights inaccuracies (eg *something wrongly spelt on an overhead projector (OHP) slide really stands out; some people delight in finding columns in tables of figures which don't add up*).

9.3 Creating your visuals

9.3.1 Important principles

There are two important principles for any visual presentation:

- the visual images should help those seeing them understand the material and clearly illustrate the points you want to make
- the visual images should engage and appeal to those seeing them.

The subjects or topics you need to present may be complex – there may be several elements to them, the ideas in them may be difficult to grasp, or there are may be many inter-connected ideas. Good visuals make complex topics simpler to understand (eg *diagrams can make the connections between things clearer; complex topics or theories may be explained by the use of 'models', often shown by diagrams*).

It can help to show your visuals to others (eg *friends, other students, colleagues*) and ask them if they understand them. Feedback from others here can be really helpful. What seems clear to you may puzzle somebody else (but remember, any work you submit for assessment as your own work needs to be your own).

9.3.2 Features of some main types of visuals

The following gives an overview of some of the main types of visual presentation, to help you think about what to use. In looking at them you could also consider:

- how important it is and therefore how much time and effort should you spend on it?
- how complicated/hard will the visuals be to create? Could you do something simpler?
- how many copies do you need? What will it cost? Could you do something cheaper?
- do you need to use it again and if so how will you store it?
- will you need to update it (eg *a portfolio*) and if so what would make this easy?
- if your visuals are valuable (eg *art or design work*) and you are sending them to somebody, do you need to insure them? How will you get them back?
- do you need to stop others 'stealing' your ideas (eg *designs*)? If so find out about copyright (library/learning centre and specialist academic staff should be able to help).

In the following 'OHP' means overhead projector, 'computer presentation' means making and presenting slides using a computer package (eg *'Powerpoint'*).

Type of work	Making it understandable to the person seeing it	Engaging and appealing to the person seeing it
Presenting and laying out written work	• Be consistent (eg *headings – same typeface for same level of heading; type of bullets; numbering*). • Number sections/paragraphs – check if this is OK for the type of work (eg *essays*) in your subject • Line space between paragraphs (or indent paragraphs for handwritten work) • Clear typeface/writing large enough to read easily • Check spelling and punctuation	• Have white space (ie with no text) – something crammed full of text is hard to look at • Attractive typeface, avoid too many typefaces in one piece of work – it looks messy • If handwriting your writing <u>must</u> be very neat and easy to read • Headings should 'signpost' points to the reader • Would using coloured paper be appropriate (eg *to identify different sections in a portfolio*)?

Type of work	Making it understandable to the person seeing it	Engaging and appealing to the person seeing it
Visual aids for presentations eg • *white/blackboard* • *flip chart* • *OHP/computer slides* • *video/film* • *objects/ models/ experiments*	• Ensure all the audience can see your visual aids • Use colours/typeface/ text the audience can see easily (eg *big enough*), ensure text can be clearly seen against background • Identify the best sort of visual aid for your purpose • Ensure the visual aid and what you say relate to each other • One slide/visual aid for each main point/'chunk' • Ensure visual aids are in the right order, number them • Use enough (eg *1 OHP/ computer slide per 2 minutes*) • As few words as possible per slide, key words/notes not full sentences (max 40 words per slide) • Word-process visual aids • Check spelling, punctuation • Simple, not over elaborate • If scale is important, ensure the visual aid shows it • Video – ensure clips complete enough to make points • Object/model – ensure big enough to see; give background information before showing it • Demonstration – make movements slow, exaggerated • Demonstrations/models – explain what is happening, check the audience is following	• Ask if everybody can see the visual aids • Make clear why you are using them • In advance, practise using them, learn to use equipment so the audience isn't bored while you sort it out (eg *focus slide projector, cue up video/film*) • Check the room in advance (eg *does it have blackout for slides, computing facilities?*) • Slides/video – use good quality • Avoid talking while looking at a screen with your back to the audience; standing between the audience and the visual aid • Turn off OHP when not referring to it as it can be noisy • Mention every visual aid • Leave things on for long enough for the audience to see but not so long that the impact is lost • Make copies of slides as handouts, tell the audience this at the start • Avoid film/video clips which are too long • Allow time to pass an object around the audience (they will stop listening to you while looking at it) • Discussion – start it after video/ film clips, blackout discourages discussion.

Type of work	Making it understandable to the person seeing it	Engaging and appealing to the person seeing it
Posters	• Use short statements, as few words as possible without losing the sense • Short lines of text • Use language the viewer will understand • Check spelling and punctuation carefully • Text and figures – clear enough to read (eg *title from across the room, text from a meter away*) • Use bullet points • If using a background colour, ensure the text can be seen on top of it • Emphasise items by using bold or increasing the size of letters • Simple and clear rather then fancy and confusing	• Check requirements (eg *size of poster, format*), some are very specific • Use colour, borders, shading/ shadows • Use a limited number of fonts (ie types of typeface) eg 2 • Use a clear font eg sans serif like Ariel (without tails on letters) is easier to read than serif (with 'tails') like Times New Roman. CAPITALS ARE HARDER TO READ THAN Words Which Only Start With Capitals. • Have white space (ie space with no text) – a poster crammed with text is hard to see • Avoid underlining – it looks messy
Presenting numerical information eg *in tables, charts or graphs*	• Title for each table/chart/graph showing what it contains, if more than one, give each a number • Give information showing scale (eg *how many in the sample*) • Label all aspects of the table/chart/graph (eg *axes*) • Avoid distorting information (eg *parts of the information on a different scale from others*) • Say where the information in the table/chart/graph came from • Big enough to read easily	• Choose a format to best illustrate your points (eg *table, pie chart, histogram*) • Use a format those seeing it will be familiar with (check for your subject area) • Be neat (eg *use a computer drawing package, or 'proper' equipment like compasses*) • Make it easy to read (eg *avoid colours which look like the same shade of grey if printed*) • Avoid overwhelming the person seeing it (eg *too much information in one table*)

Type of work	Making it understandable to the person seeing it	Engaging and appealing to the person seeing it
Presenting evidence of your visual work eg *in a portfolio*	• Use photos to show 3 dimensional objects • Avoid distracting/irrelevant things in photos, colour photos may show more detail • Scale – photograph an object next to something (eg *a person*); use a key to scale on drawings; describe size • Slides – mark each one to show right way up • Number items; give a contents list with information about each item by number • Give a description beneath each item • Have clear labels (eg *order of clips and running time on showreel/video/CD*) • Give a commentary (eg *what you did in a group activity*) • Make it (eg *a portfolio*) easy for the viewer to see and for you to move it around (eg *size*)	• Use good quality material (eg *paper/video, commercially produced portfolio, pockets for slides*) • Unless you have wonderful handwriting, word-process • Ask if gimmicks will work. Who will look at it? Will 'whizzy' appeal or irritate? • If it starts to look well used and grubby, tidy/clean it up

You could highlight any of the above items you need to take special note of in your work.

9.4 Checking the presentation of your visuals

You need to check your work to make sure it:

• is clear and understandable to the person seeing it
• will appeal to the person seeing it.

Feedback from friends before you use your visuals in the 'real situation' is always very helpful.

You could use Section 9.3.2 above as a list against which to check your work. However, there may be other requirements specific to your course/subject/topic. Check again any instructions you have been given (eg *your brief*) and assessment criteria. In the box below you could add any other items you may need to check, not included in the lists in 9.3.2 above.

✍

9.5 Improving your visual communication skills

9.5.1 The effectiveness of your work

How effective do you think your visual work is:

- for the subject/topic?
- for the purpose it is being used for?
- for those seeing it?
- for the situation in which it is used?

You may want to look at any feedback you've had on your work, or to ask friends or tutors what they think, or to show your work to a specialist and ask what they think of it.

You can make notes in the box below. It might help to think about some recent pieces of work you have had to do.

✍

9.5.2 Improving what you do

What do you need to do to improve your visual communication skills? This may include getting training (eg *how to make a presentation using a computer*), finding out about resources or asking for help.

Actions needed	Resources, help, training needed	By (date)

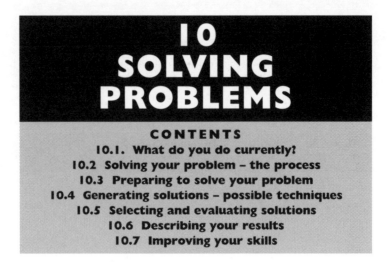

10
SOLVING
PROBLEMS

CONTENTS

This chapter aims to help you solve the problems likely to be encountered on your course.

Being able to solve problems is very important in all professional areas. How can systems or processes operate more effectively? How can difficulties between people be resolved? How can transport, or medical, or engineering problems be solved?

Courses include assignments or activities designed to help students develop the ability to solve problems (eg *case studies, projects, experiments*). Improving your skills in this area will help you get better grades or marks.

We suggest you use this chapter:

- **in relation to a particular assignment or activity which involves solving a problem**
- **before you start work on that assignment or activity**
- **then whilst you are working on it.**

When you have completed it, you should be able to:

Explore problems
- review your current approach to solving problems
- recognise a complex problem exists and select/use different methods to explore it (eg *divide it into sub-problems, analyse its features*)
- identify criteria to judge solutions against
- select/use different ways of tackling the problem
- compare main features of each possible solution, including risk factors, and justify the one chosen.

Plan and implement options
- plan how to tackle the problem and implement your plan
- review progress and revise plans if needed.

Check, describe results and review approach
- identify and use ways of checking if the solution meets the criteria
- draw conclusions and describe the results
- review your approach to the problem and identify alternative methods and their likely effectiveness.

(Based on QCA Key Skill specifications, QCA 2000)

10.1 What do you do currently?

Here are three problems. Spend 5–10 minutes getting as far as possible within the time in solving one or more of them. Use the check list below to note what you are doing. This will help you identify how you tend to solve problems. Doing the exercise in pairs, with one person problem solving and the other recording the process could be useful.

Problem 1   You keep seven pairs of socks unsorted in a drawer. If you just pull out a pair at random they never seem to match. What is the minimum number of socks you would have to pull out to be sure that you get a matching pair?

Problem 2   How long will it take to complete an assignment you currently have to do (eg *the one you are using this chapter for*)?

Problem 3   Your notes are so disorganised that you can't find those you need. What system would help you find notes more easily?

✔

Calculating	
Mentally picturing	
Sketching	
Writing a list	
Thinking about something else entirely	
Feeling anxious	
Please add other items which describe what you do	

Which methods did you use to solve the above problems? Which others are you familiar with?

✔

	In this exercise	Familiar with
The logical approach – definite steps you go through		
Follow a hunch/your intuition		
Discuss with others		
Trial and error – try ideas until one works		
Creative idea generation – think of lots of ideas		
Rationally choosing from alternatives – weighing up the advantages and disadvantages		
Other methods (please specify)		

We each have **preferred** approaches to solving problems and there can be a tendency to think our way is the only way. However, there is a range of different approaches and the method chosen depends to some extent on the type of problem; problem 1 above had a right answer, whereas the other two problems did not.

10.2 Solving your problem – the process

With the exception of those areas which require you to follow a set procedure (eg *in a lab*), there is normally no one best way to solve a problem. However, there are common elements in solving problems.

Whatever your starting point, at some stage you need to give attention to the following aspects. This is presented in a circle rather than in linear form, since it is important to acknowledge that there is no one right way.

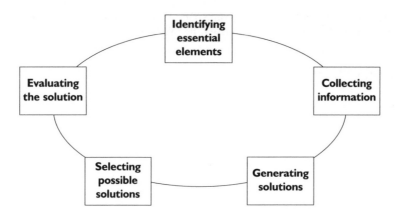

You may find that you move backwards and forwards between these elements (eg *think of a solution, realise you need more information, think of more solutions*).

It may be helpful to try out an approach which is different from the ones you normally use. You can then see if it works better, whether you prefer your usual approach, or if you could merge the approaches in some way.

Using an approach which is totally alien can inhibit your creativity – but so can not trying new ones.

Sections 10.3–10.5 work through the above process.

10.3 Preparing to solve your problem

10.3.1 Defining your problem

You need to define the essential elements. Some problems you deal with may be quite complex, and you may need to manage a range of information/ideas. You might have to identify underlying issues and make links between different aspects of the problem. It could help to break down your main problem/question into a series of sub-problems/questions.

What are the basic elements of your problem?

What have you been asked to do/decide/solve?

Who for?

Why?

By when?

Different questions will arise from different problems – you will need to identify the essential elements. You might ask yourself the following.

What makes it a problem?

What are the sub-problems?

Who will need to use/apply the solution? Who is involved? Who will it affect?

Who has vested interests in it?

Others (please add)

What does the solution have to achieve?

How will you know you have successfully solved the problem? What **criteria** will you use to judge the solution? (eg *completed within two days, cost less than £5, satisfies your tutor, agreed to by others in your group*).

What does the solution need to achieve?	Criteria by which to judge it

10.3.2 Planning and reporting

What will you actually do? What methods will you use? When? What resources will you need?

It may help to draw up a plan. This could include notes on:

* the nature of the problem
* the tasks and sub-tasks needed (it helps to break down large tasks into smaller, more manageable ones)
* which methods and techniques you will use (eg *to gather information, to generate solutions, to help you decide which solution to select, to carry out the tasks*)
* resources or facilities needed (including people who can help and any likely costs)
* deadlines and timescales (allowing for the unexpected)
* if you are solving problems in a group, plan for who will do what.

You might find it helpful to look at the Chapters 18 and 32 on 'Action Planning'.

Your problem:			
Main elements of the problem	**Actions/methods to deal with this element**	**Resources/support**	**Deadlines**

How will you monitor your progress with solving the problem? Reviewing how you are doing as you carry out your plan will help you revise your ideas and actions as needed. It will be useful to keep notes about what you do and decisions/actions you take.

10.3.3 Collecting information

Have you got enough information about the problem to help you begin to solve it?
Context – what do you need to bear in mind about the situation surrounding the problem? What are the constraints, ie what might limit any solutions? Cost? Time? Physical limits of space or size? What other information do you need?

10.4 Generating solutions – possible techniques

There are different approaches to generating solutions – the following briefly describes some of them. You could adapt them to the problem you are currently dealing with.

10.4.1 A design process

This six-stage approach is often used to design manufactured products and organisational systems.

Stage 1 – Needs evaluation
What is the purpose of the object or system?
What are the user's needs?
What are the circumstances in which it will be used?
What might be the benefits of having or using it?

Stage 2 – Design specification
What are the requirements of the design:

- cost factors?
- how will it be used?
- safety standards?
- quantities required?
- facilities/resources needed to produce it available?

Stage 3 – Concept or solution generation
This is the creative part of the process, generating a wide range of possible solutions.

Stage 4 – Solution evaluation
Detailed consideration of how well each solution or concept satisfies the needs identified and design specifications.

Stage 5 – Detailed design
Makes sure the selected solution works.

Stage 6 – Review

Ensures that the solution meets the needs identified in Stages 1 and 2 above, before putting it into practice.

10.4.2 The GRASP ®* (getting results and solving problems) scheme

This sequence is recommended by the Comino Foundation (1990).

Stage 1

Select the purpose or objectives and the criteria for success:

• Have you pictured the situation you would like to bring about?
• Are you clear what you are trying to achieve and why, as opposed to what you would like to do?
• How will you know when you have succeeded?
• Are you committed to act and succeed?

Stage 2

Generate different ways of achieving the objective and select the best:

• Have you identified as many ways of achieving the objectives as possible?
• What constraints must be observed in any action you take?

Stage 3

Put the chosen plan into operation and control the process:

• How will you control the course of events and stay on the right path?

Stage 4

Review continually each operation and the results:

• Is the original purpose still valid?
• Is the original course of action still valid?
• Are the criteria too loose or rigid?
• Are you receiving sufficient feedback and are you acting on it?

* GRASP ® is the registered trademark of the Comino Foundation

10.4.3 Following set procedures

For some areas, particularly where safety is involved, you need to follow set procedures accurately. This may apply to laboratory work.

You need to clarify anything you don't understand with your lecturer or tutor. If you fail to find a solution you may need to backtrack to see if you have followed the procedure correctly.

10.4.4 Trial and error

If you find it difficult to get started or become anxious when faced by a problem, it can help to first try something, anything, to remove the block.

Do it now. Jot down ideas immediately then later go back and review them.

'Quantity not quality'. Get plenty of scrap paper and write as many ideas and thoughts about the problem as possible.

Warning. Trial and error in certain situations may be dangerous (eg *when electrical experiments won't work*). Using trial and error can also take up more time than thinking things through in advance.

10.4.5 Creative idea generation

Brainstorming

This works well with a group but you can do it alone. If you are in a group, get one person to write down whatever is said on a board or flip chart where all can see it. It can help to set a time limit (eg *10 minutes*).

'Rules' are as follows:

* write down **any** ideas however unusual, impractical or rude
* do not discuss or make judgements about the ideas. This stops the flow of ideas and your aim at this stage is to generate ideas creatively.
* 'piggy backing' is encouraged (adding ideas to other people's ideas, even if they may at this stage seem away from the point).

When you have finished generating ideas:

* if in a group, check what people meant
* whether in a group or alone, sort ideas into ones which appear similar
* discuss the ideas
* judge which ones look suitable and which ones don't.

Left brain/right brain

According to some theories, our brains have two ways of handling information.

LEFT BRAIN	RIGHT BRAIN
Connects with the right hand.	Connects with the left hand.
Analyses, abstracts, counts, marks time, plans step by step procedures, verbalises, makes logical, rational statements.	Understands metaphors, dreams, creates new combinations of ideas, makes gestures to communicate.

The aim in **creative** problem solving is to encourage the right brain process.

* Work at the best time and in the best place for creative thinking. You will have to work this out by experience. Some of us work best after midnight, others at 6 am, some while listening to music, others in silence.
* Use a different communication process (eg *if you have been talking about a problem, stop talking and draw, mime, generate computer images*).
* **Don't** think about it (eg *go to sleep, for a walk, ideas often emerge when you least expect them*).
* 'Reframe' the problem or look at it from another angle (eg *look at a problem object upside down or see the spaces or voids in an object rather than the solid parts*).
* Use unrelated objects to 'unstick' yourself (eg *after brainstorming a problem for a time, add one or two completely unrelated objects. How could these objects be used to solve the problem?*).

10.4.6 Have you generated a range of possible solutions?

Which technique will suit you and your problem? Having used them, what solutions have you come up with? At this stage it helps to identify as many as possible

✏️

10.5 Selecting and evaluating solutions

10.5.1 Selecting

Having generated a range of solutions, how do you choose between them? You could:

- identify any general rules which might help you select solutions, or limit the solutions which are possible

    eg *problems between people: general rules – people like being consulted; people like being listened to.*

    eg *design problem: general rule – the solution must meet the needs of the user*

- do a SWOT analysis – list the **S**trengths, **W**eaknesses, **O**pportunities and **T**hreats of each possible solution

- according to Edward de Bono (1982) we tend to make decisions about problems in an emotional way. He suggests listing possible solutions to a problem under three headings – **plus**, **minus** and **interesting**. (By 'interesting' he means any consequences of the decision that are neither negative or positive.)

- identify the costs and benefits of each solution and weigh them up against each other

- identify the risks involved in choosing a solution. Give points from 1–5 for each solution according to how risky it is, and points from 1–5 according to how likely the risk is to happen. The solutions with the highest scores are the most risky. You can then identify what you could do to reduce the risk.

- refer back to the criteria you identified in 10.3.1.

Possible solutions?	Why have you chosen it?	Likely consequences (positive and negative)	What are the risks?

If selecting a solution is difficult, what else could help you? See Section 10.3 for possible ideas.

What are the difficulties?	What would help you?
eg *two solutions seem appropriate*	• *Talk it through with a friend* • *Do a SWOT analysis*

If your problem is causing stress, look at Chapter 14 on 'Coping With Pressure' in Part I.

Which solution for your current problem seems most likely to meet your criteria? Can you justify that solution?

✍

Solution	Justification

10.5.2 Evaluating the solution

Is your solution is a good one? If not, why not? You could:

- check the results against the criteria you identified in Section 10.3.1
- get feedback from others (eg *friends, tutor, family*)
- talk it through with someone else.

✍

10.6 Describing your results

If your problem is for an assessed task and you are unsure what is required, check any instructions/guidance or ask your tutor.

Who will you tell about your solution and what will make it clear to them? Will you describe it:

- in words (eg *see chapters on 'Essay Writing'/'Report Writing'*)?
- visually (eg *see chapter on 'Visual Communication' in Part I*)?
- verbally (eg *see chapters on 'Oral Presentation'*)?

Will you need to describe how you solved the problem? You may need to justify your solution and to give evidence for your choice. If so, what sort of evidence is needed (eg *your action plan*)?

You may need to show the stages of your problem solving, or the range of possible solutions. The activities you have carried out in this chapter will help you do this.

10.7 Improving your skills

10.7.1 Reviewing your approach

Was your approach effective? What other methods could you have used? Would they have been more effective?

What methods did you use? Were they helpful? Why/why not?

What adaptations did you/would you need to make to improve the solution and help you meet your criteria?

What other approaches could you have used? How effective would they have been?

10.7.2 Action plan

What do you need to do to improve your skills in solving problems?

Actions needed to improve	Resources/support needed	Deadline

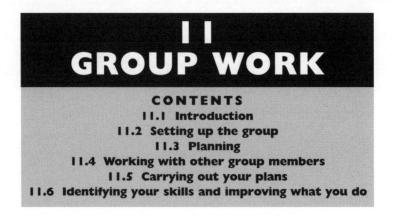

11
GROUP WORK

CONTENTS

Group work can cover any activity involving working with others (eg *group projects, lab work, seminars, tutorials*). Your course may assesses your skills in this area.

Group work means being able to share resources, ideas and abilities. Students can learn from and help each other.

Group work effectiveness depends not on luck and who is in your group, but on individual member's skills in dealing with each other. These skills can be improved by practice. The key to success is to focus not only on end results but on how to get there.

Courses include group work because employers see evidence of group work skills as very important when recruiting graduates or higher diplomates. All jobs involve working with others.

We suggest you use this chapter:

- **right at the start of any group work**
- **as you continue, to help improve your work and avoid problems.**

When you have completed it, you should be able to:

Plan work
- agree realistic aims and targets in working with others on various tasks, including complex ones
- agree responsibilities and working arrangements (eg *roles appropriate for the individuals involved and the context*)
- agree resources, timescales and actions needed.

Work towards agreed objectives
- meet your responsibilities (eg *in meeting agreed outcomes, working safely*)
- obtain and effectively use resources
- work co-operatively with others (eg *exchange information to help in meeting targets, agree how to overcome difficulties*)
- agree and carry out amendments to plans.

Review work
- evaluate the effectiveness of the outcomes and the process, identifying factors which influenced both
- identify ways of improving work with others.

(Based on QCA Key Skill specifications, QCA 2000)

11.1 Introduction

What sort of groups have you operated in up to now? Sporting? Social? Family? Work? Identifying what you liked or disliked about them may give you clues about areas you will enjoy (and may do well) or find difficult (and may need to improve) in course group work.

Type of group	Likes	Dislikes

11.2 Setting up the group

11.2.1 Ground rules

It is very helpful to have a set of rules ('ground rules') for how your group will operate, to set up good ways of working and to avoid problems. Following ground rules can make activities (eg *meetings*) run smoothly, and gives you some control if group members are difficult. You could use the following ground rules as they are, or agree as a group to change, add or remove items.

You could put your ground rules on the wall where all can see them, or take it in turns to monitor them.

Suggested ground rules. amend or remove items, or add new ones
Turn up to meetings
Agree an agenda for meetings
Nobody to speak for longer than 3 minutes at a time
No interrupting
No putting others down. Criticise the ideas not the person
Encourage everyone to speak
Start and end meetings on time
Set deadlines and stick to them
Everyone to do what they agree

11.3 Planning

Look at 11.3.1 and 11.3.2 below before completing the plan in 11.3.3.

11.3.1 Group goals

Being clear about group goals (results or outcomes of your work) is essential. You can prevent later problems by asking each member what they think the group is supposed to be doing and achieving (eg *look carefully at any instructions you have been given*). You may need to ask your tutor to clarify what is expected.

What do you need/want to achieve as a group (goals, results, outcomes)?	What do you personally need/want to achieve?
(eg *related to the task or to how you work together*)	(eg *learning something, a good grade*)

11.3.2 Planning actions and allocating tasks

On university/college courses, you may need to handle complex matters, with many elements. Planning how to manage this and how to meet your goals will avoid wasted effort and problems, and make the most of your resources. The following questions may help:

- What tasks do you need to complete to meet your goals? Where you are dealing with a complex issue (eg *with several strands or a difficult problem to solve*), have you identified all the possible tasks?
- How can the main tasks be sub-divided into smaller manageable tasks?
- By when must each sub-task be completed?
- Who will do which sub-tasks?
- What will you do about the sub-tasks nobody wants to do (eg *negotiate, draw lots*)? If you can't agree, see Chapter 13 'Negotiating and Assertiveness'.
- Is the workload evenly distributed between group members?
- What resources do you need to carry out the sub-tasks and will you be able to find and use them in the time available (eg *sources of information, computers*)?
- Can you carry out the tasks in the time you have? If not, how could you amend your plans?
- If you carry out all the sub-tasks by the time agreed, will your goals be met?

To plan work, see also Chapter 3 'Organising Yourself and Your Time', and Chapter 10 'Solving Problems'.

11.3.3 Group work plan

Task	Resources needed	To be done by (person)	Deadline

How will the group monitor progress to check everybody is doing what they agreed? How will you ensure you do what you agreed? Could you turn this plan into a 'contract' signed by all the group members?

11.4 Working with other group members

11.4.1 Meetings

It avoids confusion if you all meet together to discuss work rather than meeting in sub-groups (eg *just two of you*). For best use of time, you need:

- an agenda (list of items to discuss) – you could agree this at the start of each meeting or beforehand
- to decide how much time to spend on each agenda item
- to keep to time and to have ground rules and to follow them (see 11.2 above)
- to make notes (called 'minutes') on what you agree (eg *'actions' – who is going to do what, by when*). Each person could make notes on different agenda items, or you could take it in turns to make notes.
- to meet where you won't be interrupted.

For help on meetings see Chapter 12 'Seminars, Group Tutorials and Meetings'; for help on writing minutes/notes of meetings see Chapter 4 'Note Taking'.

You could note here how you will handle meetings (eg *where you will meet, how often, how you will organise the meetings*).

11.4.2 Listening skills

Listening effectively to others means you can benefit from their ideas and expertise and makes them feel valued, important if you are to work as a team. You could:

- make notes on what they say to help you concentrate on what they are saying
- check with them if you have understood what they meant, or summarise what you think they meant
- look at their 'body language' for clues on how they are feeling
- avoid interrupting them
- focus on what they are saying rather than on what you are going to say next.

11.4.3 How you behave in groups

The following list, from Turner (1983), describes how people may behave in groups. You could use it to make notes on how you behaved in a particular group situation (eg *a group meeting*).

		Notes
Task roles	• initiates • seeks opinions • gives opinions • elaborates • co-ordinates • summarises	
Maintenance roles	• encourages • 'gate-keeps' (keeps the group to the task) • sets standards • expresses group feelings/reactions	
Task and maintenance roles	• evaluates • diagnoses • tests for consensus/agreement • mediates • compromises • relieves tension • jokes	

You could also use the following list, from Turner (1983), to identify anything you do which may be unhelpful in a particular group situation (in some group situations self-confession, competing or seeking sympathy may be appropriate but not in others).

✔

Being overly aggressive	
Blocking (rejecting ideas without due consideration, going off at tangents)	
Self-confession	
Competing	
Seeking sympathy	
Special pleading (for own concerns or interests)	
Horsing around	
Seeking recognition (excessive/loud talking, unsociable behaviour)	

Which of these things would you like to change? It might help to try to do two things:

- monitor how often you do it (being aware of something can help you stop doing it)
- think about why you do it. Could you change something about that (eg *your attitude*)? Some of the above items relate to getting things to happen as you want them to, or to being liked – but do they really do that (eg *others may be amused by 'horsing around' for a while, but may get fed up of it if it interferes with what they need to do*)?

11.5 Carrying out your plans

11.5.1 Monitoring your plans

Students say that in course group work it is very important for members to do agreed work by the deadline and to do work to an adequate standard. How will you make sure as a group that these things happen? You could:

- agree times when you will meet to review progress
- agree to tell each other regularly (eg *by email, at meetings*) of progress or difficulties with your part of the work
- if things are not going to plan, ask why this is rather than jumping to conclusions (see 11.5.2 below for ideas)
- see if you need to change your plans (all group members need to know about any changes to avoid confusion). Things rarely go exactly as planned and being flexible is important in group work.

11.5.2 Dealing with difficulties

Identifying the cause of a difficulty can often help the group solve it. The following are examples of typical problems and suggested ways of dealing with them – they are suggestions only and you may have other ideas.

Problem	Possible Solutions
Uneven workload, 'passengers', people not pulling their weight	Agree who does what at the start, and write it down to avoid confusion. Ask those not doing their work why not – they may have a good reason. Tell them the effect it is having on the group. Use Chapter 13 'Negotiating and Assertiveness'.
Too much work involved	Look again at the project brief together – have you misunderstood? Are there more efficient ways of doing it? Use Chapter 3 'Organising Yourself and Your Time'.
Resources not available	Plan for this right at the start. Use Chapter 3 'Organising Yourself and Your Time'. Identify other resources or ways of doing things. Ask for help from resource providers (eg learning centre, library, computer support services). Amend your goals and plans.
Confusion	Discuss your goals as a group and keep referring back to them. Use Chapter 10 'Solving Problems'.
Quiet group members	Ask for their views, encourage them to speak, be positive about their comments.
Disruptive group members eg *clowning around, negativeness, over talkative, aggression*	Possibilities include ignoring jokes; asking 'talkatives' to let somebody else have a say; pointing out when somebody is negative and asking for positives. Use Chapter 13 'Negotiating and Assertiveness'.

Many difficulties can be solved by good communications between you. If you or your group tries to deal with a problem but is unable to do so you may need to seek help from your tutor. Your tutor needs to be know if things are not going well.

11.6 Identifying your skills and improving what you do

This chapter focuses not on other people's behaviour but on how **you** work with others. Your behaviour influences their behaviour and you have a better chance of changing what **you** do.

11.6.1 Evaluating what went on in the group

What is going or went well or less well in your group? This could be in terms of the results/outcomes of your work or your processes (how you are/were doing things).

What is going/went well	What is not going/did not go well	What affected this? What is/was my part in this?

11.6.2 Your behaviour

Does or did **your** behaviour help the group be effective? Score yourself using the following scale of 1–4 where 1 is 'very helpful' and 4 is 'very unhelpful'. You can use it again after a time lapse, to see if you have changed what you do.

	1	2	3	4	
Listening to others, asking for clarification (eg *did you mean…?*)					Interrupting, putting others down
Expressing relevant views positively					Being negative, disrupting, being irrelevant
Contributing equally					Keeping quiet, dominating
Asking what others think about your contributions					Unconcerned about others' views
Pulling your weight, doing an equal part of the work					Letting others do the work, not turning up
Meeting deadlines					Missing deadlines

11.6.3 Improving what you do

You could ask other group members or your tutors what they think about how you did the work and about how you behaved in the group.

Aspects I enjoy, things I'm good at in groups and want to repeat

Look at the references at the end of the book for some resources you could use to help you improve.

Aspects I find difficult, things I need to improve in groups	Actions I need to take	Resources or help I need	By (deadline)

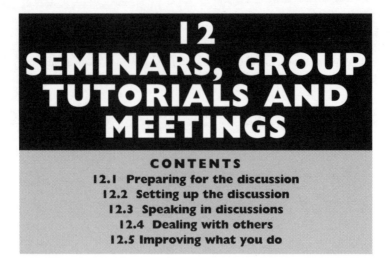

12
SEMINARS, GROUP TUTORIALS AND MEETINGS

'Seminar' and 'group tutorial' may mean a similar class, ie discussion based. You may be asked to prepare in advance (eg *by reading something*). There may be a presentation by a tutor or student, followed by discussion, or discussion without a presentation. Such classes help students to:

- look at a topic in more depth than in a lecture
- learn from each other's views
- develop skills in explaining and putting forward a case ('arguing a case')
- ask questions and explore issues with the tutor.

Meetings are common where people work together (eg *on a project*) to help them communicate.

You may take part in other discussions during your course (eg *a debate or a forum*). There may be special rules about them, but this chapter should help you take part in any discussion.

We suggest you use this chapter:

- **when you need to take part in seminar or tutorial groups**
- **when you take part in meetings**
- **if, when applying for jobs, you must take part in a group discussion at an assessment centre.**

When you have completed it, you should be able to:

Plan work
- identify what you want to get from a discussion (eg *aims*)
- do advance preparatory work
- identify your responsibilities (eg *for contributing*)
- agree ways of working within the group.

Work towards objectives
- exchange information
- vary how and when to participate to suit your aims, allowing for context (eg *other group members, topic, role of the leader*)
- listen and respond sensitively and help others to contribute
- contribute relevantly for the topic, participants and purpose
- establish and maintain co-operative relationships (eg *anticipate needs of others, act assertively, deal with difficulties/conflict*).

Review work
- identify factors affecting the outcomes
- identify how to improve.

(Based on QCA Key Skill specifications, QCA 2000)

12.1 Preparing for the discussion

12.1.1 What would you like to get from the discussion?

Whatever sort of discussion it is (eg s*eminar, group tutorial, meeting*), it helps to identify beforehand its purpose and what you would like to get from it (ie your aims). Your aims may relate to (eg *the topic; your skills in taking part; end results, such as grades/marks; making or keeping friends*). They may affect what you do in the discussion.

For a discussion you are taking part in or about to take part in, you could note here its purposes and your aims (what you want to get out of it).

The purpose of the discussion	Your aims

12.1.2 Responsibilities

It helps to be clear about who is responsible for what.

In seminars/tutorials the tutor is responsible for planning the class and encouraging participation.

In a meeting, either the whole group or a chairperson is responsible for running it (see Chapter 11 'Group Work' for more guidance).

Discussing ideas/information is a valuable way of learning and you are responsible for taking part in a way which helps your own and others' learning. No tutor, no matter how good, can force you to speak, to listen or to learn.

12.1.3 Preparatory work

You may be asked to do work beforehand (eg *read something*). Doing it will help you to get the most from the discussion and to meet your responsibilities to the group (see 12.1.2 above). If you don't do it, the discussion may be poorer.

What else could you do to get the most out of the discussion? Would any other preparation help you meet the aims you noted in 12.1.1 above? Further preparation might include:

- find out more about the topic – read about it, watch TV/films on it, look out in the media (eg *newspapers*) for issues related to it
- jot down any questions you would like answering
- jot down any issues you think are interesting or could be discussed
- talk about it beforehand with friends, to sort your ideas out
- for a meeting, agree an agenda beforehand (ie the items to discuss in the order in which you will discuss them).

12.1.4 What sort of group is it

How you behave in a discussion depends on its purpose, on your aims (see 12.1.1 above) and on those taking part. Who are they (eg *other students/not students, men/women, ethnic mix, young/older, level of knowledge about the topic, experience, background, interests*)?

Characteristics of those in the discussion (eg *seminar/tutorial/meeting*)	What might they want to get out of it?	What does this (ie your notes in the first two columns) mean for you?

12.2 Setting up the discussion

The tutor may be responsible for setting up the discussion. However, you may be asked to lead a seminar, or to start a discussion, or you may have a meeting without a tutor there – if so it helps to agree and make clear at the start how it will operate.

Are you clear about the discussion's purpose? If a tutor is leading it, you could politely ask (eg *'What are we hoping to get out of this discussion please?'*). If there's no tutor, you could discuss this as a group (eg *'Do we all want to find out more about...?'*).

If you are leading a discussion it helps to:

*   make clear what will happen (eg *I'm going to speak for 10 minutes, please leave any questions until I've finished. We'll then have 10 minutes for question and a further 20 minutes for discussion'*).
*   give them something to discuss (eg *questions or topics on a handout*) – expecting people to have a discussion without this can lead to silence or chaos
*   to encourage people to talk, ask them to discuss the issues/questions in pairs for 2 or 3 minutes before asking them to talk about it in the whole group.

'Ground rules' for how to operate are helpful. You could discuss these at the start - if a tutor is 'in charge' and does not suggest this, perhaps you could do so? This is an example, but it depends on what your group needs (see 12.1.1 and 12.1.4 above):

*   *keep to the point*
*   *nobody to speak for more than 2 minutes*
*   *encourage everybody to take part and speak*
*   *avoid interrupting*
*   *argue about ideas, rather than making personal remarks*
*   *avoid putting down what others say.*

You may find it helpful to look at Chapter 11 'Group Work'.

12.3 Speaking in discussions

12.3.1 How much do you speak?

How much do you speak in a discussion? You could note how often you speak, perhaps compared with others. If you don't say much, why? If you talk a lot, why?

What do you do?	Why do you do it?

12.3.2 If you don't speak much

Do you find it hard to speak because you don't feel confident about the topic? If so, prepare thoroughly – see 12.1.3 above. If it is difficult to sort out your ideas on the spot you could:

- make notes beforehand on points you'd like to raise
- makes notes during the discussion on what others say or you could say
- when you speak, admit your thoughts aren't clear and that you are trying them out.

If it is hard to 'get into' the discussion which of the following could you try?

✔

Raise a hand when you'd like to speak	
Catch the eye of the tutor/chairperson (look as if you want to speak, sit up, look alert)	
Wait for a small pause and quickly speak	
Speak more loudly	
After the discussion, tell the tutor it is hard to 'get in' to the discussion, suggest (politely!) other ways of doing things (eg *time in pairs or small groups*)	
Ask the course representative to tell the tutor it is hard to 'get in' and to make suggestions to help	

If you are nervous, you could:

- build your confidence by making short contributions
- set yourself targets (eg *'I'll say one thing today'*)
- ask why you feel nervous and challenge your assumptions (eg *for how long will people really remember what you say*) - your answers to 12.3.1 above may give you clues
- accept that having your ideas challenged helps you learn.

Would any of the above ideas help you? What else might? Talking to others about this may give you ideas.

✍

What do you feel nervous about?	What might help you deal with this?

12.3.3 If you speak a lot

This may be OK, your comments may be helpful, but no matter how helpful they are the point of a discussion is that everybody takes part, that several heads are better than one. If you talk a lot it may be hard for others to speak. If you may do this (ask the tutor/others in the group for feedback) you could:

- set yourself a limit on how often you speak
- make notes on what you might say and ask yourself if it is really important to say it
- wait to see if others make the point first
- really listen to others – make notes to help you focus (see Section 12.4.1 below)
- encourage others to speak (eg *ask what they think*)
- look out for the reaction you are getting (eg *enthusiastic, bored*).

12.3.4 Getting yourself heard

You will be more easily heard if you:

- sit where others can see you (it is easier to hear if you can see a speaker's mouth)
- avoid speaking with your hand over your mouth
- avoid speaking too fast
- speak up
- look at the person you are speaking to, and scan everybody.

12.3.5 Engaging with/interesting others

To communicate well you need to consider who is in the discussion (see 12.1.4 above), and what they may want to get from it. What will appeal to them, or offend or annoy them? For example:

- *what sort of language will they understand or relate to?*
- *what sort of examples will they understand?*
- *what will interest or motivate them?*

What may others want to get from the discussion?	What will appeal to or interest them?	What will offend or annoy them?

12.3.6 Making your point

Identifying what helps **you** understand can help you to see how to present things to others.

What helps you understand other people?

To make your points clearly which of the following could you try?   ✔

Avoid too much detail (the listener may get confused)	
Summarise your points first, then talk about each point in more detail	
Use language the group will understand (see Section 12.1.4 above), avoid jargon, avoid or explain abbreviations	
Use examples (eg *from your experience*)	
Describe how an idea could be applied in practice	
Use an analogy (ie saying 'It's rather like...')	
Describe any clear steps or stages	
Break a difficult idea into parts	
Ask the listeners if they have understood	

12.3.7 What will you do?

Which ideas from sections 12.3.1–12.3.6 will you try? You could consider this in relation to:

- the purposes of your group and your own aims (Section 12.1.1)
- the people in the group (Section 12.1.4 and Section 12.3.5).

Which ideas will you try? What else have you tried which worked well?

You need to vary what you do in different situations. Thinking about how things went in a discussion helps you develop ideas on what works when and with whom. You could now think about a completely different discussion group. Would you need to do anything different for that group? What? Why?

What I would do differently	Why?

12.4 Dealing with others

12.4.1 Listening and attending to others

Active listening is about understanding what somebody means, not just being able to repeat what they said. You could:

- concentrate on what they say (making notes while they speak can help)
- avoid interrupting them
- ask them to explain anything you do not understand
- check you understand by summarising what they said (eg *'Did you mean...?'*).

Feedback from others helps. How would you rate yourself on a scale of 1–4, where 1 is being a great listener and 4 is being a poor one? You could ask others (eg *friends, relatives, other students, tutors, workplace supervisor*) to rate you on the same scale. Does your rating agree with theirs? You could ask them why they rated you like that, and to be specific (eg *do you look at people when they talk?*).

Do you look for non-verbal signals? If there are others around you now, how are they sitting or standing? What does this suggest about how they feel? Non verbal signals include:

- mirroring - if you and another person relate to each other well, you may both sit in the same way
- signs of boredom – yawning, slumping, fidgeting, looking at a watch, reading something unrelated to the discussion
- signs of interest – sitting up or forward, alert face, looking at the speaker
- signs of anger – pointing fingers, distorted face

A person's non-verbal signals do not always match what they are saying, and this can give clues as to their real feelings. If they sound angry but are smiling, why?

Being aware both of what people say and of how they are feeling is essential if you are to communicate well.

12.4.4 Co-operating with others

What do others do which makes you want to co-operate with them?	What do they do which makes you not want to co-operate with them?	What do you do to co-operate with others?

What does this tell you about what you need to do in discussion groups?

Some basics can help, such as being polite, being considerate (eg *making sure others can see or get round the table*), and doing preparatory work (see Section 12.1.3 above).

12.4.3 Encouraging others

Everybody in a discussion has a responsibility to encourage others to speak. Which of the following do you do?

Looking interested (eg *looking at them*)	
If you agree with them, saying so	
Avoiding put-downs	
Avoiding off-putting reactions (eg *facial expressions*)	
Asking them what they think	
Avoiding dominating the discussion	

12.4.4 Dealing with conflict

In a good discussion you expect debate and disagreement, but heated arguments are unhelpful. It helps to:

* refer to a group member's ideas, not their personality
* avoid using very emotional (or 'bad') language
* keep a reasonable voice level
* focus on relevant points
* avoid a back and forth discussion (eg *stop the discussion and ask what others think*).

What do you think works in dealing with conflict or with somebody who is angry?

✍

How can you avoid becoming angry?	What do you (or could you) do which is helpful when others become angry?

Look at Chapters 13 and 28 'Negotiating and Assertiveness' for more help.

12.4.5 Questioning

Asking and being asked questions helps you to understand and to hear others' views.

Asking questions
You could prepare beforehand by: identifying what to ask; making notes during the discussion of questions to ask; phrasing your question clearly.

Being asked a question
You could: check you have understood it; in replying, keep to the point (avoid 'waffle' or going on too much). If you don't know the answer, you could: say you do not know; attempt an answer, to find out if it is correct or to see what others think.

What do you tend to do? Which of these suggestions could you try?

✍

Asking questions What you do and what you could try	Being asked a question What you do and what you could try

12.5 Improving what you do

It might help to think about the last discussion you were in, or several recent discussions.

✎

What did you do which worked well?	What did you do which did not work well?	What factors affected what you did?

You could now identify what you need to do to improve.

What or who could help you?

You could work through this chapter again before your next discussion. Chapters 13 and 28 'Negotiating and Assertiveness' can help if you need to be more assertive, as can Chapters 14 and 29 'Coping with Pressure'. You could talk to the tutor, or others in the discussion, or friends, or get more feedback.

✎

Aspects to improve	Actions I can take	Resources/help needed	By (date)

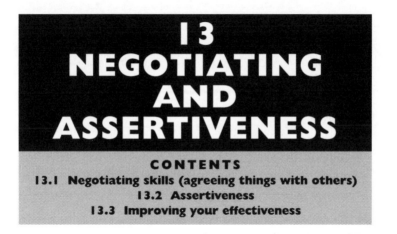

13
NEGOTIATING AND ASSERTIVENESS

CONTENTS
13.1 Negotiating skills (agreeing things with others)
13.2 Assertiveness
13.3 Improving your effectiveness

- Negotiating is the process of coming to an agreement with others.

- Assertiveness is about getting what you want, whilst respecting the needs of others.

We continually find ourselves in situations where we need to negotiate or be assertive: socially (eg *'Which film should we go to see?'*), at home (eg *'Who will do the washing up?'*), on courses (eg *'How can I ask for help?'*).

These skills are important for students to get the most out of a course and get good grades or marks (eg *ensuring all pull their weight in group work; setting up placements or projects*). In employment these skills are often vital – most jobs involve agreeing matters with others, and in many negotiating is a major aspect (eg *management; buying; selling; legal work; surveying; project management etc*).

This chapter is based on the view that how you behave influences how others behave, that you are responsible for how you deal with others and that you can learn to deal with others in ways which meet both your needs.

We suggest you use this chapter:

- **when you face a situation where you need to negotiate or be assertive.**

When you have completed it, you should be able to:

Plan work
- identify the features of assertiveness and effective negotiation
- identify your approaches to agreeing matters with others and to assertiveness
- identify realistic needs and goals
- identify your own and others' responsibilities
- identify possible ways of proceeding.

Work towards agreed objectives
- anticipate the needs and goals of others
- use assertiveness techniques to achieve goals (eg *exchange information*)
- accept your responsibility in agreeing matters with others
- reach agreement (eg *resolve difficulties*).

Review work
- identify how far goals have been met, and factors affecting the outcomes
- identify how to improve in the future.

(Based on QCA Key Skill specifications, QCA 2000)

13.1 Negotiating skills (agreeing things with others)

13.1.1 Your approach

How do you normally try to reach agreement with others? What is the result? Does it work? What effect does it have on others?

Ways I use to get agreement	Results and effects

Why do you think you sometimes fail to agree things (with friends, at home, at work)?

✔

	Often	Sometimes	Never
I don't like the other people			
I'm scared of or wary of the other people			
The other people seem difficult			
I try to please others too much			
I get side-tracked			
We seem to misunderstand each other			
I get annoyed			
They get annoyed			
I don't know what I want			
I find it hard to think of ideas for solutions			
I find it hard to make decisions			
I don't want to lose face			
I'm more interested in what I want than what they want			
Others? (please add your own)			

13.1.2 Possible approaches to negotiating

There are various approaches to negotiating. This chapter assumes that using force or 'tricks' to get agreement is not good practice. We may need to work again with those with whom we negotiate, the organisation we represent may need to maintain goodwill or an ethical reputation, and our behaviour influences that of others.

Force or 'tricks' can include bullying or pressurising (eg *'if you don't agree then…'*), use of emotion (eg *'I've struggled here on this broken leg, the least you could do is…'*), 'brinkmanship', 'divide and rule', or 'deliberate misunderstanding' (Steel, Murphy, Russill 1989 – the examples are our own).

13.1.3 A suggested approach

One approach is suggested below – based on a book by Fisher and Ury (1987). Throughout this section we use our own example:

> *Five students are working on a group project. 'A' has not written a section of the group report as promised.*

After each suggestion there is a box for your notes on how you could use it in a situation facing you. It will help to now identify a situation you want to think about while working through this – one where you need to agree something with somebody.

Suggestion 1. Separate the people from the problem

* Identify problems and issues (rather than focusing on personalities).
* Look at the other's point of view. How do they see things? You don't have to agree, but acknowledging this can help. How do they feel? Involving them can encourage commitment (eg *not 'this is what we'll do' but 'how should we do this?'*)

Example

Problem: *What work still has to be done for the group project? When is the deadline? What are the difficulties? Why hasn't A done it?*

People: *How do we, and A, feel about it (worried, guilty, angry, not bothered)?*

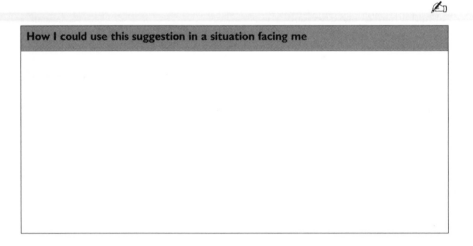

How I could use this suggestion in a situation facing me

Suggestion 2. Focus on interests, not positions

If you, or others, take up a position on an issue it can be hard to shift as you may lose face (eg *'if you don't do X, I'll do Y' – what happens if they don't do X and you don't want to do Y?*). Instead, ask others what matters or is important to them, then list these 'interests' and see where there are agreements and differences between you. You could ask them 'why?' or 'why not?'.

Example

What matters most to the members of the group? A good grade? Sharing work equally? Maintaining friendships? This may influence the option you choose.

How I could use this suggestion in a situation facing me

Suggestion 3. Think of options before making decisions

Having a number of options can mean better decisions. Think of as many options as possible before evaluating them, then decide on a few possible ones, perhaps in order of preference.

Try to avoid:

* looking for one answer
* assuming the situation can't be changed
* seeing the problem as 'theirs'
* making decisions too soon
* having a 'bottom line' which limits your thinking (although a 'bottom line' can mean you all work to the same end, eg *a deadline*).

It helps to know what you'll do if you don't reach agreement (the better the alternative, the greater your power – eg '*I don't really need to sell the house, I could rent it out*').

Example

The options for dealing with the group work problem may depend on the group members' interests, and the reasons for A's not doing the work. Possible ones are: A does it; the others do it and it is submitted as from all five, or it is submitted as the work of four people minus A; the report is restructured to remove A's section; the report is submitted without A's section; the matter is referred to a tutor.

How I could use this suggestion in a situation facing me

Suggestion 4. Agree criteria against which to judge outcomes

Agreeing in advance how to judge if the outcome is successful can avoid problems (eg *if you agree that everybody doing work on time is a criterion by which to judge success, everybody knows what is expected – and you have comeback if somebody does not deliver*). It can also change the way you see things (eg *not 'did you win or lose', but 'was the end result of our project good'*).

Example

How will the members of this group project judge their success? A good grade/mark? Sharing work equally? Maintaining friendships? This may affect the option chosen.

How I could use this suggestion in a situation facing me

Yes... but

What if there is a row, or A won't talk to us about the group project, or we daren't broach the subject, or we just put up with it? This is where assertiveness comes in.

13.2 Assertiveness

13.2.1 What is assertiveness?

People may behave in different ways in different situations. Which of the following do you do and when (or with whom) – on your course or in other situations?

Behaviour	If you do this, when (with whom)?	Why?
1 I allow others to get what they want, even if it's not what I want		
2 I tell others what to do, even if it's not what they want		
3 I get what I want by ways which aren't straightforward (eg 'scheming', 'tricks')		
4 I ask for what I want without imposing it on the other person		

In the box above:

1 is **passive**. Allowing others to get what they want, not expressing your needs (eg *'You have the cake'*).

2 is **aggressive**. Imposing your will or needs on others (eg *'Give me that cake'*).

3 is **manipulative**. 'Scheming' to get what you want (eg *'No, no, you have the cake, I'll go without'*).

4 is **assertive**. Expressing your needs openly without imposing on the other (eg *'I like cake, do you? Should we divide it up?'*).

What you do can affect how other people behave:

- If you are **passive** others may feel powerful or frustrated.
- If you are **aggressive** others may feel angry or intimidated.
- If you are **manipulative** others may feel powerless or taken advantage of.
- If you are **assertive** others know where they stand and feel respected. It encourages them to be assertive as they are not on the receiving end of one of the other behaviours.

Do you need to be more assertive? Looking at two main areas may help:

- why you behave non-assertively
- assertiveness techniques.

13.2.2 Reasons for not behaving assertively

There are many reasons for not being assertive. We may think others are better than us ('You're OK, I'm not OK') – or we are better than them ('I'm OK, you're not OK'). Assertiveness is about thinking 'I'm OK and you are OK' (Harris 1973). We may not know what we want – or just think about what we want and not what others want.

Look back at your notes in 13.2.1. If you can identify why you may not be assertive, it may become clear what you could do about it.

For example *if you are not assertive:*

* *when you feel negative about something – try to rephrase negative thoughts positively*
* *when you are under stress – identify what causes the stress and how you could reduce it (see Chapter 14 'Coping with Pressure')*
* *by trying to please others – you could begin to also think about your needs.*

Reasons why I am not assertive	Possible solutions

Sometimes people behave non-assertively because they have never considered the alternative. The following 'bill of rights' may help.

> I have the right to:
>
> 1 express my thoughts and opinion
> 2 express my feelings and be responsible for them
> 3 say yes to people
> 4 change my mind without making excuses
> 5 make mistakes and be responsible for them
> 6 say I don't know
> 7 say I don't understand
> 8 ask for what I want
> 9 say no without feeling guilty
> 10 be respected by others and respect them
> 11 be listened to and taken seriously
> 12 be independent
> 13 be successful
> 14 choose not to assert myself.

From Townend (1991)

You could now consider the above 'rights'.

* Do you agree with them or disagree with any?
* Do you find any of them difficult? Why (your culture may mean you may not want to follow all the 'rights' all the time)?
* What ideas does it give you about what you are responsible for and what others are responsible for?
* What effect might your view of these 'rights' have on how you deal with others?

My view on the 'rights'	Actions I could take

13.2.3 Goals and needs

To behave assertively, you must know what you need and want to happen. For a situation currently facing you, can you identify your needs and goals?

My needs	My goals (results/outcomes wanted)

Are your needs and goals realistic? Could you achieve them? Are they too difficult to achieve, or have you set them too low?

Being assertive is about accepting that others have needs and goals and that all parties should feel OK about solutions. What are the needs and goals of the others involved?

Their needs	Their goals (results/outcomes wanted)

13.2.4 Assertiveness techniques

Being assertive is partly about attitudes and partly about behaviour. If we begin to behave in a way which is assertive, even if we don't **feel** assertive, it starts to 'rub off', builds confidence and make us feel different. The following techniques can help.

As an example we use the group work situation given in 13.1.3 above. In this example *A should have produced a graph for a group project but has not done so.*

'Broken record'
This means repeating what you want without getting drawn into an argument.

Statement	Response
'You agreed to produce a graph, and we need it for our presentation tomorrow'	'I haven't got time'
'Yes, but we need it for tomorrow'	'I've had a lot of other things to do'
'I appreciate that, but the presentation is tomorrow'	'Can't somebody else do it'
'We agreed that you would do it, and tomorrow is the deadline'	'OK, I'll do it tonight'

If you do get drawn into an argument you are lost. For example:

Statement	Response
'I haven't got time'	'You've had as much time as us'
'No I haven't'	'Yes you have' etc, etc

Acknowledging criticisms

Accepting criticisms, but without grovelling, can defuse matters.

> *'That's right I should have produced the graph'*

Accepting compliments

Statement	Response
'That graph looks good'	*'Thanks' (not 'It's not as neat as I want!')*

Asking for clarification

If others criticise in a vague way, ask them to be specific.

> *'How have I not pulled my weight?'*

Avoiding preambles

They can confuse the listener and weaken the statement.

> *'We don't want to trouble you, and I know you are very busy, and there was the concert, and I know you've had a cold but please could you do the graph'*
>
> *Better to be direct 'Could you do the graph please?'*

Acknowledging and recognising your feelings

It is important to recognise your feelings.

> *'I feel bad about this, but I can't do the graph on time'*

It can help to note your initial gut reaction to being asked to do something (pleasure? panic?). What do those initial feelings tell you about what you want?

'Going up the gears'

If you don't get what you want first time be increasingly firm, as opposed to starting off at a maximum position.

> *Start by asking where the graph is, then make clear when it is needed by, then ask what the problem is, then firmly ask A to do it, then refer the matter to the lecturer.*

Being aware of your appearance

How you are dressed can increase confidence. Non-verbal signals send messages to the other person about how you feel.

> *If you face the other person and are at the same level you can look more assertive (if the other person stands while you sit they may appear dominant).*

Examples

Non-assertive	Assertive
stooped posture	*upright posture*
no eye contact	*eye contact*
voice (soft, angry, loud, volume)	*firm clear voice*
gestures (pointing fingers, biting nails)	*relaxed gestures*

Practise saying no

Practise saying no without excuses. It'll get easier.

13.3 Improving your effectiveness

13.3.1 Your effectiveness

How effective are you in meeting your goals and needs and allowing for those of others? Are you agreeing things with others (negotiating) effectively? Are you being assertive? The following can help you monitor and review what is happening.

Goal	
What I did	
Effect on me (and factors affecting this)	
Effect on others (and factors affecting this)	

13.3.2 Planning to improve

What I need to change	Actions to take, including resources and support to help me	Deadline

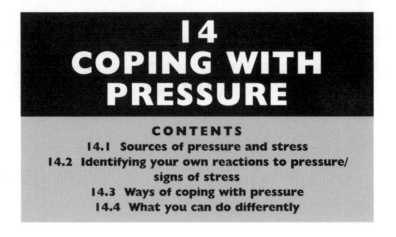

14
COPING WITH PRESSURE

Being under pressure carries both advantages and dangers. Human beings respond to and are encouraged by challenges, and a certain amount of tension is positive. Great advances have been made by individuals dealing with and over-coming challenges or problems.

However, the human body's biochemical processes deal with danger by releasing noradrenalin into the blood – the 'fight' or 'flight' hormone. This is a natural response.

Modern society's rules of behaviour often prevent us from fighting or fleeing, so there is no release of tension and this causes stress. We all experience stress and deal more or less effectively with it.

Certain illnesses can be stress related (eg *heart disease and high blood pressure*). Long before we reach that extreme stage stress can impair how well we operate.

People react to stress differently but common responses include: changes in sleep patterns; irritability; loss of temper; worrying about things, recurring minor ailments. Common physical symptoms of stress include: butterflies in the stomach; shallow breathing; minor illnesses such as sore throats or more serious ones like ulcers.

If you are not sleeping well, are falling out with those around you, or taking days off ill you will not get the most out of studying and enjoying life at university or college.

It may help to talk to others about how they feel about pressure, and how they deal with it.

We suggest you use this chapter:

- when a pressurised time is coming up (eg *exams*)
- when you are in a difficult situation
- to handle ongoing course pressures.

Agree targets
- identify your own reactions to pressure (positive and negative)
- identify possible sources of pressure (current and future)
- identify and select possible strategies to cope with pressure
- plan actions to cope with pressure, with timescales and resources/support needed
- identify factors which might affect your plans (eg *predict future pressures*).

Use your plan
- prioritise actions needed for improved coping with pressure
- carry out plans, monitoring and revising them as needed, to deal with any difficulties and changed circumstances
- seek and use feedback and support to cope with pressure.

Review progress and achievements
- identify how you coped with pressure and what affected this
- identify ways of improving your skills in coping with pressure in the future.

(Based on QCA Key Skill specifications, QCA 2000)

14.1 Sources of pressure and stress

Generally we feel stressed by:

- things which are very important to us
- changes which impose new pressures
- continually facing situations or people we don't know how to handle.

Increasing your awareness of what creates pressure and stress in you helps you to see what you can do about it.

Different people react differently to pressure and even have different views on what causes it (eg *some students positively enjoy exams while others are unable to think straight in them*). It is our perception of our ability to cope in a given situation that matters, not the situation itself. The following table, however, shows what people commonly find stressful.

Excessive stress may be caused by one or two major things or several small ones.

Look through the list below and add your own ideas of stressful events or situations you have experienced in the right-hand column (eg *getting a place on an HE course, leaving home for the first time, making new friends, coping with examinations, going for placement interviews*).

Events/experiences	My stresses (experienced within the past year)
Death of a partner	
Divorce/separation/break-up of relationship	
Death of a close family member/friend	
Marriage	
Marital reconciliation	
Sex difficulties	
Children leaving home	
Difficulties with relatives	
Partner starts/stops work	
Making new friends	
Prison term	
Personal injury/illness	
Pregnancy	
Outstanding personal achievement	
Change in living conditions	
Moving house/finding lodgings	
Change in recreation activities (eg *sport*)	
Change in personal habits (eg *sleeping/eating*)	
Holiday/Christmas	

Events/Experiences	My stresses (experienced within the past year)
Loss of job (eg *dismissal/redundancy*), retirement	
Balancing work and study	
Change in work (eg *different work, responsibilities, workload*)	
Begin or end school/college	
Difficulties with work	
Change in work hours or conditions	
Change in financial state	
Large mortgage, debts, no grant	
Foreclosure of mortgage or loan	
Small mortgage or loan	

Use the following to make notes on your current pressures (eg *on your course or in your life at university/college or outside*).

On my course or in my life at university/college or outside what is particularly important to me at the moment?

What do other people want from me and who wants it?

What is happening that is new or different in my life?

Has my workload or level of activities changed?

Are there people who upset or annoy me? Why?

What might cause pressure in the future?

14.2 Identifying your own reactions to pressure/signs of stress

Increasing your awareness of how you react to pressure and stress helps in starting to identify what you can do about it.

In what positive ways do you tend to react to pressure? It is worth reminding yourself of your strengths. How will you know if you are reacting negatively and feeling stressed?

14.2.1 Positive reactions to pressure

When under pressure I...	
think clearer	∨
work faster	∨
dump what is unimportant	✓
take a step back, think before acting	✓
see the pressure as an opportunity	
see the pressure as a challenge	∨
enjoy meeting targets	
Other reactions: add your own items	

14.2.2 Stress – negative reactions to pressure

What are your symptoms?   ✔

How often do you:	Often	Sometimes	Rarely	Never
feel irritable?		⌄		
feel restless/ talk fast/ walk fast/ feel in a rush?		⌄		
feel angry?				
feel frustrated at having to wait for something?		⌄		
slump?				
become easily confused/have memory problems/find it difficult to concentrate?			✓	
Have emotional outbursts/have marked mood swings/feel weepy?				
think about negative things without wanting to/worry?			✓	
smoke?				
drink too much alcohol?				
eat too much/eat when you are not hungry/go off your food?		⌄		
not have enough energy to get things done?				
find it difficult to fall asleep/hard to get up/wake early?				
feel you can't cope/feel sorry for yourself?				
find it hard to make decisions?				
feel you have lost your sense of humour?			⌄	
take tranquillisers/non-prescribed drugs?				
have minor accidents?				

We all feel or do most of these things from time to time, but if most of your ticks are in the often or sometimes columns perhaps it is time to review things. It is easy to get into habits of behaviour, accept them as 'normal', and not realise they are indicators of stress which can be removed or reduced.

How many ticks did you have in the 'Sometimes' column	How many ticks did you have in the 'Often' column

When you are stressed what are the most significant signs for you?

14.2.3 How are you reacting to current pressures?

How are you reacting to current pressures and what are the advantages or disadvantages (eg *putting things off may make you feel better in the short term but cause longer term problems*)?

It may help to discuss with friends how they think you react to pressure. What advantages or disadvantages can they see about your reactions?

Source of pressure	My reaction	Advantages	Disadvantages

14.3 Ways of coping with pressure

Different people find different things helpful. The following suggests a range of strategies. Some may help in some situations, some in others – pick and choose. They need practice especially if they are new ways of doing things. You could refer back to your notes on current pressures in Section 14.1.

14.3.1 Remove the cause of the pressure

You could get out of the situation (eg *if you live in a shared flat and can't work because of other's noise – move out and find others who are quieter, or live alone*).

However, sometimes it may be better in the long term to stay and sort it out, and you may not be able to get out of a situation easily.

14.3.2 Find a better way of dealing with the pressure

What could you do differently? You could:

* be clearer about what you want and tell people in an assertive way (see Chapters 13 and 28 on 'Negotiating and Assertiveness')
* prepare: if you've got an interview think it through in advance; if you've got an exam, plan ahead (use Chapters 15 and 30 on 'Revising and Examination Techniques'); if you have been 'last minuting', try forward planning (see Chapters 3 and 20 on 'Organising Yourself and Your Time')
* take a fresh look at the situation. Write the problem down and list the options, then think about other approaches (see Chapters 10 and 26 on 'Solving Problems')
* talk about it with somebody to help clarify things.

14.3.3 Keep fit

You are more likely to cope if you feel well. Regular exercise can use up 'fight and flight' hormones, and it does not have to be strenuous – little and often is the key. Walking short journeys instead of catching the bus may make the difference between feeling tense and feeling relaxed.

Eat healthily – there is evidence that certain foods cause stress. The healthy diet advocated nowadays is lots of fruit and vegetables, and less 'junk food'.

It may not feel like it at the time but drinking alcohol and smoking increase stress. They are stimulants which add to the agitation caused by the 'fight and flight' hormones.

14.3.4 Distract yourself

If you are constantly thinking about whatever is causing you stress, you may make it worse (eg *by getting it out of proportion, getting yourself into such a state that you can do nothing*).

One way is to distract yourself (eg *go to a film, go out with friends – but don't discuss your problem*). Do something to make you laugh (eg *not a weepy film*). Humour is therapeutic (it creates helpful chemicals in the body).

This does not mean ignoring the problem. At other times, you will need to talk about it, or deal with it quickly. It means giving yourself a break from it – this may also get it into perspective.

14.3.5 Treat the symptoms of stress

Some simple techniques can reduce the symptoms of stress.

Breathing exercises – if you are anxious you may breathe shallowly, only using the top of your lungs. This should reduce butterflies and calm you down:

- Breathe fully out pulling your stomach in.
- Then breathe into the bottom of your lungs by letting your stomach out, then into the chest, and finally into the top of your lungs.
- Breathe out to a count of 4, 6, or 8 and in to the same count.

Relaxation exercises – lie down or sit in a comfortable chair. In turn, tense and then relax your muscles. Start with your foot, then your calf muscles, and then go round the body.

Other forms of relaxation include meditation, massage and yoga. There are yoga classes around and being in a group can make it easier to get involved.

Think about something pleasant – a place you've been on holiday, a room you like. See it with your 'mind's eye' and concentrate on it.

If you can't sleep, **count backwards aloud from 500** to stop your mind racing. Keep a pad by the bed and write down what you are thinking about.

14.3.6 Change your way of thinking

This can be hard. It doesn't happen quickly and you have to work at it. It can be frustrating if others say 'stop thinking like that', 'snap out of it', or 'cheer up'. This section isn't meant to be like that.

Ways of changing how you think can include:

- write it down: how you feel; what the opposite view is; challenge your assumptions (is it really like that?).
- decide on a different way to think about it and talk to yourself, looking at it from that perspective. Stop thinking negative or worrying thoughts by making yourself think about other things.
- talk to yourself out loud (you'll need to pick your time!) – you can't think one thought while speaking about another. It might take 20 minutes to stop yourself thinking about unpleasant things, but it does work.
- look at the situation differently and put things into perspective.

What is the worst that could happen?

How important will it be in a year?

Are there positive things about it?

How would somebody else, who wasn't involved, see it?

What would the opposite way of thinking about it be?

What are the positives in the rest of your life?

14.3.7 Seek help

If you feel under stress you could seek help, eg:

- consult friends: 'a problem shared is a problem halved'
- join others with similar concerns (eg *a support group*). The Students Union or a library may have lists of groups – or form one yourself (eg *mature students'/women's/gay groups, etc*)
- consult your tutor/lecturer: may help you understand a subject or plan your time better
- use other chapters in this book (see conents) (eg *'Group Work', 'Negotiating and Assertiveness'*)
- take a study skills course
- consult a Careers Service: can help you think about what to do at the end of your course, or with interview and self-presentation techniques
- consult a Counselling Service: can provide support and an opportunity to talk things through
- sports activities (at 'competitive' and 'fun' levels)
- visit your Medical Centre or doctor: can help if the symptoms have made you ill – or help you stop them making you ill
- consult specialists (eg *a Disability Unit: provides support for disabled students*).

14.3.8 Use feedback

It may help to ask others for feedback about how you cope with pressure. There are many different types of feedback (eg *written comments from your tutor/employer, informal feedback from friends and fellow students*). It helps to ask specific questions.

'How do you think I coped with the pressure of the exams?' could elicit useful information (eg *'You seemed to leave things until the last minute and then got quite tense about it'*).

'Can I cope with stress?' is a more general question which may lead to sweeping statements in reply. It invites judgmental comments which may be less helpful (eg *'Yes, very well'*, *'No, you go to pieces'*).

When seeking feedback it helps to:

- listen without interrupting or defending
- check that you have understood (eg *'Do you mean that...?'*)
- weigh up which aspects of the feedback you agree with and what to take note of (you may think the other person is wrong or has misunderstood the situation).

For more information on asking for and using feedback, look at Chapter 17 on 'Reflecting on Your Experience' in Part I.

Which of the suggestions above (14.3.1–14.3.8) would be most useful to you now, for a situation you are currently facing?

14.4 What you can do differently

14.4.1 Planning to cope

It could help to review this chapter and your notes on it, to summarise the main areas you want to change, what actions you could take and who or what might help.

What factors might affect your plans (eg *an exam or interview coming up*)? Try to allow for this as you complete the following action plan.

Who could give you feedback and support on how you are coping (eg *friends, other course members, family, personal tutor*)?

Areas to change	Actions to take	Sources of support (people or materials)	When?

What will you do first? What is most important at the moment? You could identify your priority areas by numbering or highlighting key actions in the table above.

14.4.2 Monitoring and revising what you do

Making notes of what you have tried and what works for you would:

- make you feel better
- build your confidence
- help you identify what to do again.

Making notes of what hasn't worked will help you see what to focus on to improve.

You could use your action plan (in the previous section) or keep a diary/log, to note:

- what you did which worked
- how you know it worked – the evidence
- what didn't work
- how you know it didn't work – the evidence
- anything which affected your plans
- what the feedback tells you about your progress. Can you use others' ideas and suggestions to help you further?

Amend your action plan regularly:

- as your skills in coping develop
- as your situation/priorities change
- if any difficulties arise as you work through it (eg *books are unavailable*).

Make allowances for yourself. Changing things like this takes time.

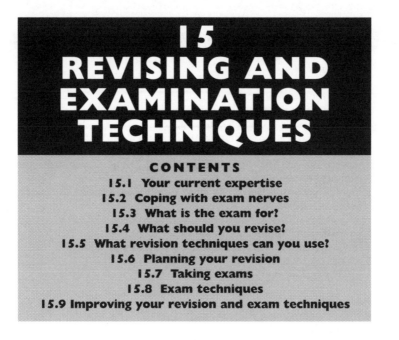

15
REVISING AND EXAMINATION TECHNIQUES

CONTENTS

Examinations are a common form of assessment at university/college. You may have considerable experience of them, or very little, depending on your route into university or college.

University/college exams may differ from those you have experienced to date, as may the type and amount of material to be revised. Given the importance of exams for most final qualifications, it is well worth considering how to improve your performance. Doing well in exams not only depends on your knowledge, but also on how good you are at revising and handling the exam itself.

Even if exams in the early stages of your course do not count towards final grades, they are important in helping you develop your revision and exam techniques. It is helpful to have developed effective strategies before your final exams.

If you have a disability which may affect your exam performance, speak to your lecturer as early as possible about alternative arrangements.

We suggest you use this chapter:

- **when you have an exam coming up to help you plan the revision for it and then to perform successfully in it.**

When you have completed it, you should be able to:

Agree targets
Revision techniques
* review your current expertise
* identify which material to revise and prioritise
* identify possible revision techniques
* identify the purpose and format of the exam and what the examiners are looking for
* make a revision plan – identify tasks with deadlines, resources and support needed
* identify any factors that might affect your plans (eg *family commitments, workload, difficulties*).

Examination techniques
* identify your own usual responses to exams and plan for this
* identify techniques to deal with the exam
* plan time allocation in the exam.

Use a plan
Revision techniques
* identify and use possible revision techniques which work well for the subject, the exam format and you
* monitor revision plans and amend them as needed, dealing with any difficulties and using feedback and support.

Examination techniques
* identify what questions mean and what is required
* identify which questions to answer in which order
* plan answers including appropriate evidence.

Review progress and achievements
* identify what influenced the outcome of the exam
* identify ways of improving revising and exam techniques in the future.

(Based on QCA Key Skill specifications, QCA 2000)

15.1 Your current expertise

Think about the last exam(s) you took.

* Did you do as well as you deserved?
* What did you do which worked well/less well?

In the following box please focus on how you carried out your revision and how you handled the exam, rather than on how well you dealt with the subject matter.

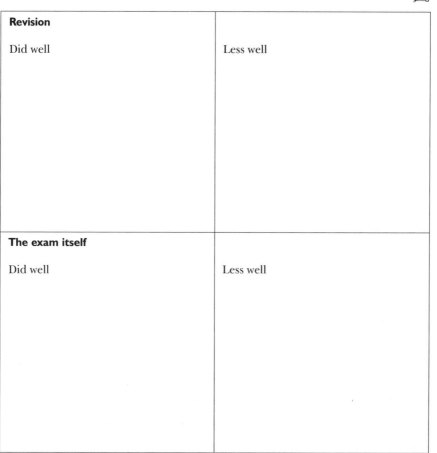

Revision	
Did well	Less well
The exam itself	
Did well	Less well

It might help to discuss your replies with (an)other student(s). What did they do which was different from what you did? You can then consider:

- what aspects of your revising and exam techniques are effective and can be built on?
- what aspects of your revising and exam techniques are not effective and need improvement?

15.2 Coping with exam nerves

Exams are stressful – but stress is not necessarily negative. You may be more mentally alert under stress, which is why you can produce so much in the short space of an exam. Research indicates that you will perform better if you view stress as positive and exams as a chance to demonstrate your abilities rather than as a way of tripping you up.

To help you reduce anxiety, you could:

- prepare thoroughly and do enough revision to make you feel confident
- find out as much as possible about the exam (eg *when/where the exam will be; how long it will be; how many questions there are, how much choice there is; what the arrangements are if you want to go to the toilet, or if you have a problem during the exam. What happens if you are ill or if you fail?*)
- find out about the assessment criteria. Do all the exam questions carry equal marks? What will get good marks?
- spend the first 10 minutes in an exam planning how to deal with it and then try to stick to the plan. It avoids the 'flitting about' or 'getting stuck' that nerves sometimes induces.
- swap experiences with others after an exam to release tension. This can be helpful in acknowledging that most people experience exam nerves, and in discussing how to avoid problems.
  Others may find this makes them more anxious. If this applies to you, leave as soon as possible after the exam.
- Use relaxation techniques, eg yoga, avoid too much alcohol, eat sensibly and get sufficient sleep. See Chapter 14 on 'Coping with Pressure' in Part I.

15.3 What is the exam for?

In order to revise and then to perform well in the exam it helps to identify what the examiner is looking for. This may vary from subject to subject and also between levels in a subject eg *between years 1 and 2*.

In the following box, tick what you think was looked for in the exams for a subject you studied in the past, and what you think the examiner will look for in your next exams.

✔

What did/will the examiner look for?	Previous exams you have taken	This course
The amount of work you have done		
The amount you can write in a given time		
How you cope with the pressure of the exam		
The factual information you know		
How well you grasp what the exam question is aiming at		
Accuracy		
Your writing style, eg *spelling, grammar, how you express yourself*		
Ability to apply conventions, eg *correct references, ways of presenting graphs or diagrams, use of scientific terms*		

✔

What did/will the examiner look for?	Previous exams you have taken	This course
The presentation of your exam paper		
Being able to apply knowledge to a particular situation		
The underlying concepts/principles you know		
Being able to argue a particular point of view		
Being able to criticise and analyse information		
Other. Please list		

If you are unsure how to complete the final column of the above box in relation to your current course you can:

- look at previous exam papers. You may find examples: in your learning centre/library; in your course/programme guide; by asking your lecturer.

  What does **the format** suggest about what they are looking for? For example, many short questions may mean knowledge of factual information is required, or a case study may mean being able to apply knowledge to a particular situation.

  What do **the type of questions** suggest about what they are looking for? For example, do the questions ask you to repeat the knowledge you have or to do something with it (eg *to present two sides of an argument, to analyse etc*)?

- ask your lecturer what is expected both by her/himself or by an external examiner.

It is worth checking out your assumptions (eg *at university/college the examiners will not be as concerned with how much you write in a given time as with what you write*).

Each exam may have different expectations (eg *some may look for an in-depth knowledge and how you apply it, others for how well you argue a case*).

What are the formal requirements? You could look in course handbooks, in a Student Handbook or ask your tutor.

Questions to ask	Your notes
Will it count towards your final degree classification? If so, by how much?	
What do you need to do to pass? What are the assessment criteria? What is the pass mark?	
What happens if you are ill, or have serious problems which could affect your performance?	
What happens if you fail? When are resits?	
What are the regulations about cheating and plagiarism?	

15.4 What should you revise?

How can you choose what to revise? This may depend partly on:

- what is likely to be covered in the exam
- what will maximise your marks.

What do your responses to Section 15.3 'What is the exam for?' imply about choosing what to revise? Have the selection methods you have used in the past worked? What are their advantages/disadvantages? Will this be appropriate for your next exam?

- How do you normally choose?
- Which other methods could you try instead?

✔

Selection method	In the past	Could try
Work through the material from beginning to end and try to cover it all		
Cover all the material to some extent but identify particular areas to focus on		
Focus on topics which seem difficult		
Focus on topics which seem interesting or easy		
Look at previous exam papers to identify what might crop up		
Ask the lecturer what is critical and likely to crop up		
Memorise as much factual information as possible		
Focus on the main principles/concepts and also the factual information which provides evidence for them		
Base your selection on the format of the exam (eg *will you only have to answer three long questions on three topics or 50 short questions on a wide range of topics?*)		
Others. Please specify		

In thinking about what will prepare you well, you could consider:

- what is likely to come up in the exam
- what will get good marks (eg *factual information or understanding principles and concepts*) – the assessment criteria
- how much time you have to revise
- what the exam format is (eg *if you need to answer three long questions on three topics, you will need to know those three topics in depth; 50 short questions mean you may need to cover a broader range of material, but perhaps in less depth*).

See the revision plan in Section 15.6.3

15.5 What revision techniques can you use?

15.5.1 What helps people remember?

The best revision techniques are active. Just reading through notes is insufficient to make you remember them. Even if you could recite them, it is unlikely to be enough. In university/college you rarely have to just repeat information in an exam, you also need to demonstrate you can use it in some way.

People are more likely to remember something if:

- **it is relevant to them**. How can you make the material more relevant to you? (eg *see revision technique (e) below*)

- **it is associated with something else** (just as we remember a person's name by remembering where we met) (eg *see revision techniques (f), (h) below*)

- **they remember things in sequence**, where one thing triggers the next element (like an actor's/actress' cue) (eg *see revision technique (k) below*)

- **they do something with the information.** All the following suggestions involve actively doing something.

15.5.2 Suggestions for revision techniques

You could consider which of the following revision techniques are best suited to the subject and form of the exam, as well as to your own way of working.

a) Before you start revising, sort out your material for each subject, so you know how much and what material you have.

b) Keep notes and other materials well organised. Go through your material each week, making notes clearer, putting in headings, checking on what you don't understand. Use coloured/highlighting pens for different topics, or coloured dividers in files. See Chapter 4 on 'Note Taking' for ideas on how to improve your notes.

c) Try to identify the central questions/issues at the heart of each subject and plan how you would answer them.

d) Test yourself. Look at some material and then jot down what you can recall. Go back to the original material and see what you remembered.

   Look at some material and write questions on it. Leave it for a few days, then try to answer the questions and 'mark' yourself.

e) When you recall your material, try to link a topic with other elements on your course, rather than revising as if the subjects are unrelated. Produce a card for each topic with notes about other topics it refers to.

f) Use patterns. Write a theme word on a page and connect it through lines to related topics. This can be more memorable than a list because it has visual impact. You can practise reproducing it from memory and if an exam question contains one of the words in the pattern you could reproduce the image in rough as a starting point.

g) Look at a section of the material and jot down a summary of the main points. Keep the summaries to use as a brief reminder.

h) Flash cards. Read your notes, make summaries for each topic and then further reduce them to a few words on a card. As the exam approaches reading through the flash cards can serve as a quick reminder.

i) Work with a friend. Test each other or summarise a topic you have just revised for each other. Explain a difficult concept to a friend and check s/he understands what you mean. Discuss what questions might crop up and how you might answer them.

j) If you don't understand your material when you come to revise, clarify it. Use a learning centre/library. Ask friends, the lecturer or tutor.

k) For science, technology or maths, go over tutorial sheets/assignments and work again through the calculations/problems, to ensure you understand each stage and can use the techniques.

l) Make lists (eg *of important sequences, vital points, steps in a process*).

m) Practise in advance. Think of likely questions and make outlines answers. Try to answer previous papers in the time allowed.

n) Tape record information and listen to it while driving or cooking.

o) Ask friends how they revise. They may have useful suggestions.

p) How long can you concentrate for? Build in breaks. Revise different subjects in one day.

Avoid distractions. Being tired or hungry can affect you. If you are distracted by thoughts (eg *what to have for tea*), write it down and look at it later. If your mind wanders you may need to stop for a while.

q) Identify the environment you work best in (eg *quiet/warm/cold/alone*). Where could you work?

r) Revising is hard work. Give yourself treats.

Which of these revision techniques would work well for your subject, the format of your exam and for you personally?

You could note below the ideas which you intend to use.

15.6 Planning your revision

15.6.1 How much time have you got to revise?

Many people put off revising and panic when they realise time is running out. Panic can mean you think less clearly and it interferes with memory. Identify what you could do in advance. For example:

2 months in advance	eg *sort out notes, ensuring that they are understandable*
1 month in advance	eg *make summaries of notes*
1 week in advance	eg *test self*
1 day in advance	eg *use flash cards*

15.6.2 Make a plan

You are expected at university/college to be responsible for your own learning. You will need to decide for yourself what to revise, how and when. You may receive very little direction about this. One of the aims of Further and Higher Education is to encourage students to be independent.

A plan might include what you are going to revise, how and when. Listing the topics you need to revise within each subject/unit means you can tick them off as you go along. You could produce a day by day revision timetable. A plan can:

- indicate if you are spending too much time on one subject
- alert you to what still needs to be done
- be a psychological boost by showing what you have already done.

What do you need to allow for in your plan?

Will you need to consider:

Personal factors	Your notes
revision for other exams at the same time?	
paid work?	
family commitments, relationships, friends?	
possible illness?	
not understanding material?	
your need to take exercise?	
how much sleep you need?	
your need for leisure activities and fun?	
Others? Please list	

Will you need to consider:

External factors	Your notes
not being able to get hold of lecturers or other specialists?	
equipment breaking (eg *computers, cars*)?	
books not being available?	
the exam format?	
any particular techniques associated with your subject?	
Others? Please list	

You are more likely to cope with pressure if you are physically fit and keep things in perspective – look at Chapter 14 on 'Coping with Pressure'.

15.6.3 Revision plan

- What are your priority areas to revise? Mark these on your plan.
- Check your plan regularly, to see how well you are doing. You may need to change it (eg *for something unexpected, revision takes longer*).
- You could check with others how you are progressing. Could anyone help you stick to your plan? Could anyone give you feedback?

Subject/what to revise	
Revision techniques	
Support/ resources needed	
By when?	
Progress/notes of further action needed	

15.7 Taking Exams

15.7.1 Your responses in exams

Think about the last exam you sat.

How did you spend the first 10 minutes of it? What did you do?

How did you feel during the first 10 minutes?

What did you do during the middle part of the exam?

What did you do during the last 10 minutes?

How did you feel during and at the end of the exam?

Section 15.8 will help you focus on what you can do to build on strengths and improve on weaker areas.

15.7.2 Types of examinations

An unseen exam
This is any exam where you do not know what it will contain in advance. Examples might be:

- **essays/problems**. Usually these require you to apply your knowledge to a particular situation (eg *to answer a particular problem or to present an argument from a particular standpoint*).

- **short answer questions**. Here you are given a number of questions which often require factual knowledge.

  Tip. It may be best not to waste time on those you cannot answer. Answer those you can and return to the rest if you have time. Avoid wasting time by giving more information than is asked for. If there are only 2 marks for an answer you won't get any more by writing more.

- **multiple choice**. Here you have to choose between several given answers.

  Tip. Answer those you are sure of and return to those which require more thought.

- **phase tests.** These are short tests of usually no more than an hour. They test that students have grasped the essential elements of a specific and small section of material (ie that covered in one 'phase' of the course).

A seen exam
This is where you are given material or questions in advance. The focus is less on remembering information and more on what you do with it (eg *analyse it, present arguments etc*). Examples might be:

- **open book exams**. Here you can take material into the exam.

- **take away**. You may be given a question in advance, to complete and return by a given date, or you may be given a question to prepare in advance but answer it under exam conditions (eg *you are given a case study in advance, on which you answer questions in an exam room, within a time limit*).

15.8 Exam Techniques

The following cover a range of exam techniques, some of which will be reminders of what you already do, while others will be new to you.

Before the exam
a) If you have a disability which may make it difficult for you to perform well in an exam, you need to discuss any special arrangements with your tutor in advance, eg *Braille or large print exam papers can be made available.*

b) Arrive at the exam in plenty of time to avoid panicking. On arrival, will it help to chat to others, or will this make you feel anxious? If so wait outside until it is time to go in.

c) Make a list of what you will take into the exam (eg *calculator, spare batteries, pens, pencils etc*). Check in advance what is allowed

d) If you are used to short exams, like phase tests, and you now face a long exam (eg *3 hours*), think what you will need to do differently (eg *in a long exam you may need to spend more time planning at the start*).

Choosing questions to answer

e) Spend 5 minutes reading the exam paper, deciding which questions to answer. Make sure you answer the correct number of questions. (If you only answer three instead of four, for example, you automatically lose 25%.)

f) What do the questions mean? Underline the key words in each question to identify exactly what is being asked, eg:

- *compare/contrast* (implies looking at two or more different perspectives)
- *evaluate* (implies offering criticisms or making judgements)
- *analyse* (implies asking why, looking at two underlying factors)
- *explain* (implies laying out each stage in a process or argument or each aspect of an object in a logical way).

A common reason for losing marks is not answering the question asked. You will not get credit for an excellent, but irrelevant answer. It is easy to misread things if you are nervous, and it can help to put the question into your own words.

g) Try to avoid questions which contain a word or phrase that you don't understand. If you guess wrongly you may get few marks.

Planning and monitoring time

h) Decide how long you will give to each question, then monitor your timekeeping. Allow 10 minutes at the end for checking.

i) Spend a few minutes planning your answers. Jot down notes and then cross them out, so the examiner knows not to assess them. You may get better marks for coherent and logical arguments than a list of ideas on a topic.

j) The first 50% of marks for a question are easiest to obtain. The next 25% are harder. The last 25% are very difficult to achieve. If you are running out of time two half answers may be worth more than one whole.

eg $^{15}/_{25} + {}^{15}/_{25} + {}^{12}/_{25} + {}^{10}/_{25}$

is better than

$^{20}/_{25} + {}^{18}/_{25} + {}^{10}/_{25} + {}^{1}/_{25}$

If you do run out of the time you have allocated for a question, jot down in rough notes the main points you still need to include while they are fresh in your mind and move on to the next question. If you have time you can return to it.

k) You could plan your answers to subsequent questions after you have finished your first answer. At this stage you are over the initial tension of the exam, but you still have time for planning.

l) Spend the last 10 minutes checking your work (eg *how you have numbered your answers, spelling, handwriting, ensuring that all the steps have been shown in a calculation etc*).

Writing answers

m) For an essay type answer, write a strong introductory paragraph showing that you understand the question, and a strong last paragraph where you draw conclusions, returning to the question. This will demonstrate to the examiner that your answer is purposeful and relevant.

n) Write clearly! A model answer will gain no marks if the examiner cannot read it. Examiners are influenced by how well work is presented (imagine marking 100 exam scripts!). Make sure you number your answers correctly, especially if you do them out of sequence.

o) At university/college, answers are expected to show a rigorous understanding of the subject. Avoid unsupported opinions and include evidence to demonstrate your points. Unless specified, this will usually not mean personal experiences, but rather evidence from research or from the literature on the subject.

p) Quantity will not gain marks. It is more important to make relevant points than to include padding, which takes valuable time to produce without improving your grade. If you think you have covered all the main points in an answer, move on.

15.9 Improving your revision and exam techniques

After the exam, it should help to ask yourself if you did as well as possible and what affected the outcome. This can be the start of your preparation for your next exam.

In what way was your exam performance affected by:
what you revised?
how you revised?
how you used your time (eg *when you started revising, effectiveness of your plan*)?
what you did in the actual exam? How (eg *not doing a plan, waffling*)?
What else influenced it?

What can you do to improve your skills? You could refer back to the action plan below when you are revising and preparing for another exam.

What do I need to improve?	Action I could take	Resources/ support needed	By when?

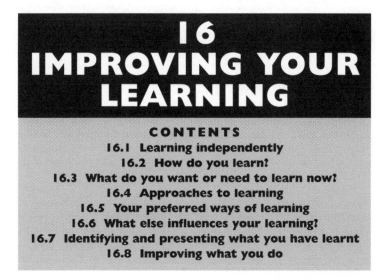

16
IMPROVING YOUR LEARNING

CONTENTS

You may think that learning is just something you do naturally, a skill which can't be learnt, or that we all learn in the same way.

The research evidence suggests that people learn in different ways, and that you can improve how you learn. Reviewing how you learn and trying out new methods can improve your learning and make you more successful on your course.

We suggest you use this chapter:

- to help you with things you want to or need to learn now
- to help you improve how you learn in general
- together with the other chapters, which are all about learning specific skills
- together with Chapter 18 'Action Planning', which will help you plan to improve and to put your plans into action.

When you have completed it, you should be able to:

- identify learning goals or targets
- study complex matters
- seek and use feedback to aid learning
- identify and use sources of support and information to aid learning
- identify, use and adapt effective ways of learning for your subject, the context, the format (eg *visual, verbal, auditory, physical)* and yourselves
- identify how and what you learned
- present information about your learning, with evidence
- identify factors, including difficulties, which influence your learning
- deal with difficulties which may affect learning
- learn independently
- identify how to improve your learning.

(Based on QCA Key Skill specifications, QCA 2000)

16.1 Learning independently

At university/college you are expected to learn independently, without constant support from lecturers and tutors. This is known as 'autonomous learning'.

It does not mean you should learn alone (many courses have group work/seminars/ tutorials to help students learn from each other), but that you know how to learn and can do so without much guidance. This may be different from school, or workplaces. You are seen as responsible for your own learning. You may think you already know how to learn, but it may be very different at university/college – and you can 'learn to learn' better.

The answer to 'how can you learn best' varies between individuals and between courses. This chapter aims to help you identify how best to learn given the person you are, your subject, the sorts of materials you will learn from (eg *visual, verbal, text, objects*) and your situation (eg *living at home, in a shared house, doing paid work while studying etc*).

16.2 How do you learn?

16.2.1 What do you do now?

We learn new things all the time: physical or practical things (eg *how to play a sport, drive, repair things or cook*); how to deal with people (eg *how not to annoy them or to persuade them*); academic subjects.

When you learn something, how do you go about it? Do you do the same thing, or different things in different situations? Here are some idea starters, to which you can add items.

✔

Possible ways of learning	Physical/ practical	Dealing with people	Academic
Watch what others do/copy examples			
Follow instructions			
Read books/information about it			
Watch videos about it			
Discuss it with others (eg *tutors, friends*)			
Try things out until something works			
Practise (do something until you get it right)			
Ask others for feedback on what you do			
Ask others for advice			
Think about it later to see what did/didn't work			
Make plans			
Others. Add your own items here			

Which of the above works best for you? Which do you find easy or hard, or like or dislike? You could go back and mark items with plus or a minus, or 'l' for like and 'd' for 'dislike'.

16.2.2 What do you think you should be learning?

On your course what do you think you are trying to learn? What do you think the lecturers or tutors want you to learn? What do you think gets good marks or grades?

✔

Remembering facts and details	
Being able to follow set procedures, such as calculations or lab procedures	
Knowing what other people say about a topic	
Understanding concepts, principles, theories, ideas	
Being able to make connections between different topics or pieces of information	
Being able to identify the principles, concepts, theories, behind the facts and details	
Relating theory to practice	
Learning to do things (eg *skills/procedures, communicating/working in groups*)	
Learning how to question, analyse, criticise, or think in certain ways	
Being able to form your own judgements	

16.2.3 Why are you learning?

Are you learning at university/college...

✔

to get a good grade or mark?	
to get a good job?	
to find out as much as you can about the subject?	
because you like learning new things?	
to develop aspects of yourself?	
Others. Add here any other reasons you might have	

16.3 What do you want or need to learn now?

At the moment, what do you most need to or want to learn on your course? This could be one thing or several things. It could be a particular topic or a way of doing something.

Why is this important to you? How will you know you have learnt it or judge your success (eg *good grade/mark; being able to do something; feedback*)? You can then work though the rest of this chapter with this in mind.

What do you want or need to learn now?	Why?	How will you know you have learnt it well enough?

16.4 Approaches to learning

It may sound obvious, but educational research shows that what you think tutors want influences how and what you learn. What may not be so obvious is the effect this may have on, for example, *your grades/marks, your understanding of a subject* (see 16.2.3 above).

Marton and Saljo (1984) identified two main approaches to learning: **surface and deep.**

In their study, some students thought they were supposed to learn facts and details and had to follow set procedures or repeat what others had said. So, this is what they did. They took a **surface approach** to their learning.

Other students thought they were supposed to look for underlying concepts and principles beneath the facts, and to make connections between different topics (eg *are there common features?*). So, this is what they did. They took a **deep approach** to their learning, looking beneath the surface details at principles.

In university/college courses you may sometimes have to follow set procedures (eg *this may affect safety in a lab or the accuracy of results*) and may need to know facts and details, but this is usually as evidence for theories and concepts. You must deal with complex topics, where there are different ways of seeing issues and there is no simple interpretation. What is needed is an ability to see the underpinning aspects and the connections between similar topics. What is wanted in university/college courses is a **deep approach** to learning.

A deep approach becomes even more important at the higher levels of a course (eg *by the final year*), when you need to make your own judgements, based on evidence (for more help see Chapter 22 'Critical Analysis'.

If you think only facts and details are wanted, but what is mainly wanted is identifying underlying principles, you may not be very successful. **Look at 16.2.2 above**. Are you taking a surface or deep approach to your work? Do you take a different approach for different topics or units?

Gibbs (1992) identified a third approach – **'strategic'**. Here students do what they think will get the best mark, taking a surface approach when they think that is needed and a deep one when that is needed. The problem here is that you may be wrong about what is wanted. At university/college it may be safest to assume 'deep' is needed.

There may, however, be different balances in different subjects/topics – in some it may be important to learn facts and details, in others less so. Because something is expected in one unit does not mean it is expected in another. To find out what is needed you could:

- ask the lecturer/tutor
- look at the learning outcomes for the course or unit/module
- look at the assessment criteria for any work you have to do
- look at past exam papers to see what sort of questions were asked
- look at the sort of coursework you are asked to do
- look at or listen to the sort of feedback you get from lecturers/tutors
- talk to other students (eg *in your year/level, in the year/level above*).

You need to know what you are supposed to be learning about in order to learn it. Look back at 16.3 above. You can note below what you think you need to learn.

What do you want/need to learn now (refer back to your notes in the box in Section 16.3)?	What should you be learning for this (eg *facts, concepts, ways of thinking, skills*)?

16.5 Your preferred ways of learning

16.5.1 Why it is important to identify your way of learning

Kolb (1984) suggested we learn by following a cycle. The following is based on, but not identical to, Kolb's cycle.

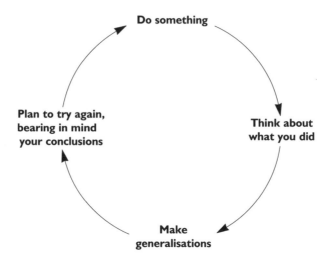

Kolb identified four main ways of learning, which relate to the stages in this cycle and which are described in Section 16.5.2 below. The ways of learning relate to parts of the cycle.

- 'Do something' relates to 'concrete' (see 16.5.2)
- 'Think about what you did' relates to 'reflective' (see 16.5.2)
- 'Make generalisations' relates to 'abstract' (see 16.5.2)
- 'Plan to try again' relates to 'active' (see 16.5.2)

To learn well you should be able to use, at least to some extent, all four ways. If you only learn in one way you won't go all the way round the cycle.

16.5.2 What are 'ways of learning'?

Kolb (1984) suggested that we each prefer to learn in a certain way. We don't **only** learn in that way, but we **prefer** to do so. There is nothing right or wrong with any way of learning – they are just different. Some people have a very strong preference for learning in one way. Others may not and can learn in various ways.

These are the ways of learning Kolb describes. Kolb also looked at what teaching methods were liked/disliked by people who have a strong preference.

Four ways of learning

Way of learning	Description of this way of learning (based on Kolb 1984, pp68–69)	What those preferring this way of learning like or dislike about teaching methods (based on Kolb, 1984, p200)
Concrete	Focus on feelings rather than logical thinking, on what is happening now rather than on theories and generalisations, on using intuition rather than systematic approaches. Tend to be good at making decisions and in unstructured situations. Value relating to people and being involved in real situations.	Like – feedback which is personal, feedback from peers/students, talking about feelings, teachers being friendly helpers, applying skills to real life problems, being self-directed/ autonomous. Dislike – reading theory.
Reflective	Focus on the meaning of ideas and situations by careful observation and description, on understanding rather than on practical application, on what is true and how things happen rather than on what will work. Good at seeing implications, looking at things from different angles, relying on own thoughts and feelings to form opinions. Value patience, being impartial, thoughtful judgements.	Like – teachers giving expert interpretations, teachers guiding or putting limits on discussions, work being judged against clear criteria, having lectures. Dislike – situations where there is a need to get a job or task done.
Abstract	Focus on logic, on ideas, on concepts, on theories, on logical thinking rather than feelings, on a systematic approach to problems rather than on using intuition. Good at systematic planning, using abstract symbols. Value precision, analysis, neat conceptual systems.	Like – case studies, thinking alone, reading theory. Dislike – group exercises, simulations, being self-directed/autonomous, feedback which is personal, talking about feelings, activities related to a professional area (eg *field trips, placements*), the teacher being a role model for the profession, judging your own work, applying skills to practical problems

Way of learning	Description of this way of learning (based on Kolb 1984, pp68–69)	What those preferring this way of learning like or dislike about teaching methods (based on Kolb, 1984, p200)
Active	Focus on influencing people and changing situations, on practical application, on what works, on doing rather than observing. Good at getting things done, taking some risks to achieve objectives. Value influencing things around them and seeing results.	Like – small group discussion, projects, peer feedback, homework problems, the teacher being a role model for the profession, applying skills to practical problems. Dislike – lectures, the teacher forcing you to do work, work being judged as simply right or wrong.

16.5.3 What is your preferred way of learning?

What is your first reaction to the above?

What does your initial reaction tell you about your preferred way of learning? If you:

- find the above table interesting, it may suggest you prefer an **abstract** way of learning
- dislike it or can't see the point, it may mean you prefer a **concrete** way of learning
- start to think about what you do, perhaps you prefer **reflective** ways of learning
- start to wonder how it could be used, perhaps you are an **active** learner.

Do you lean towards one of the four categories, or could you fit into more than one, or even all four categories? You could use a highlighting pen to mark which parts of each category seem to apply to you and which do not.

If you think you prefer some over others, how would you rank them in order of which you prefer most and least, 1–4:

Concrete	
Reflective	
Abstract	
Active	

16.5.4 How could you improve what you do?

Which of the ways of learning do you most need to develop – what or who could help you do this? The following are suggested working methods for each way of learning. You could highlight any which are new to you which you could try.

Way of learning	Suggested methods
Concrete	Ask for feedback Talk about feelings Tackle real life problems Focus on what is happening now Listen to your intuition Use trial and error approaches (see Chapters 10 & 26 'Solving Problems') Just get on and do it Draft written work straight off Direct self (make own decisions about what to do) Be autonomous (work independently) Make quick decisions (see Chapters 10 & 26 'Solving Problems')
Reflective	Listen Observe Ask why Look at things from different angles Trust own judgement Use patience Look at things impartially (look at them from other perspectives) Take time to think about things Edit and improve written work Think about things afterwards, what went well/badly Use assessment criteria Use Chapters 17 & 31 'Reflecting on Your Experience'
Abstract	Read theory Think alone Look at things logically Produce logical arguments (eg *in written work*) Use a systematic approach to solving problems (see Chapters 10 & 26 'Solving Problems') Plan ahead (do plans for written work) Use case studies Use diagrams or models Check for accuracy, be precise Be neat Use Chapter 22 'Critical Analysis'

Way of learning	Suggested methods
Active	Take part in group discussion (see Chapters 11 & 27 'Group Work') Ask for feedback from peers (other students) Tackle practical problems Influence people (see Chapters 13 & 28 on 'Negotiating and Assertiveness') Ask people for help (see Chapters 13 & 28 on 'Negotiating and Assertiveness') Change situations Do things Take some risks Try things out (eg *pilot things*) Focus on results and targets (see Chapters 18 & 32 'Action Planning')

On your course, do you need to learn from:

- text, written material (eg *books, on the web*)?
- visual material (eg *art work, films, photos, plans, drawings*)?
- others speaking (eg *lectures, seminars/tutorials, audio tapes*)?
- physical objects (eg *skeletons, models, lab equipment, computers*)?

You may need different learning methods for different types of material. You may forget what people say if you don't make notes, whereas you can look at written material again. Visual material needs good observation skills. You may need to use an object to learn about it.

For the things you now need to learn (see Section 16.3 above) which of the above methods could you try first (see what you highlighted)? What might help (eg *which chapters, who could give feedback/help you set targets/could you discuss things with*)?

Do you need to adapt any methods to suit you, your subject, or your material? If your course uses ways of learning which you find hard, which do you most need to develop?

Methods I will try	What might help me

16.5.5 Learning styles

Kolb (1984) identified four learning styles which are related to the ways of learning.

When looking at these, beware of putting yourself into a 'pigeon hole'. You may not fit exactly into a style. You may prefer one. You may be a mix. You can change and develop.

Learning style	Characteristics
Convergent	Problem solving; decision making; actively experimenting; likes situations where there is one single correct answer. Prefers dealing with technical tasks and problems rather than social ones and issues between people.
Divergent	Imaginative ability; awareness of meaning and values; see things from many angles; interested in people and feelings.
Assimilative	Drawing conclusions or creating concepts by looking at details and evidence; can create theoretical models; less focus on people and more on abstract concepts and ideas; like theories which are sound and precise rather than practical.
Accommodative	Concrete experience; doing things; trying things out; trial and error; getting involved in new experiences; seeking out new opportunities; risk taking; can adapt to changing circumstances; rely heavily on people for information.

16.6 What else influences your learning?

What else has an effect on your learning? What could you do to build on positive influences and to improve where influences are negative. The following makes suggestions, but you may want to add in other personal influences

Influence	Sources of help
Understanding the subject	Library/learning centre reference books and other materials, library/learning centre staff, lecturers, tutors, other students
Your time management and organisation	See Chapters 3 & 20 'Organising Yourself and Your Time'
Your work environment (eg *where you study*)	See Chapters 3 & 20 'Organising Yourself and Your Time'
When you study	See Chapters 3 & 20 'Organising Yourself and Your Time'
Access to resources	Check to make sure when they are available. Plan ahead. See Chapters 3 & 20 'Organising Yourself and Your Time'

Influence	Sources of help
Other people • interruptions to your study by them • attitudes of others (eg *other students, family*) • support from others	See Chapters 3 & 20 'Organising Yourself and Your Time' See Chapters 13 & 28 'Negotiating and Assertiveness' Set up your own support group with other students, email them, computer conferences
Getting and using feedback	See Chapter 17 'Reflecting on Your Experience' for a section on feedback
Your social life	See Chapters 3 & 20 'Organising Yourself and Your Time'
Paid/voluntary work	See Chapters 14 & 29 'Coping with Pressure'
Domestic responsibilities	See Chapters 14 & 29 'Coping with Pressure' See Chapters 13 & 28 'Negotiating and Assertiveness'
Motivation to the subject or course	Visit your university/college or other Careers Service to discuss whether you are on the right course
Being away from learning for some time before the course	All the chapters in this book
Others. Please list	

How could you deal with these influences? Would any of those methods suggested in 16.5.4 above help, or could you adapt any of them?

16.7 Identifying and presenting what you have learnt

You may be asked to identify what you have learnt in a particular situation and to provide evidence for this. Some people find this difficult (especially those who find reflection hard). The following might help – but see also Chapters 17 and 31 'Reflecting on Your Experience'.

Think of a recent activity you were involved with on your course, such as an assignment or a class you attended (eg *a lecture, seminar/tutorial, lab, IT class, workshop etc*).

What information did you know at the end of it you didn't know before (eg *facts, theories, principles etc*)?

What did you learn or realise about other people?

What did you realise about yourself?

What did you do? How did you do it? What skills did you use?

What influenced or affected what you learnt or what you did (both good and bad)?

How could you prove or show what you learnt or realised? What evidence could you give (see the following list of possible sorts of evidence)?

Possible types of evidence

• notes (eg *lecture notes, lab notes etc*) • essay, report, other written work • poster • presentation • speakers' notes/handouts/visual aids for presentation • successive drafts of something showing how it changed • minutes of meetings • audio/video tapes	• artefacts (eg *models, objects, works of art*) • drawings, sketches, plans • photos • logs/diaries showing what you did • written feedback on what you did from others (eg *others in the group, a tutor*) • testimonials/signed declarations from work colleagues/clients, reference from an employer

If you are asked to say what you learnt and how, you need to be explicit. It is not enough just to include evidence, you need to say clearly what you want the evidence to show.

Example:

In producing this essay I learnt about theories on how people learn, I learnt to use the library online catalogue and found materials, I learnt how to extract information from those materials. From looking at feedback on the essay I learnt the grammatical errors I tend to make.

Evidence.
The evidence I am including is as follows

Evidence	What it shows
The essay itself	*My grasp of the educational theories* *My use of the materials I looked at*
List of references/bibliography	*The results of my using the online catalogue and evidence of the range of materials I looked at*
Notes I made on the materials	*My use of the materials. The information I extracted from them*
Feedback on the essay	*The grammatical errors I tend to make*
Action plan	*How I plan to improve my grammatical errors*

16.8 Improving what you do

What would most help you improve how you learn? This could be building on/doing more of what works well, developing new ways of doing things, or improving what you do.

You can use this box to make an action plan (but see also Chapters 18 and 32 'Action Planning').

What I need to focus on	Actions to take	Support, help, resources needed.	By (date)

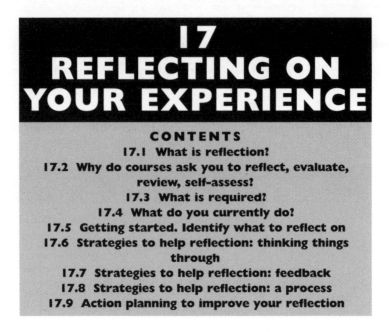

17
REFLECTING ON YOUR EXPERIENCE

CONTENTS

Being able to reflect is essential to learning. It is not just common sense, it is more than that, it is a skill you can improve.

Reflection improves your learning and your performance on your course, by helping you identify what you do well (and how to make the most of it) and what to improve.

Some people find it easy to think about what they have done, said, or thought, while others find this uncomfortable or difficult. This chapter should help both. It aims to:

- explain why reflection is so important, and why courses ask you to do it
- help you get better grades or marks for assessed work requiring reflection
- help you develop ways of reflecting on your experiences.

We suggest you use this chapter:

- **when a tutor asks you to reflect on something, evaluate your actions as part of course work, or self-assess**
- **to reflect on something personally important to you on the course or in a course related activity (eg *a work placement*).**

If you like to reflect in different ways, you could use the margins to note what would work better for you. The chapter focuses on reflection on the course, but you could also use it, if you wish, to think about personal matters.

When you have completed it, you should be able to:

Agree targets
- identify main features and purposes of reflection
- identify your current practice in reflecting
- identify and select possible strategies to reflect.

Use your plan
- use your reflection strategies, monitoring and revising them as needed
- seek and use feedback and support, as part of reflecting on an experience
- use feedback and support to improve reflection skills
- identify appropriate evidence for claims about your performance.

Review progress and achievements
- when required, produce a summary of the results of your reflection, with appropriate evidence
- review your reflection process, and identify any factors influencing performance
- identify ways of improving in the future.

(Based on QCA Key Skill specifications, QCA 2000)

17.1 What is reflection?

'Reflection', here, means **looking back on an experience and making sense of it to identify what to do in the future**. It helps you repeat what worked and learn from mistakes. Most of us think about experiences afterwards. We may re-live something enjoyable or be concerned about something (*'Our team played well today because…'; 'I wish I hadn't said…'*). We may reflect soon afterwards or later, when something triggers a memory.

Reflection is a skill needed at work. Professionals need to know they are doing a good job. It is encouraged via appraisal schemes, and by professional bodies' Continuing Professional Development schemes.

Taking action as a result of reflection assumes you are responsible for your learning, and that you can do things differently, that 'old dogs' can learn 'new tricks'.

17.2 Why do courses ask you to reflect, evaluate, review, self-assess?

Reflection helps you:

- reinforce your learning
- learn concepts and principles
- identify, while in a situation, the best action to take.

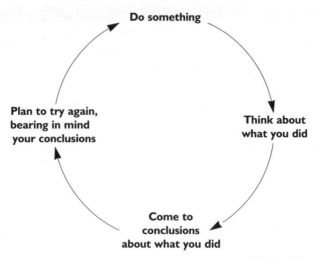

(derived from Kolb 1984)

Some learning theory (Gagne 1985, Kelly as described in Bannister and Fransella 1971, Kolb 1984) suggests that we sort information, feelings and sensations into categories. When we meet new situations which seem to fit the same categories we recall our original thoughts and feelings, eg *one recall method is to associate one thought with another, such as remembering somebody's name by remembering where you met.*

Reflecting helps to make sense of an experience and 'categorise' it so that learning from it can be used again. Without it we may do things the same old way, not thinking what works, what doesn't and what to do differently (*'Why do I keep doing that!?'*).

Reflecting helps you understand concepts and principles ('deep learning') as well as knowing facts ('surface learning' – Gibbs 1992) (eg *reflecting on the practical experience of project work or a placement can help in understanding theory*).

Being effective is not just repeating what you did in another situation – each situation must be weighed up to see what is appropriate. Schon (1987) suggests that if you make sense of something afterwards ('reflection on action'), you are more likely to be able to work out what to do whilst **in** a situation, to think on your feet ('reflection in action').

17.3 What is required?

17.3.1 What sort of reflective work will you meet on your course?

You may be asked to reflect on, review, evaluate or assess what you have done. The following are strategies used by courses to help you reflect. If they are assessed, check what will get a good grade – but also use them to help you learn and improve.

Work	Points to consider
Reflective log or diary	Records what happens. A reflective log/diary also makes sense of it. It might include what: you did well; you did less well; you learned or realised; you might do differently in future. Some professional bodies require one to show your professional competence.
Evaluation of work carried out	This may be evaluation of your own work or that of a group you were in. This means not just recording what happened or who did what, but what: was good or went well; could have been improved; could be done differently in future; was learnt/realised.
Reflective portfolio	In a portfolio you place evidence of what you learnt and how (eg, *written work, audio/video tapes, visuals*). You make clear what each item demonstrates, and include a commentary, saying what you want your evidence to show and how or why.
Critical incident	Here you identify an incident which helped you realise something. You briefly describe the incident but are much more concerned with what it showed, what you learned or realised, and why.
Stories/fictional writing	You may be asked to write about an experience in a way which turns it into a story.
Report eg, *a placement report*	A reflective report does not just cover your experience, but evaluates the experience and your role in it.

NB See Chapters 7 and 24 'Report Writing'.

17.3.2 Evidence

In assessed work you usually need to produce evidence for your reflections – so the assessor knows you can prove/support what you claim (eg *evidence of your ability to work well in a group might be: minutes of meetings; work produced by yourself for the group – a log/diary can show what you did; feedback from other members about your performance*).

17.3.3 What is the lecturer looking for?

The lecturer or tutor will want to know:

- what you did or what happened and what your part in it was
- what you thought was good/went well, why, what you achieved
- what could have been better, why, how, what was not achieved, what you could have done differently
- what links you see between theory and what happened (eg *does what happened agree/disagree with theory?*)
- honest opinions. They are interested in how well you interpret the situation, rather than how well the situation went. Identifying what went wrong and what you could do differently indicates that you have learned, not that you made a mistake
- what you learnt and will do in future (an 'action plan') – this may involve how you will go about it and how you will judge if you have improved or performed well.

Your lecturer or tutor will not want:

* just a straight description of what you did with no analysis
* a lack of honesty, making everything sound fine or terrible (there are few situations when everything goes perfectly or where something positive doesn't happen)
* excuses (explanations are OK) or blaming others. They will want you to acknowledge what you are responsible for.

17.4 What do you currently do?

17.4.1 How do you usually respond to experience?

What do you normally do when you have dealt with others, carried out an activity, or read/seen/heard something? You may tend to reflect in the same way regardless of the experience, or to think about different sorts of experiences differently. ✔

Way of reflecting	Very rarely	Sometimes	Usually	Always
Tend not to reflect much				
Think about it on my own				
Talk about it to somebody else				
Write it down (eg *in a diary*)				
Repeat it as it happened (eg *replay conversations*)				
Focus on things I feel good about				
Focus on things I feel bad about				
Imagine what I wish had happened				
Blame somebody (myself or somebody else)				
Consider how other people involved felt or were affected				
Identify the essentials of what I read/saw/heard or of what happened				
Identify what aspects are similar to those in other situations				
Identify how to use new realisations				

It might help to consider:

* which of the above might encourage learning (eg *'blaming' can lead to resentment or guilt, not to learning*)?
* which might build confidence or reduce it?

17.4.2 When do you reflect?

Your initial reaction may change as you think about something, talk to people, see or read things, and your views may change. Do you tend to:

✔

have an initial reaction and then forget about it?	
have a reaction some time later?	
find it difficult to let the matter drop?	
think so much about it that it stops you taking action?	
vary what you do depending on the experience?	
none of these (when do you reflect)?	

Possibilities for doing things differently include:

- set regular time aside to think things over
- if you can't let a matter drop, distract yourself by an enjoyable activity, or by talking aloud to yourself about something else (you can't think of one thing/talk of another)
- ask friends what they do.

17.4.3 Could you do anything differently?

You could keep a note of how effective your reflection strategies are. If needed, you could try other ideas.

What are the advantages/disadvantages of how/when you tend to reflect?	What could you do differently?

17.5 Getting started. Identify what to reflect on

For Sections 17.6, 17.7 and 17.8 below it will help to have in mind an experience to reflect on, and to complete the boxes in relation to it.

It may help to use a simple experience to reflect on (eg *a small project, a group meeting, an essay/report/lab session, a work activity*). You can then work though the sections again reflecting on something more complex (eg *a large project, a term/semester*).

To identify an experience to reflect on for the rest of this section, consider:

- are you pleased interested, curious, excited about something which has happened?
- do you feel uncomfortable or bad about something?
- do others seem to do things differently in a situation?
- what does your lecturer/tutor think is important for you to reflect on? If in doubt, ask.
- if your reflection is assessed, what will they be looking for? If in doubt ask.
- who will see your reflection, what is appropriate for them/what is private to you?
- does a 'critical incident' stand out (eg *something that changed things/had a big impact on you*)?

What are you going to reflect on while using this chapter?

17.6 Strategies to help reflection: thinking things through

The following suggest ways to think about the issue you want to reflect on. This chapter is for all students in all subject areas – keep an open mind on the ideas, even if they seem strange (or obvious) to you on your course. Which could you try?

Talk to somebody...

- explaining it gets it clearer in your own mind
- hearing yourself speak puts things into perspective
- the person might have useful questions, similar experiences, new ways of looking at it, be reassuring
- ask others involved in the same situation what they felt/thought.

Write, draw...

- write about it; re-reading it later helps you see it as somebody else might
- write a letter (you don't have to send it), a play, a newspaper report, a poem
- make a drawing, picture, diagram
- make lists of pros/cons, likes/dislikes
- if you can't sleep, get up and write it down to get it off your mind
- writing/drawing makes you feel you've done something and can reduce anxiety or anger.

Think about it on your own...

- give yourself time and space... on the bus, walking, in the bath....

Look at it in new ways

- replay it as it happened (or repeat it as you read, heard or saw it)
- to give new insights – read books/poems/newspapers, look at pictures/films/TV
- think about what might have been....what you wish had happened
- think of what else you could have done, however unusual or uncharacteristic of you
- think about it in the opposite way from how you normally would (eg *'I liked...' instead of 'I didn't like...'*)
- describe it as somebody else might
- identify your feelings about it (what was your gut reaction?)
- ask yourself questions (eg *why do I feel angry/upset?*)
- identify the main or crucial aspects of the situation.

What other ways do you use (or do your friends use – you could compare notes)?

Which of the suggestions could you try to use for the issue you identified in 17.5 above?

17.7 Strategies to help reflection: feedback

17.7.1 Seeking feedback from others

Verbal or written feedback from others is very helpful and gives useful evidence of your skills.

Who could you get feedback from? You could jot in the right-hand column names and notes on what they could give you feedback about.

Suggestions	Your notes
For course activities • tutors • other students • technicians • other specialists (eg *library/learning centre, computing support staff*) • others (who?)	
If you are in employment • your boss/supervisor • colleagues at your level • colleagues above/below your level • clients/customers • others (who?)	
Other areas of your life • family members • friends • people in eg *sporting or social clubs* • others (who?)	

How can you get helpful feedback and encourage people to give it to you again?

- Explain why feedback is important and what will help you
- Ask for feedback as soon after the event as possible
- Ask specific questions (eg not *'what did you think of it'* but *'could you understand what I wrote?'*) – this gives more specific information to act on
- Listen without interrupting or defending
- Check you have understood
- Make it easy for them – don't take up too much time
- Thank them and accept it without arguing or disputing.

17.7.2 Recording feedback

Are you aware of and do you take notice of feedback:

- from tutors? Do you understand it (if not, ask them to explain it)?
- from other students (eg *about how they do things differently from you*)?
- others such as library/learning centre or computing support staff or technicians?

Do you make a note of feedback to help you in the future? You could:

- keep a diary
- keep tutor feedback sheets together in a folder – to help you note any changes
- use an action plan to help you improve (see Section 17.9)
- use the following format – practise using it for some feedback you recently had.

Feedback received	Key points to consider	Actions to take

17.7.3 Using feedback

You need to weigh up feedback to see if you agree with it. There are dangers in:

- believing what everybody says (eg *they may be wrong, in a bad temper, not know the facts, have a distorted view*). You may do so if you lack confidence.
- not believing what anybody says (eg *they may know more than you, have a different view, be more experienced*). You may do so if you are over-confident or defensive.

Feedback may be particularly worth noting if:

- more than one person gives you similar feedback
- the person giving feedback is knowledgeable/an expert
- the other person is important to you (eg *an assessor*)
- the feedback confirms something you thought
- the feedback makes sense to you
- there is evidence (proof) to support the feedback.

If you disagree with the feedback, why?:

- did you misunderstand what was wanted in the first place (eg *in assessed work*)?
- could the other person have misunderstood what you did?
- is the other person biased, do they have a vested interest?
- is their view less accurate than yours?
- are you being defensive or avoiding facing up to things?
- have you got any evidence (proof) that the feedback is inaccurate?

Try to discount personal comments and identify the key points beneath them (eg *'You are a real pain, you never do the work for the group'*).

Key point – if you don't do the work you cause problems for the group.

Discount – *'You are a real pain.'* It doesn't mean you are a pain in every situation, or that all group members think so.

Seeing it like this means you can do something about it. Seeing it as a personal insult may harm your confidence or cause problems between you and others.

You could complete the following in relation to feedback you have recently received.

Feedback points I agree with	Evidence

Feedback points I disagree with	Evidence

17.7.4 Giving feedback

If you are asked for feedback from somebody else:

- give it as soon after the event as possible
- be specific (not *'You are OK in meetings'* but *'When you chaired you kept to the agenda but you overran a bit on time'*). This tells them what to do about it.
- give feedback on things they can do something about (eg *they may not be able to alter how they speak*)
- avoid judgement words (eg *'rubbish'*)
- if you point out something negative make sure you also include positives
- avoid generalised personal comments (eg *'You are a pain.'* What can they do with this? They don't know why and it will just upset them)
- calmly keep to the point if the other person is defensive (see the 'broken record technique' in Chapter 13 'Negotiating and Assertiveness')
- check they have understood and that you have been specific enough for them.

17.8 Strategies to help reflection: a process

In this section it will help to have in mind something you want to reflect on (see 17.5 above) and to complete the boxes in relation to it.

This section questions: what happened; how you felt; how others reacted; what was good/did you achieve; what needed improvement/did you not achieve; what choices you made and what effect they had; what will you do in the future.

If any of the questions don't apply to your issue change them, pass over them, or add others which do apply (eg *for a technical issue you may need technical questions*).

Complete the boxes in an order that makes sense to you (not necessarily in the order given). If the process seems too structured, what would work better for you? Each box gives an example of a student on a group project. This is not intended to limit your thinking, the situation you are thinking of could be completely different.

17.8.1 What happened

Who did/said what, what did you do/read/see/hear? In what order did things happen? What was the scale of it (eg: *how much work, time taken; costs*)? What were the circumstances (eg: *at home; in class; at work; lots of people around*)? What were you responsible for? What evidence (proof) do you have for what happened?

✍

> **Your record**
> **Example.** *Group project. Used the library to get information for my part. Library very busy. Found some information, couldn't find rest immediately (computers all being used). Got information in end but after deadline.*

17.8.2 How did you feel?

What was your initial gut reaction, what does this tell you? Did your feelings change, how, why, what does this tell you? What evidence (proof) do you have for how you felt?

✍

> **Your record**
> **Example.** *Panicked at first. Worried about what others in group would say about me missing the deadline. Once completed it felt better. Pleased. Want to pull my weight.*

17.8.3 How did others react?

Is what other people thought or how they reacted important/relevant? Did they react like you or differently: how? Who had which reactions, and what does this tell you? How did their reactions affect you? What evidence (proof) do you have for how others reacted?

✍

> **Your record**
> **Example.** *One group member wasn't bothered (missed deadline too). Another (normally gets very high marks) was fed up. Others probably fed up too. Once I'd done it they were relieved and pleased with my work. I felt bad and want to avoid that in future.*

17.8.4 Identifying the positives

What pleased, interested or was important to you? What went well, how, why? What/who was helpful? What skills/qualities/ abilities did you use? What evidence (proof) do you have for the positives?

✍

> **Your record**
> **Example.** *Found most of the articles in the end. Used computerised data bases. Took good notes. Tidied up notes at home and filed them. Produced a summary for the group project report, and my bit got a good mark.*

17.8.5 Identifying negatives, or things which could have gone better

What made you unhappy? What didn't go well, didn't you achieve/do? What difficulties were there, who/what was unhelpful? Why? What needs improvement? What evidence (proof) do you have for the negatives?

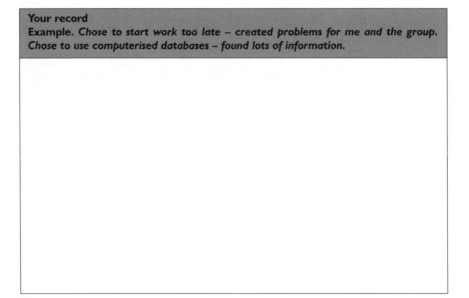

> **Your record**
> Example. *Books out on loan. Wasted time in library chatting. Had to break off to go to bank. Didn't start work early enough or allow for others using the information or getting on computers.*

17.8.6 What choices did you make and what effect did they have?

What choices did you make in this situation? What effect did they have? What evidence (proof) do you have for your choices and their effects?

> **Your record**
> Example. *Chose to start work too late – created problems for me and the group. Chose to use computerised databases – found lots of information.*

17.8.7 What have you learnt for the future?

What you have learnt from the experience, what are the main points? What similarities or differences are there between this and other experiences? What in the future might be the same/different? What you would do next time?

Note. The other chapters in this book can help put your actions into practice.

✍

Your record
Example. *Carry on with current system for organising notes. Start work earlier next time. Allow longer to do things/build in leeway. Plan at start of each week so can do jobs like going to bank at best time. Sit in library away from people I know.*

17.9 Action planning to improve your reflection

This section is about your skills in reflecting.

What do you need to do to improve your reflection, both to get good grades for reflective work and to improve your learning? It will help to look back over the chapter.

✍

What reflection strategies have you tried?	How well did they work? What influenced or affected this?

What do you need to improve in your reflection?	What action can you take to improve this (include help from others)	By (deadline)

Acknowledgement

Thanks to Jo Mackett, Combined Studies student at Sheffield Hallam University, who evaluated an earlier draft (upon which this chapter is based) as part of a final year independent study unit (1996–7).

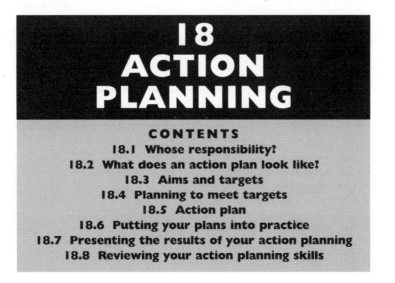

18
ACTION PLANNING

Action planning helps you to be organised, to meet all your course commitments, and can make you more successful. Students new to university/college often find it difficult to get all their work done on time.

Action planning is important:

- for course work (or other activities) to identify what you need to do, by when and how
- for skills you are trying to develop, to identify what you need to do, by when and how
- where others are involved (eg *group work*), so everybody knows what they should be doing
- to help you monitor what you are doing against your plans.

It may seem formal, but it is a valuable tool to help you achieve what you want. You are very likely to need it in employment (eg *for handling projects*).

We suggest you use this chapter:

- **when you have course work to do or exams to prepare for, to help you plan**
- **to help you plan how to develop your skills for any of the topics in this book.**

This chapter focuses on action planning related to your course, but you could also use it to think about other areas of your life (eg *work, social, domestic, family*).

When you have completed it, you should be able to:

Identify plans
- identify targets and methods to meet those targets
- identify factors (including difficulties) which might affect your plans
- identify and use sources of information, support and resources to achieve targets.

Use the plan
- prioritise actions to achieve targets
- deal with difficulties
- revise and amend the plan
- seek and use feedback and support.

Review progress and achievements
- present the outcomes of the action planning, with evidence
- identify factors affecting the outcomes
- improve your action planning.

(Based on QCA Key Skill specifications, QCA 2000)

18.1 Whose responsibility?

At school/work others may help you plan work or chase you to do things. This is unlikely at university/college. Tutors and lecturers will suggest you do things, give you work and deadlines, but how and when you do it is up to you. Feedback from them may suggest skills you need to develop, but unless a skill is taught as part of the course it will be up to you to improve it. It is your responsibility.

Planning ahead is essential. You may have several deadlines close together at the end of a semester/term. Inexperienced students often think the deadline means **when** to work, rather than being the end point for it, and leave it too late. If you have several deadlines together you need to plan, so your work is done on time and spaced out, to prevent stress (see Chapter 14 'Coping with Pressure').

If you are working in a group, action planning helps clarify who is responsible for what and helps you, as a group, monitor how you are progressing.

18.2 What does an action plan look like?

See Section 18.5 below for an example of one possible layout.

18.3 Aims and targets

This is the starting point for an action plan. An aim is what you are heading towards. A target is a specific end point – you can clearly see when you have got there. For example

Aim. *Improve my skills in dealing with people.*
Target. *Listen to people.*

18.3.1 Long-term aims

Where are you heading? What are your long-term aims? Identifying this can help you see if you putting effort now into the right areas, ones which will help you achieve your long-term aims. You can add your own items to the box below.

✔

A good degree/diploma	
A higher degree	
An interesting job	
A job with power or status	
A well-paid job	
To pursue particular interests	
Good relationships, family, friends	
A balanced life (work/leisure/family)	
Other. Please list	

You may have sub-aims eg, *if you want a well paid job, your sub-aims might relate to the class of degree you want, or to finding relevant work experience*.

18.3.2 Immediate aims

What are your immediate aims? They might be to get course work done, or to achieve a certain grade, to learn how to do something, or to achieve something.

What might your targets be (eg *to get course work done; to get it done by a deadline; to a certain standard*)? If you are working with others, these might be both targets for the group and targets for you individually.

✍

What are your immediate aims?	What are your targets for these?

18.4 Planning to meet targets

Where you are working with others, you will need to discuss and agree about the issues raised in the following sections.

18.4.1 Actions and methods needed

What must you do to meet your targets? Identifying the actions or tasks needed to do so makes it easier to manage (eg *if your target is to write a report, you may need to gather information, draft it, produce a final version of it*).

You can then think about the methods you will use to carry out the action or task.

You then need to identify the resources or help to carry out your methods. For an example this might be:

Action, task	Methods	Resources, help, support
gather information	• *use a library/learning centre to find material* • *use and make notes on the materials* • *sort notes out*	• *library/learning centre online catalogue* • *library/learning centre staff* • *books, databases, Internet* • *Chapters 5 'Gathering and Using Information', & 4 'Note Taking'*
draft the report	• *find out what format the report needs to be in* • *draft it (word-process)*	• *tutor, other students – ask about report format, Chapter 7 'Report Writing'* • *examples of similar reports (eg in library/learning centre)* • *a computer* • *IT materials (see Pettigrew and Eiliott 1999)*
produce a final version of it	• *re-draft it (word-process)* • *edit, proof read and spell check it* • *add references in correct way*	• *IT materials (see Pettigrew and Eiliott 1999)* • *spell checker on computer* • *dictionary, thesaurus* • *Chapter 5 'Gathering and Using Information'*

If you are working in a group, you will need to identify who will do what. Agreeing this in advance helps to avoid group members not pulling their weight.

18.4.2 Deadlines and timescales

Setting deadlines by when you need to complete each action or task helps you focus. A deadline may be given to you for the overall work, in which case you need to set deadlines for each task you must do to complete the work on time.

Estimate how long each task will take (eg *how long will it take you to find information and to use it; if you need to read three books, how long will that take?*), then add on half again. It always takes longer than you think.

Work backwards. If you have to meet deadline Y, when do you have to finish task X? For example:

Action, task	Start work	Finish work (deadline)
hand in report		*12th Dec*
gather information	*1st Nov*	*20th Nov*
draft the report	*20th Nov*	*5th Dec*
produce a final version of it	*6th Dec*	*11th Dec*

18.4.3 What might affect your plans?

Things may arise which influence your plans. Try to identify these in advance to help you re-consider the methods you use and how long it will take. Which of the following could affect your plans? You could add your own items. ✔

Availability of books or other learning materials	
Availability of computers	
Computers crashing	
Other people doing/not doing what they say	
Domestic responsibilities or problems	
Social life	
Illness	
Holidays (eg *Christmas or bank holidays*)	
My own skills (eg *in using materials, computers, dealing with people*)	
Other, please list	

What methods could help you deal with these possibilities (eg *find other computer resources; use the library/learning centre at times when it isn't very busy*)? How much time should you add to your estimates to allow for them?

If you lack some of the skills needed to use the methods, you may need training or advice, or it may take you longer. Sources of help include computing support staff and library/learning centre staff.

It's also worth adding time on for things you can't foresee.

18.4.4 Prioritising

To achieve your target, some tasks may be more important than others, or you may need to do some before others. In your action plan you could:

* list your tasks from most to least important
* list them in the order in which they need to be done
* add numbers to each item showing their priority (eg *1 high priority; 2 medium priority; 3 low priority*). If they all come out as 1, look again. What **must** you do as soon as possible? (It may tell you you've left things too late, in which case note when you need to start work in the future!)

For more help on prioritising see Chapter 3 'Organising Yourself and Your Time'.

18.5 Action plan

You can now complete this action plan for your own targets. You could copy it and use it again, or make a version for yourself on the computer.

You may want to complete it in relation to a skill you want to develop, rather than something you have to produce. For example:

Note here your target			Deadline to meet it	
Improve my self organisation			*31st Dec*	
Task	**Methods**	**Resources, support, help**	**Start date**	**End date**
devise new filing system	• *sort notes under headings* • *create list of topics/files* • *make new files*	• *Chapter 4 'Note Taking'* • *filing cabinet* • *files, file dividers* • *see above*	*1st Nov*	*20th Nov*
sort out workspace	• *put all notes into new filing system* • *re-organise top of desk* • *improve lighting*	• *'pots' and boxes for pens, paper clips, other 'bits and pieces'* • *new lamp*	*21st Nov*	*1st Dec*

If you are working in a group you will need another column, for 'who does what'.

You could take copies of the following page, one for each target.

Action plan

Target			Deadline to meet it	
Task/actions needed	Methods	Resources, support, help	Start date	End date

18.6 Putting your plans into practice

If you are working with others, you need to consider the following as a group.

18.6.1 Reviewing your plans

You need to review and update your plan. Circumstances change. It helps to keep notes of progress, particularly if you need to present the results of your action planning to others.

You also need to check if your methods are working. Chapter 17 'Reflecting on Your Experience' can help you think about this. If the methods aren't working you may need to amend them or try others.

18.6.2 Using feedback

Feedback from others can help you review your plans. You could:

- check with others at stages whether what you have done so far is OK (eg *with tutors, friends, library/learning centre staff, computing support staff*)
- look at all the feedback you've had for work you've done this year – what does it suggest about the areas you need to focus on?
- look at the feedback you get on a piece of course work – use it to plan how to improve future work of that kind.

18.6.3 Dealing with difficulties

Things rarely go completely to plan. Section 18.4.3 above looked at identifying in advance what might go wrong, but if you are in the middle of your plan and have problems, what can you do? Possibilities include:

- talk things over with friends, they may have ideas
- talk to your tutor
- ask specialists (eg *library/learning centre staff, computing support staff, technicians*)
- use books or other resources for suggestions
- review your targets and your plan, to see what you could amend
- cut your losses and try a new approach
- use Chapter 10 'Solving Problems' or any other relevant chapter.

Chapter 3 'Organising Yourself and Your Time' also has guidance on dealing with difficulties.

18.7 Presenting the results of your action planning

The result of your action planning might be a piece of work which you hand in (eg *a report*). If so, you need guidance on how to present that type of work, and other chapters can help.

However, for course work you may be asked to produce an action plan, with evidence for how far you achieved your targets (eg *to show how you tried to develop a skill*).

Check here what tutors are looking for. Are they more interested in whether you met your targets, or in how you used the action planning process? This will affect what you present. Possibilities for presenting your action planning are:

- the action plan itself, possibly with earlier versions to show how you amended it. You could add notes on why you amended it.
- describing how far you met your targets
- presenting evidence that you met your targets (eg *minutes of meetings, pieces of work, statements from other people about what you did*). You could add notes explaining what the evidence shows.
- an evaluation of your methods (what worked, what didn't, what affected this). See Chapter 17 'Reflecting on Your Experience'. Evidence might be a diary or log showing what you did.

18.8 Reviewing your action planning skills

The focus in this section is on the action planning process itself, and on you as an individual (not on any group you were in). How well can you:

- identify targets?
- plan actions or tasks and methods?
- identify and meet deadlines?
- plan for and deal with difficulties?
- review and revise your plans?
- present your plans and their outcomes?

What do you think affected or influenced your action planning? Were these factors over which you had control or not?

What factors affected your action planning? How?	What could you have done about this?

What do you need to do to improve your action planning?

Actions to take	Resources, help, support needed	By (date)

PART II

DEVELOPMENT LEVEL

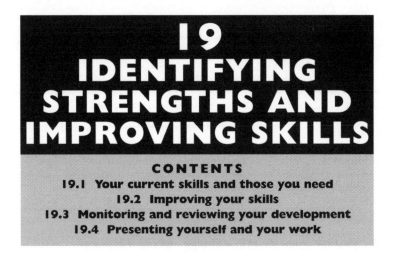

19
IDENTIFYING STRENGTHS AND IMPROVING SKILLS

CONTENTS

This chapter assumes that you have some experience of identifying your skills in order to improve your performance. If not, see Chapter 2 on 'Identifying Strengths: Improving Skills' in Part I.

It is not easy to judge our own performance. Often we prefer to get on with a task rather than to think **how** we are doing so.

Identifying what you have done well and where to improve helps you learn. On courses and in professional life, giving attention to how you do something can improve the result.

Identifying strengths and improving skills is part of the Continuous Professional Development seen as vital by many professional bodies. Identifying strengths is crucial in applying for placements or jobs – employers want to know what you have done, how well, and what you are capable of.

We suggest you use this chapter to:

- **identify your current skills and their level – our skill levels change continually**
- **identify the skills you need**
- **identify how to continuously improve your performance**
- **identify other chapters in this book which could help you.**

When you have finished it, you should be able to:

Develop a strategy
- review your own current strengths and areas to improve, identify skills you particularly want to develop in the future
- identify opportunities to build on strengths and address weaknesses
- select personally relevant strategies to develop skills
- produce action plans for improvement, specifying deadlines and resources/support needed.

Monitor progress
- take responsibility for implementing plans and your own performance
- critically reflect on your own performance, seeking and using feedback and support and monitor changing performance
- adapt plans for skills development and adapt performance as needed.

Evaluate strategies and present outcomes
- evaluate the effectiveness of strategies for self-evaluation and for developing skills
- identify ways of further developing your own skills in self-evaluation and in developing self.

(Based on QCA Key Skill specifications, QCA 2000)

Confidentiality

This chapter is designed for your use alone, although you can show it to others if you choose. You can keep it and extract information from it in the future (eg *if you need to provide evidence of your abilities on your course – students on some courses need to do so in portfolios, or for a placement or job application*).

19.1 Your current skills and those you need

This chapter assumes that although there are sources of help and support, it is up to you to identify what you wish to improve and then to take action – this is your responsibility. It is important to begin by identifying your current skills.

19.1.1 Getting started

It is easier to identify your current level of a skill if you think about it in relation to a particular activity. If you feel uncertain about this process, look at Section 2.1 of Chapter 2 'Identifying Strengths and Improving Skills' before proceeding.

We suggest you:

- identify the activities likely to be encountered on your course (eg *class activities, or assessed work such as projects or a dissertation*)
- identify activities you may encounter in the job area you may enter. If you have no clear idea about the profession you wish to enter, think of activities likely to occur in any job (eg *attending meetings, meeting deadlines, writing letters/reports etc*) or activities you would **like** as part of a job (eg *practical activities, managing others etc*).

You can then consider your skills and how to improve them in relation to those course and job activities.

Course activities	Job activities

19.1.2 Evaluating yourself

Seeking feedback
Feedback can give you useful evidence of your skills and is essential if you are to accurately evaluate your skills. You could ask for feedback from different sources (eg *tutors, friends, other students, employers, work colleagues*).

For more information on asking for and using feedback, see Chapter 17 on 'Reflecting on Your Experience' in Part I.

Your own attitudes and motivations
These might affect how well you judge or rate yourself on your performance of a skill. It can help to consider the following questions:

Which skills/tasks do you find easy/like? Why? Identify areas you can build on?

Skill	Enjoy/like	Why?
eg *oral presentation*	eg *producing visual aids*	eg *good at identifying main points, good at visual layout*

Which skills/tasks do you dislike or find difficult? Why?

Skill	Enjoy/like	Why?
eg *oral presentation*	eg *feel nervous dealing with questions*	eg *in case asked something can't answer*

Does your attitude to a skill affect how you judge how good you are at it (eg *if it is very important to you, are you over-critical of yourself*)?

19.1.3 Identifying your needs

The following Skills Evaluation will help you identify:

* which skills you need for your course and any job area you may enter
* your current level of skill. Identifying strengths can be a real confidence booster.
* where you want to improve. Identifying areas which need improvement is an important first step.

In the first column on the Skills Evaluation, list the skills you need to focus on.

The following is a list of skills covered by other chapters in this book. You could use this list to select skills to consider, and could also add other skills important for your course or for prospective job activities.

Action planning	Oral presentation
Coping with pressure	Organising yourself and your time
Critical analysis	Reflecting on your experience
Essay writing	Report writing
Gathering and using information	Revising and examination techniques
Group work	Seminars, group tutorials and meetings
Improving your learning	Solving problems
Negotiating and assertiveness	Visual communication
Note taking	

In the following Skills Evaluation please consider:

* your need for these skills (or any others) for the activities you identified in Section 19.1.1 above
* your current skill level. How well have you used that skill in course (or job) activities up to now? How much are you likely to need it in future?
* which skills you most need to improve. For example, where the skill will not be needed to a great extent either in the course or future jobs, it may be unimportant for you to give attention to it, even if your current level of the skill is low. On the other hand, you may be quite good at a skill, but it is so important for your course or future jobs that you feel you still need to improve it.

You could take copies of the Skills Evaluation sheet if needed.

Skill	Course activities needing this skill	Level needed 1–4 (1 = high)	Job activities needing this skill	Level needed 1–4 (1 = high)	My current skill level 1–4 (1 = high)	How important is it to improve? (1 = most important)

19.2 Improving your skills

19.2.1 Identifying targets

Identifying targets to aim for and areas to improve is essential. What targets are important for you, your course/work? These might be:

- things you identified as priorities in Section 19.1.3
- skills you will need to use/demonstrate soon (eg *for assessed work, a job interview*)
- skills you need to frequently use (course, social or work related)
- areas your tutor/others suggest (eg *from feedback*).

Imagine your weaker areas are now your strengths. What would you be doing differently? What could you do now to move towards that position?

Skill	What I'd do differently	How to get there	By (deadline)
eg *oral presentations*	eg *answer questions confidently*	eg *identify possible questions in advance*	eg *next week*

19.2.2 Doing things differently

To identify what you could do differently, it helps:

- to know what you are good/not so good at
- to know what the situation requires.

You can then put the two together to work out what you will be good at in a particular situation, and what you need to improve.

Ways of doing things differently include (*the examples all refer to an oral presentation*):

- build on positives (eg *be well organised on the day*)
- use another strategy (eg *if you are good at visual aids emphasise them – the audience can focus on the visual aids rather than on you*)
- change your attitude (eg *see the audience as on your side/making allowances for nervousness/interested in the topic rather than in you*)
- improve the areas you feel poor at (eg *prepare well, practise in front of friends or on tape, anticipate the questions you will be asked, avoid fidgeting*)
- avoid or minimise situations requiring the skill (eg *avoid jobs that require a lot of presentations*). You may have to weigh up how important it is to you to be in the situation (eg *you may need to do oral presentations for assessment, or a job may have many features you like, but also require oral presentations*)
- focus on your motivations (eg *if the job is very important to you, you might apply, even though it means making presentations*).

19.2.3 Using opportunities, resources and support

Opportunities to build on strengths and improve your skills will not just arise on your course. You will be developing skills (eg *communication, solving problems, working in teams*) in many other contexts – social activities, work (paid or voluntary). Once you have identified what you are going to work on, think about the range of possible opportunities to practise/develop further and build this into your action plan.

Unexpected opportunities will arise and you need to take advantage of them. You could keep notes when you monitor and review your progress (see Section 19.2.5).

Resources and support can come from:

- **others,** eg *your* **lecturers/tutors** *(they may be able to spend time in class on particular skills)*
- **friends and other students** (either from your year or in later years). What ideas do they have for improving the skill? Support from others can be very important.
- **materials/information** eg *chapters in this book, a learning centre/library.*

19.2.4 Choosing strategies

It will help to use methods which will suit you. What will help you most?

✔

Method	Will it suit you?
Talking about or sharing ideas	
Doing something practical	
Thinking through possible actions	
Listening (to others/tapes)	
Watching others (in person or on video)	
Getting feedback	
Trying things out	
Reading books/electronic information (eg *other Skill Packs/Key Skills Online*)	
Other ideas	

You may find it particularly helpful to look at Chapter 16 on 'Improving Your Learning' in Part I.

19.2.5 Make an action plan

We suggest that you complete the action plan below, using the guidance in other sections of this chapter. The final column is for a record of how well you are meeting your targets.

🖎

Skills I wish to focus on	Targets/actions to take	Resources/support needed	When?	Progress notes
Essay writing	*Concentrate on structuring an argument*	*The chapter on 'Essay Writing'*	*next week*	
		Relevant material in a learning centre/library	*next week*	
	Check spelling and punctuation	*Look at other essays (ask tutor for examples of good ones)*	*in 2 weeks*	
		If others also find it difficult, ask a lecturer to cover it	*2 weeks*	

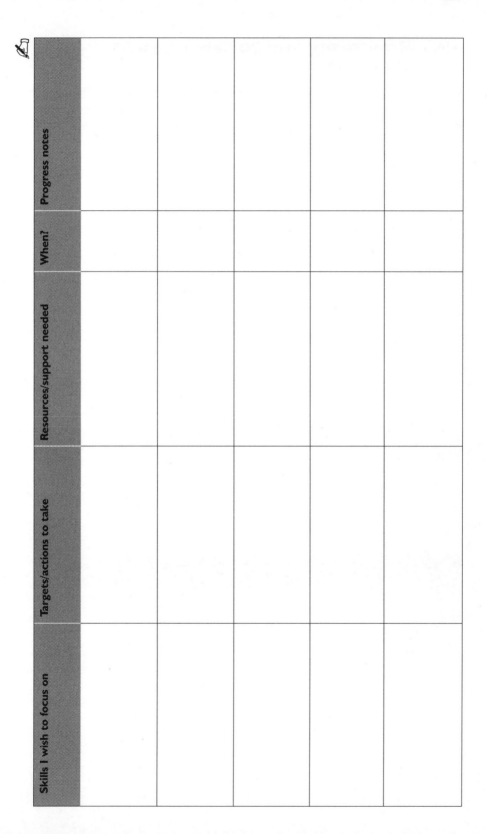

Skills I wish to focus on	Targets/actions to take	Resources/support needed	When?	Progress notes

19.3 Monitoring and reviewing your development

You are responsible for improving your own learning and performance and for implementing your plans, and presenting the outcomes, if required (eg *for assessment, interview*). Are you progressing as well as you can? Is your performance improving? Are your strategies working? If not, why not? What needs to change?

19.3.1 Regular review of action plan

You need to regularly review your action plan:

- as your skills develop and change
- as the situations or activities facing you change.

You could set aside a regular time each week to do this, making sure you adapt your plan as needed.

When monitoring your progress, you could ask others for feedback on your performance (eg *tutors, friends, other students, employers*). They may have suggestions to help you further.

19.3.2 Little progress?

If you find when you reach a deadline set for a particular action that you haven't made it, it helps to ask why.

- What is stopping you?
- Was your deadline or target unrealistic?
- Do you need a new approach?
- Do you need training, or advice?
- Do you need to change your attitude?
- Changing the way you do things can be difficult. You might need help and you might need to make allowances for yourself. Acknowledge that it's hard and give yourself credit for how far you **have** got.

Unmet target	Why?	Progress which has been made	Further action needed

19.3.3 Developing your strategies for evaluating yourself

How effective are the strategies you use to evaluate your skills and performance? Are your judgements about yourself realistic and supported by evidence (eg *feedback from tutors/employers, observing others, reading material on skills*)?

What do you need to do to improve your skills of self-evaluation?

What could you do to improve?	What resources/support is needed?	By when?

19.4 Presenting yourself and your work

You may be asked to present the outcomes of your self-evaluation and/or the process you have been through (eg *course-related: a reflective piece of work; work-related: an appraisal/review or job application*).

Style and format
You need to select the most appropriate format and style to suit your purpose and audience. You may find it helpful to look at other chapters, in particular:

- 'Reflecting on Your Experience'
- 'Oral Presentation'
- 'Report Writing'
- 'Visual Presentation'.

Evidence
You may need to provide evidence (eg *of your skills, the process you used to improve them, your evaluation of that process, the outcomes of your action planning*). You could ask yourself:

- who is this information for (eg *a tutor, interviewer, other students*)?
- how will this affect what you do?
- what are the criteria they will use to make judgements?

Possible sorts of evidence include:

- action plans, including progress notes and amended plans, with dates
- logs/diaries showing the work you did
- written evidence from others, commenting on aspects of your work/development (eg *from employers, group members, clients*)
- your self-evaluations. You could use the activities/exercises you've done in this chapter (and the equivalent one in Part I).

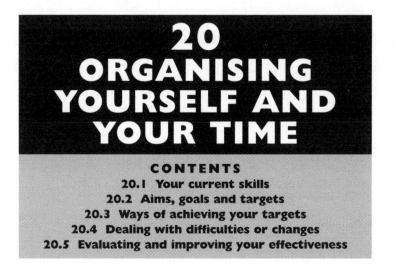

20
ORGANISING YOURSELF AND YOUR TIME

CONTENTS
20.1 Your current skills
20.2 Aims, goals and targets
20.3 Ways of achieving your targets
20.4 Dealing with difficulties or changes
20.5 Evaluating and improving your effectiveness

This chapter aims to help you to make the most of opportunities, by being well organised and using time well.

You can achieve more. Your performance on the course is likely to be much better if you are well organised. In addition, employers need employees to prioritise and meet deadlines. This is a skill area they look for when recruiting graduates or higher diplomates. If you are well organised, you are more likely to be able to cope with pressure and less likely to succumb to stress.

We suggest you use this chapter:

- **to make the most of your time and opportunities**
- **in conjunction with course activities**
- **at the beginning of a semester or a busy period, to help you plan and monitor your actions.**

When you have completed it, you should be able to:

Develop a strategy
- review current practice and identify factors about yourself which influence the ability to organise yourself and your time
- identify what you want to achieve in the future (long-term targets/aims) and the criteria against which to judge the standard or quality of those outcomes
- set realistic targets
- select methods which will achieve the targets and are personally relevant.

Monitor progress
- take responsibility for your time management and meet deadlines
- cope with unexpected demands
- critically reflect on your practices, note choices made and judge your effectiveness, adapt your time management strategies.

Evaluate strategies and present outcomes
- evaluate how well you met deadlines and targets, and managed your time
- identify ways of further developing this skill.

(Based on QCA Key Skill specifications, QCA 2000)

20.1 Your current skills

The chapter on 'Organising Yourself and Your Time' in Part I covers the following. How would you rate your current skill level against each item? If you feel you need to improve on any of these areas, you should refer to that chapter. The following uses a scale where 1 is 'very well' and 4 is 'needs considerable attention'.

✔

	1	2	3	4
Being aware of my strengths/weaknesses in how I currently organise myself/my time				
Identifying targets				
Estimating how long work will take and planning ahead				
Prioritising				
Reducing time wasters				
Meeting deadlines				
Having a well-organised workspace				
Having easy to use filing/recording systems				

Is the way you spend your time helping you study effectively? Do you need to change anything?

It can help to keep a diary of all your activities over a week, to see what you spend your time on (see the chapter in Part I for a template to use).

You could ask yourself the following questions:

- Why did I spend my time in that way?
- Is the way I spend my time helping me to study effectively? What is good about how I use my time?
- Am I surprised by anything?
- Do I need to change anything? What?
- Is there anything I really can't change? What?

It is your responsibility to make the most of your time and opportunities. Activities can be affected by other people and circumstances, as well as your own preferences and ways of doing things. What matters is how you deal with this.

Being autonomous means deciding what you do yourself, rather than others directing you.

20.2 Aims, goals and targets

Your long-term aims will affect what your more immediate aims are – see Chapters 18 and 32 on 'Action Planning'.

20.2.1 Immediate aims and targets

What immediate targets do you have or things you must do? How long will each take to achieve? Can each target/task be broken down into more realistic sub-tasks? How long will each sub-task take (estimate this, then add on half as much again, as most of us seriously underestimate time needed).

It might help to include not only course targets but others too: domestic; work; social. These may affect your course work.

How will you judge the outcomes? How will you know if the results of your work are good? Identifying this before you start helps keep you on track. Use the box below to note the tasks and sub-tasks you want or need to achieve, and then identify criteria you will use to know if they are the right quality or standard.

Target/task	Sub-tasks	Time needed	Deadline	Criteria to judge success
Eg *prepare a presentation*	*Gather information (learning centre/library Internet, from companies)*	*10 days*	*4 weeks*	eg *clear, well-structured presentation*
	Sort and order material	*1 day*		*understandable and clear OHPs*
	Plan the structure and audience activities	*1 day*		*audience understands and participates*
	Create visual aids/handouts	*1 day*		*questions handled well*
	Practise delivery	*1 day*		

20.2.2 Realistic targets

In considering what is realistic, think about the time and resources available and your skills/abilities.

Targets need to be SMART:

- **Specific** (eg *'to improve my time management' is not specific, 'to plan each week how to spend my time' is specific*)

- **Measurable** (eg *'to improve my time management' is harder to measure than 'plan each week' – you either planned or you didn't*)

- **Achievable** (eg *you may not be able to improve all your time management now, but you can start planning for each week*)

- **Realistic** (eg *it is more realistic to make a start by planning each week, than to try to improve all your time management at one stroke*)

- **Time-bound** (eg *given deadlines – you will start weekly planning next week*)

20.3 WAYS OF ACHIEVING YOUR TARGETS

20.3.1 Prioritising

Nobody can do everything which comes their way. Effectiveness is improved by deciding what should be done now, what later, and what can be left. It helps to be clear about your aims, to help you to decide priorities (see Section 20.2).

What are your long, medium and short-term priorities? You could see Chapters 18 and 32 on 'Action Planning'.

Identifying them may help you plan ahead and not just deal with what arises day to day. This can lead to feeling out of control. Not planning ahead can mean not making the most of new opportunities (eg *self-employed people need to allow time to get new business as well as to carry out current business*).

In prioritising for the long term it can help to identify:

- what would determine your future
- what might influence your future to some extent
- what would have little effect on your future
- what would have no effect on your future at all.

In prioritising for the short term it can help to identify what is:

1. Urgent and important
   – do it
2. Urgent and not important
   – do it if you can
3. Important but not urgent
   – start it before it gets urgent
4. Not important and not urgent
   – don't do it.

You could return to the box you completed in Section 20.2.1 and add notes indicating priorities.

What if you have prioritised, but still have too much to do in too short a time? Possibilities are:

- make a list of what you must do. Estimate against each how long it will take and add on half again. If it adds up to more time than you have – reprioritise.
- make a list of what is to be done in order of priority. If after three days items are still on the list put them at the top or discard them.

20.3.2 Using resources and delegating

What could make things easier and reduce effort? Possibilities include:

- using a computer (but beware, computers don't always save time), eg
  - time word-process work – it's easier to correct work and edit it
  - use computers to process information (eg *to make tables, create databases*)
  - identify which computer applications could save you time – it might be worth investing some time in learning to use them well
  - use a computer to store notes

- find out what resources there are to help you with a task (an hour doing this could avoid future time wasting). Identify who would know (eg *learning centre/library, computing support staff, lecturers, friends*)
- reduce the time you spend on other activities (eg *travelling*). Could you share out domestic tasks?
- share a task with other students (beware – if you need to produce an individual piece of work, then it must be done by you to avoid accusations of cheating.).

20.3.3 Saying no

Being unwilling to say no to others' requests can increase demands on you enormously. This might include social events you don't like to turn down, requests for help from other students, the needs of family members. It may be helpful to ask yourself the following about a current request from somebody.

Have I got time to do this?

Do I want to do this?

Do I have to do it? Could somebody else do it? Does it really need to be done?

What would happen if I didn't do it?

> How does it fit with my long-term goals and immediate targets?

If you find it hard to say no, it might help to look at Chapters 13 and 28 on 'Negotiating and Assertiveness'.

20.3.4 What will suit you?

You need to take responsibility for managing yourself and your time – you need to meet deadlines and targets. The methods you choose need to work for you, and help you achieve what you want – the working methods used by others may not suit you.

You could:

- identify your preferred working environment (eg *at night/warm/music playing*) and way of organising (eg *lists, highlighting pens, box files of notes*).
- clarify your long and short-term targets (refer back to Section 20.2 and see Chapters 18 and 32 on 'Action Planning'.
- talk to others about what they do (eg *friends, tutors*) – try some of their methods to see if they work for you
- look at Chapters 3 and 20 on 'Organising Yourself and Your Time' for ideas
- use feedback from others about how effectively you are managing yourself and your time.

20.4 Dealing with difficulties or changes

20.4.1 Dealing with the unexpected

What about the sudden crisis, the additional piece of work, the breakdown of equipment? What do you normally do when faced by the unexpected?

Possible strategies

- Allow time for the unexpected. Going for an interview? Allow for the train to be late. Need certain books? Allow time for inter-library loans. Need to use a computer? Assume there will be a queue.
- Try to anticipate what might happen and plan for it. Identify how likely it is to happen/how important it is, before spending time on planning for it.
- When estimating how long a task will take always add half on again.
- Delegate work to someone. Who? Why might they agree?
- Share a task with other students (eg *researching information, domestic jobs*).
- Identify resources or people who could help with current or future pressures.

Resources/people	How they might help

20.4.2 Conflicting demands

What if you have conflicting demands (eg *needing to do different things at the same time*)? You may need to:

- prioritise (see Section 20.3.1)
- identify other ways of meeting one of the demands. Could anybody else do it? Could it be done on a different day? Could it be done in any less time? Could it be done in advance?
- stop doing something else.

20.4.3 Adapting what you do

As you work through your plan, monitor your progress. Think about a current piece of work you are doing. Are you doing it as you intended?

Has anything changed since you decided how to do it?
What factors are influencing what you are doing?
What choices have you made and what effect are they having?
Is the way you're doing it working well? Why? Why not?
What could you do differently/better?

It helps to think in this way about any work or other activities you are involved in. You need to be flexible and adapt/change how you do things.

20.5 Evaluating and improving your effectiveness

In order to make the most of your time and opportunities, you need to review how effective your strategies have been.

Did you meet your deadlines and targets? If not, why not? What could you do differently/in addition/better?

Strengths in organising myself and my time	Actions needed to build on these	Resources/support needed	By when?

Weaknesses in organising myself and my time	Actions needed to build on these	Resources/support needed	By when?

How do you like to organise your time? Could you find other, effective ways which would suit you? Which of the ideas in this chapter could you try?

If you organise yourself and your time you will hopefully not often feel under too much pressure. If you do feel under pressure, you might find Chapters 14 and 29 on 'Coping with Pressure' helpful.

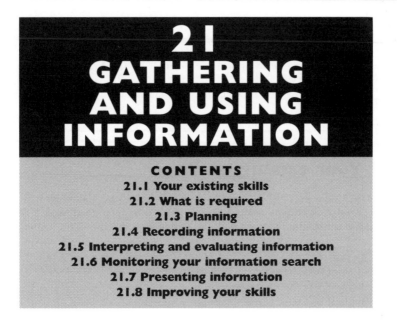

21
GATHERING
AND USING
INFORMATION

CONTENTS

21.1 Your existing skills
21.2 What is required
21.3 Planning
21.4 Recording information
21.5 Interpreting and evaluating information
21.6 Monitoring your information search
21.7 Presenting information
21.8 Improving your skills

Skills in gathering and using information are vital for academic success (on your current course, in a higher degree), and in future employment. All organisations need to base decisions on accurate and up to date information.

In this chapter we use an example to illustrate points: *finding information about policies on cigarette smoking.*

We suggest you use this chapter:

- to help you carry out a particular piece of work, such as a project or assignment.

When you have completed it, you should be able to:

Develop a strategy
- identify hoped for outcomes and the criteria against which to judge the standard or quality of those outcomes
- plan to use information skills over an extended time (eg *for a project or dissertation*)
- identify and select relevant resources, including current research/academic publications/appropriate primary sources, and methods (eg *IT resources, people, visual/audio sources, recording information*).

Monitor progress
- critically analyse information/data, identifying inaccuracy, opinion, bias and distortion
- synthesise information/data
- make judgements about information/data and present your interpretation
- monitor and review the effectiveness of own information strategies, making adaptations as necessary (eg *to overcome difficulties*)
- use feedback to review information strategies
- note choices made and their effectiveness.

Evaluate strategy and present outcomes
- organise and clearly present information
- evaluate your effectiveness in information strategies and the factors that affected it
- plan to further develop your information skills.

(Based on QCA Key Skill specifications, QCA 2000)

21.1 Your existing skills

Chapter 5 'Gathering and Using Information' covers the following basics. Rate yourself against each item using a scale where 1 is 'very good' and 4 is 'needs considerable improvement'. If you need to reconsider any items, see Chapter 5. ✔

Basic information skills	1	2	3	4
Identifying why you need the information				
Identifying who you need it for				
Analysing the task (your research questions)				
Identifying when you need it by				
Recording information (your filing system, citing/referencing material)				
Identifying where you might find the information				
Using information (eg *understanding it, covering a lot of it, answering your research questions, analysing it, knowing you have enough*)				
Understanding plagiarism				
Being aware of copyright				
Putting information into an appropriate format				
Reviewing your skills, what affects them, and how to improve				

21.2 What is required?

It will help to use this chapter in relation to some work you are doing now. What are you trying to achieve in gathering information for this current piece of work? ✔

a) Collecting factual information	
b) Proving how much work you've done	
c) Making sure you've covered every possibility	
d) Focusing on what is really important	
e) Looking for proof of an idea or hypothesis	
f) Criticising ideas	
g) Looking for underlying meanings	
h) Clarifying your own views	

All these are important and their appropriateness may vary with the task. Sometimes you need to cover every possibility, sometimes to focus on a small area. However, at higher levels of courses interpreting and evaluating information (items d–h) become more important, and are expected of all students by the end of their courses.

21.3 Planning

Planning ahead, rather than plunging straight in, saves time and effort. Sections 21.3.1–21.3.5 below help you think about the plan you can complete in Section 21.3.6.

21.3.1 What do you want to achieve?

What outcomes do you want for this piece of work, in relation to information? How will you know you have achieved them? Your answer may be 'a good grade' and 'I'll know by the grade I get' – but what will get a good grade (Section 21.2 above may help)?

Examples

Outcomes	Criteria which will tell me I have met this
Cover a wider range of up to date sources	*Number of references at the end of my work, dates of my references*
Produce work which is rigorous	*There is evidence for all my claims, the evidence can be traced, it is accurate*
Clearly explain concepts I've discovered	*Others can understand my explanations, all steps/ stages/essential ideas covered.*

You can make notes in the following box in relation to your own work. ✍

Outcomes	Criteria which will tell me I have met them

In your information search, you can keep returning here to see if you are on track.

21.3.2 What sort of information do you need?

As well as identifying your purpose, who the information is for, and your research questions (see Chapter 5 Section 5.1.4), considering the sort of information you need can help you see where to look for it.

- What is the subject: the broad subject area or a specific area; special aspects of the subject; a subject applied to another area (eg *IT in marketing or medicine*)?
- Do you need: a starting point (eg *an introduction or summary*); a detailed analysis; primary research; statistics, surveys, company/product information, visuals (eg *picture, graph*)?
- What type of resource is needed: book; journal; databases referring you to sources or ones giving complete articles; web sites; individual people; organisations?
- What you expect the information to look like (eg *visual image, print, numerical*)?
- How up to date does it need to be or what time period should it cover?
- What methods are needed to find it (eg *asking people, searching computer databases, doing an original investigation such as a survey*)?

What sort of information do you need?	Where might you find it? Do you need help from anybody to find it?	Do you need training to find it? In what? Who could train you?

21.3.3 Using imagination and initiative

Using our cigarette smoking example, a standard approach might be to do an online catalogue search under 'cigarette smoking'.

You could also jot down any ideas (no matter how daft they sound) on who would be interested in your topic. Then identify where you would find information produced by them. For example:

Who might be interested in smoking as an issue?	Possible sources of information
Politicians	*Hansard, newspapers (also on CD ROM).*
Health Service	*Local NHS HQ, leaflets in doctors' surgeries, Health Statistics, Medline CD-ROM, ASSIA CD ROM, CTI PLUS CD-ROM*
Employers	*Employers you've worked for, local Chamber of Commerce*
Trade unions	*Directories, Industrial Society, TU offices*
Tobacco manufacturers	*Advertising directories, trade directories*
People with tobacco related illnesses, or their relatives	*Directory of Pressure Groups, Charities Digest*
Civil liberties groups	*Directory of Pressure Groups*
Pubs, transport companies, fire brigade etc	*etc*

In addition to the above the Internet is a source of information covering almost any topic you can think of.

To become more aware of sources of information, you could:

- talk to friends or contacts (eg *people you've met at work or on placement*)
- be alert to the media (eg *newspapers, TV, radio may spark off ideas*)
- ask specialists, such as library/learning centre staff or lecturers.

Being imaginative may not be enough without initiative – you need to 'get up and find it'. People can be a great source of information. If you feel hesitant about approaching them, see Chapters 13 & 28 'Negotiating and Assertiveness'.

You could see your information search as a problem to solve. Chapters 10 & 26 'Solving Problems' may help.

21.3.4 Research methods

You may need to collect information from an original source (eg *from experiments, surveys, interviews, observations etc*).

This chapter does not focus on such methods. It focuses on information which already exists in a published form, rather than on information you create yourself.

Libraries/learning centres have information on research methods. Either look for 'research methods' in an online catalogue, or look for a particular method (eg *questionnaire*), or ask library/learning centre staff or your lecturers.

21.3.5 Planning time

Use your experience of gathering and using information to estimate the following.

Task	Time it will take (eg *2 hours, a day, 2 weeks?*)
How long will it take to find information from your sources? NB: Writing for information, allow at least 2 weeks for replies (include a stamped-addressed envelope); inter-library loans take on average 2 weeks.	
How much information may you have to look at? What methods will you use to cover it all? How long will this take?	
How long should you allow for problems? NB: A borrower with a book you want may be able to keep it for 3 weeks (check with your library/learning centre).	
If you are unfamiliar with computerised systems, how long will it take you to learn to use them?	

You may also need to consider:

- how to fit this information search in with searches for other work?
- how important this piece of work is. How much of your time/effort is it worth?

See Chapters 3 and 20 'Organising Yourself and Your Time'.

21.3.6 Plan

Sources of information can include people: library/learning centre staff; friends and other students; lecturers; technicians (eg *those working on IT*).

Tasks to do/areas to investigate/questions to answer	Sources to use and methods needed to use them	By (deadline for this)

21.4 Recording information

As you progress through your course you are likely to need more information for a piece of work (eg *for a dissertation*), and may need the information for different purposes (eg *an essay, a report, a presentation, an exhibition, a poster*).

In considering how to record information, you need to think how you will use it (see Section 21.7). You may also need to consider ethical and legal issues.

- Copyright. How much of the material can you reproduce? Ask library/learning centre staff
- Plagiarism. To avoid accusations of copying other people's work, you must acknowledge your sources (see Chapter 5 'Gathering and Using Information')
- Integrity and reliability. Is it true? Is it accurate? Who says?
- Is it confidential? To whom? Whose permission is needed to use it?

How will you use the information? How will you present it?
Do you need it for this assignment only, or might you need it again? What for?
What ethical and legal issues should you consider?

Given your notes in the above box, what are the best ways to record your information?

Chapter 5 'Gathering and Using Information' suggested simple manual and computerised storage systems. You could now think about further possibilities to save time and effort (eg *you may wish to transfer information from a database to another computer package, such as a spreadsheet*). Library/learning centre staff or computing support staff should be able to help.

It may help to review your current recording system.

- Does it take up as little time and space as possible?
- Would it a computer software package help, or not (will it save time/take more time to set up, make it more/less flexible)?
- Can you find information easily and quickly?
- Is your system cheap and simple?

See Chapter 4 'Note Taking'.

Ways in which I could reorganise my system

21.5 Interpreting and evaluating information

21.5.1 Analysing and criticising information

At higher levels of courses this is more important, as is giving evidence for your criticisms. For guidance on this essential area, see Chapter 22 'Critical Analysis'.

21.5.2 Interpreting information

Having analysed information you need to interpret it. In the following 'relate to' means making links between or looking at what is the same or different.

What you do may vary with the type of information (eg *factual information, theories, creative work*). Giving your own interpretation includes using your critical analysis to:

- look at what the information means and make sense of it (eg *identify essential elements – see Chapter 22 'Critical Analysis'*).
- identify which aspects you agree or disagree with and why (making judgements)
- relate the information to your topic
- relate the information to any original research you have done (eg *surveys, experiments*)
- relate the information to your own experience
- relate the information to any other evidence you have
- draw conclusions.

21.6 Monitoring your information search

You need to monitor how you are getting on with your information task and ways of dealing with difficulties (you are bound to have some). Some difficulties are easy to anticipate and can be solved by planning ahead or allowing enough time (eg *book out on loan; computer system crashes; people don't reply by your deadline*).

21.6.1 What if you can't find information?

There are various possible reasons for not being able to find information. You need to know which one it is, so you know what to do about it.

Reason	What to try
People make decisions about how to organise information and they may have looked at it from an angle which is different from yours.	Try looking for it under other related subjects. Try identifying other possible key words. Ask library/learning centre staff.
The information might not exist.	Finding this out may mean you have to collect information from scratch yourself. Researchers always start by looking for what information already exists to avoid duplicating it.
The information might exist, but not be available (eg *it might be confidential*).	This might be very useful to find out, especially if you could identify reasons for this.

21.6.2 Using feedback

Ask for feedback from others:

- have you found the best sources of information?
- is your information relevant?
- is it good quality?

Who could give you feedback?:

- library/learning centre staff
- lecturers/tutors
- other students (but remember individual work must be your own)
- employers
- professionals with an interest in the area.

21.6.3 Dealing with difficulties

What do you tend to do when faced with difficulties in any situations (eg *seek help; try to find solutions yourself; have a break and try again; give up*)?
What difficulties have you faced up to now when searching for/using information?
Will your usual ways of dealing with difficulties work when you are searching for and using information? What do you need to do differently?

For help, see Chapters 10 and 26 'Solving Problems', 14 and 29 'Coping with Pressure', and 13 and 28 'Negotiating and Assertiveness'.

21.7 Presenting information

In deciding how to present information you could consider:

• what will make it clear (eg *labelling, titles*)
• what will ensure it looks accurate (eg *visuals to scale*)
• what will ensure you avoid plagiarism and make your sources of information clear
• if comparing two or more sets of information, how to make the comparisons clear
• if it would help to present it visually (eg *graphs, diagrams, maps, photographs*)
• if details need to be in the main body of your work or could go in an appendix (for written work) or a handout (in a presentation)
• if your layout makes it clear (eg *headings, sub/headings*).

Useful resources to help include:

• Huff (1977) on presenting statistics accurately (an old book but still useful)
• dictionaries, a thesaurus (gives alternatives for a word)
• computer packages with presentation features
• examples of work in your subject in similar formats (eg *how journal articles/ reports/posters present information; how lecturers present information*)
• friends can look at your work to see if it is clear (but individual assessed work needs to be your own)
• other chapters on particular presentation formats (eg *'Report Writing', 'Oral Presentation'*).

21.8 Improving your skills

21.8.1 What affected what you did?

For a current (or recent) piece of work, what affected your searching for and using information? This could be a factor outside yourself (eg *resource availability, other people, domestic situation*), or in yourself (eg *time management, persistence*), or related to the choices you made (eg *aspects to focus on, sources to use*).

What was helpful, made your information search/use better? What choices worked well?	What was unhelpful, made your information search/use worse? What choices did not work well?

In completing the box in 21.8.3 below, you could think about how to build on or repeat what helped and how to avoid or deal differently with what was unhelpful.

21.8.2 Your effectiveness

How would you rate your skills (1 is 'very good', 4 'needs considerable improvement')?

	1	2	3	4
Identifying what you want from your information search (your outcomes)				
Analysing the task, ie identifying research questions, why you need the information and for whom, when you need it by				
Planning your information search and use				
Identifying where to find information (the sources)				
Recording information				
Referencing information				
Covering a lot of information and knowing when to stop				
Finding out about aspects/terms you don't understand				

✔

	I	2	3	4
Analysing, criticising, interpreting information				
Providing evidence from your information				
Presenting information				
Monitoring your information search/use and dealing with difficulties				

21.8.3 Action planning to improve

The following will help you plan to improve.

Aspects of my information skills to improve	Actions to be taken	By (deadline)

Thanks to Aileen D. Wade of the Learning Centre and Phil Bannister of the LTI at Sheffield Hallam University for their contributions to a version of this chapter in *Key Skills Online*.

Based on an original pack by Sue Drew/Rosie Bingham/Andrew Walker/Aileen Wade.

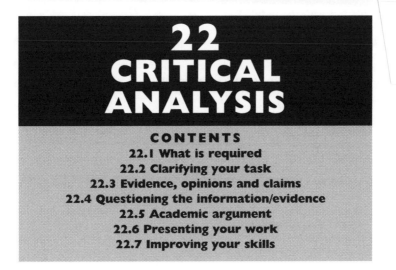

22
CRITICAL
ANALYSIS

CONTENTS

On university/college courses it is important to use the skill of critical analysis, even more so at higher levels (eg *towards the final year*), and to use it in a way which is generally acknowledged to be 'academic'. This chapter aims to:

- explain what is meant by critical analysis in a university/college context
- help you to be critical and analytical in your coursework
- and therefore to help you with your assessed work.

We suggest you use this chapter:

- **when you begin work on an assignment (eg *project, dissertation, presentation, report*) and then while you are working on your assignment**
- **in relation to any published information you use, whatever the format (eg *written, oral, visual, electronic*)**
- **in relation to any information you have collected (eg *from surveys, interviews, experiments, field work*).**

You may find it helpful to practise this skill by using this chapter first with a short piece of written work in front of you (eg *an article*).

This chapter is linked to Chapter 21 'Gathering and Using Information', and it is suggested that you use them together. You will find it helpful to begin with Chapter 5 'Gathering and Using Information'.

When you have competed it, you should be able to:

Plan and use strategies
- identify opinion, unfounded claims, assumptions
- identify the relevance and significance of any aspects related to a topic, critically analyse information/data, identifying inaccuracy, opinion, bias and distortion
- identify what makes evidence/proof appropriate in a particular context (eg *sufficiency, validity, currency, accuracy, relevance, reliability, completeness*)
- question, in an appropriate way for a context, the evidence or proof for claims
- identify, explain and analyse different perspectives on a topic

- make connections between elements (including perspectives) of the same or different topics in order to identify common themes, models or theories
- justify any links and connections identified
- summarise and synthesise information/data coherently
- make and justify judgements
- interpret information in relation to a particular context and purpose
- analyse and criticise an academic argument.

Evaluate strategy and present outcomes
- organise and clearly present information
- devise and sustain an academic argument supported by appropriate evidence
- evaluate your effectiveness in critical analysis strategies and the factors that affected it
- plan to further develop your information skills.

You should be able to do this in relation to information which may be complex, unpredictable/uncertain, incomplete, or ambiguous.

(Based on QCA Key Skill specifications, QCA 2000)

22.1 What is required?

22.1.1 What is critical analysis?

'To analyse' is to break information into its elements. 'To be critical' (in an academic sense) is to make careful judgements about information and to evaluate its quality.

22.1.2 What is not critical analysis?

Critical analysis is **not:**

- a straight description of something
- making assumptions without checking them out
- making generalisations which are not supported by evidence
- accepting information without questioning it
- giving information with mistakes in it or which is misleading
- saying 'This writer says this, that writer says that' without also giving your views on what the differences are between what the two writers are saying.

22.1.3 What your tutors expect

It is important not only to find information but to use it in ways which are understood by academic staff to be 'at an academic level'. You may track down everything on a topic, but this on its own will not get a good mark/grade.

What is required is the ability to be critical of information and to make your own judgements about it, well supported by evidence.

Perry
The work of an American researcher called Perry (1970) may help to clarify what tutors expect. From talking to American students he identified nine stages of 'ethical and intellectual development'. These stages can be summarised as:

Summary of stage	Our example
1. The authorities know	eg *'the tutor knows what is right and wrong'*
2. The true authorities are right, the others are frauds	eg *'my tutor doesn't know what is right or wrong, but other tutors do'*
3. There are some uncertainties and the authorities are working on them to find the truth	eg *'my tutors don't know, but somebody out there is trying to find out'*
4. a) Everyone has a right to their own opinion b) The authorities don't want the right answers. They want us to think in a certain way	eg *'different tutors think different things'* eg *'there is an answer that the tutors want and we have to find out what it is'*
5. Everything is relative but not equally valid	eg *'there are no right and wrong answers, it depends on the situation, but some answers might be better than others'*
6. You have to make your own decisions	eg *'what is important is not what the tutor thinks but what I think'*
7. First commitment	eg *'for this particular topic I think that...'*
8. Several commitments	eg *'for these topics I think that...'*
9. Believe own values, respect others, be ready to learn	eg *'I know what I believe in and what I think is valid, others may think differently and I'm prepared to reconsider my views.'*

You may be at different stages in different areas of your life (eg *at stage 9 for academic issues, but at stage 1 when learning to drive a car*). In your academic work, tutors will want you to be at the higher stages by the end of a course.

The middle stages in Perry's scheme may cause anxiety and confusion. You no longer think others have the right answers, but have not yet decided on your own views. You may feel that the more you learn about something the more it seems you don't know.

Bloom

Bloom developed a hierarchy of cognitive (thinking) skills. Bloom's (1979) *Taxonomy of Educational Objectives* has 'knowledge' at the lowest level, the hierarchy moving through several stages until the highest level, evaluation. It can be summarised as:

1. Knowledge
    – of specifics
    – of processes
    – of concepts

2. Comprehension
3. Application
4. Analysis (eg *of elements, of relationships between elements, of principles*)
5. Synthesis (putting elements together eg *plans, proposals for operations, creation of models to explain data*)
6. Evaluation (making judgements)

(From Bloom, B. (ed.) *Taxonomy of Educational Objectives*, copyright 1979 by Allyn & Bacon. Adapted by permission.)

By the end of degree courses, for example, you are expected to be able to show all those levels.

22.1.4 Your current skills

What 'Perry stage' are you are at in this course? Are you at different stages for different units or topics?	What 'Bloom stage' are you are at in this course? Are you at different stages for different units or topics?

22.2 Clarifying your task

What do the instructions for your assignment mean? Your assignment may explicitly tell you what to do, or it may imply that you do certain things without explicitly saying so (eg *if you are asked to make recommendations that implies you have to evaluate something and draw conclusions*).

It helps to:

- break the task into its elements
- identify explicit instruction words
- see if the topic implies other instruction words; use dictionaries to identify what instructions mean
- rewrite the instructions in your own words.

If in doubt, ask your tutor.

Chapters 5 and 21 'Gathering and Using Information' help you to clarify your task as do the other chapters.

Instruction	What is meant
clarify	identify the components of an issue/topic/problem/; identify the main points; make the meaning plain; remove ambiguities or misunderstandings; restate something in your own words
analyse	break information into constituent parts; examine the relationship between the parts; question the information
be critical	identify what is good and bad about the information and why, probe, question, identify inaccuracies or shortcomings in the information, estimate the value of the material
evaluate, weigh up	as above but also – come to a conclusion (see below) about the information
balance	look at two or more viewpoints or pieces of information; give each equal attention; look at good and bad points; take into account many aspects and give an appropriate weighting to those aspects
compare	consider the similarities or dissimilarities; implies evaluation (eg *which aspects of two or more topics/subjects are most valuable*)
identify trends	identify patterns/changes/movements in certain directions (eg *over time or across topics/subjects*)
argue	put the case for/against a view or idea giving evidence for your claims/reasons; attempt to influence the reader to accept your view
conclude/draw conclusions	the end point of your critical thinking; what the results of an investigation indicate; arrive at a judgement by reasoning
develop a view	decide what you think (based on an argument or on evidence)
justify	make a case for a particular view; explain why something is like it is/why there is a certain view on it; give reasons; show adequate grounds for something
give evidence	evidence from your own work or that of others which could be checked by a third party to prove/justify what you say
summarise	briefly identify the main points or aspects of the information, remove unnecessary detail
review	similar to summarise (see above) but usually includes evaluation (see above), an overview, a reconsideration of something

22.3 Evidence, opinions and claims

22.3.1 Evidence

Material (either published or your own work) should include evidence for what it claims. Evidence is proof for something (think of 'evidence' in a TV crime programme). To identify if evidence is appropriate for a situation, consider if it is:

* valid, ie does it prove what it claims to prove
* current, ie is it up to date, or is the date appropriate (eg *for historical issues*)
* accurate
* relevant
* reliable, ie can you trust it
* complete
* sufficient, ie enough evidence to prove something.

22.3.2 Opinions

An opinion is an idea for which there is no evidence. In academic work it is bad practice to give an opinion without evidence (unless you clearly state that it is only an opinion). It is particular important to identify opinions without proof if they are central to an argument (see Section 22.5 below).

Within a subject area, some ideas may be so well accepted by subject specialists that they are seen as 'truths' and it is not necessary to keep repeating the evidence. It may take quite a lot of subject experience before you know what these 'truths' are. Until you get to that point, it may be safer to check there is evidence for them.

For practice, look at a piece of information and identify any statements which are opinions (ie which have no evidence or proof).

22.3.3 Claims

A claim is a statement of something you believe or you have discovered (eg *a hypothesis*). It must be supported by evidence or proof – otherwise it is an opinion. In a piece of work the proof or evidence may not always be next to the claim – it may appear later.

For practice, you could look at a piece of information and identify the claims made and the evidence.

Claims	Evidence

The following sections will help you decide whether the evidence is believable or acceptable.

22.4 Questioning the information/evidence

Sections 22.4.1– 22.4.4 consist of questions to consider in relation to information. You could add your own questions to the lists and use them whenever you have to critically analyse information. When others (eg *assessors*) look at your work, they will ask similar questions about it, so you could use the following sections as 'checklists' when editing your own work.

22.4.1 Analysing the information

Question	Your notes
What are the essential elements?	
What are the most important points made?	
What concepts lie beneath the factual information?	
Are there any recurring themes?	
Is all the information relevant to the topic?	
Is the information significant (ie is it noteworthy or important for the topic)?	
Is the evidence believable?	
Your own questions (please add)	

22.4.2 Accuracy, completeness, currency, bias

Question	Your notes
Is the information accurate? Do figures add up? Are the statistics misleading (see Huff 1973)?	
How selective is the material? Is it complete? What more is needed? Does it (perhaps deliberately) omit any information?	
How up to date is the information? Is the date important? Has the information been superseded by more recent information?	
Is the source of the information reliable or reputable? Can you trust what they say?	
Might the source of the information be biased? Have they got a vested interest?	
Your own questions (please add)	

22.4.3 Questioning and checking for assumptions

Question	Your notes
Why do those giving the ideas/opinions/claims think as they do? Why was the information prepared? What were the underlying assumptions?	
Is it necessarily so? Could there be reasons other than those suggested?	
Are the ideas/opinions/claims based on values/attitudes? What are they? Do they relate to a specific group (eg *gender, social class*)? Would the ideas/opinions/claims look different with different values/attitudes?	
Do you agree/disagree with the concepts/ideas? Why?	
Have you accepted the ideas/opinions/claims because they confirm what you think, rather than because there is good evidence for them?	
Are there other situations where the ideas/opinions/claims should also apply and do they? What exceptions might there be?	
What would people unfamiliar with the material ask about it? What will your audience or reader make of it, or not understand?	
Your own questions (please add)	

Ruggiero (1996) suggests the following reasons for these producing the information making mistakes or distorting information:

- their perceptions (eg *being over positive or over negative*)
- how they made their judgements (eg *irrelevant criteria, stereotyping, oversimplifying*)
- their reactions to the topic (eg *discomfort may lead them to attack individuals, or to explain things away*).

22.4.4 Comparing information

Question	Your notes
Are there any connections between aspects of the information?	
How does what one author/source say compare with what others say? Are the similar/different? How?	
Do most authors/sources agree? If one disagrees, how, what are their views based on (eg *new information; different values or perceptions*)?	
What do other authors/sources say about one particular author/source?	
Which author/source do you agree with? Why? What is the evidence for what you think?	
Your own questions (please add)	

22.4.5 Some examples

The following gives examples of critical analysis, in relation to some of the points in sections 22.4.1–22.4.4 above .

Issue	Example
Checking and questioning assumptions	*'Business Process Re-engineering' assumes that businesses have processes which can be re-engineered; 'the economy depends on having a skilled workforce' is an assumption unless information which proves the statement is given.*
Claims should be supported by evidence	*Evidence might include quotations; summaries of information from the literature; results of investigative work you have carried out; statistics.*
Are there any other explanations for information?	*If figures for shipments of personal computers (PCs) have increased is it because more PCs are shipped or because the collection of data is more efficient?* *Do statistics on the connections between cigarette smoking and health conceal other factors, eg about social class?*
Reasons for bias should be identified	*IT strategy writers may have a vested interest in asserting that IT strategy works.* *A report on cigarette smoking may be selective in the information it presents about the dangers, if written by those in favour of smoking.*
Information and how it is presented should not be misleading	*Examples of misleading information: using percentages when the base numbers are very small; drawing graphs which are not to scale.*
Dates of information may be important	*Information on the connections between cigarette smoking and health may have been produced before certain medical evidence emerged.*

22.4.6 Giving evidence for your criticisms

It is not enough to give criticisms, you must provide evidence for them (eg *other writers' criticisms of a concept, or factual information which contradicts an argument*). If you have found evidence of bias or distortion you need to identify the reasons and justify why you consider the bias to exist. You must provide accurate references for information. Who said it? When?

22.5 Academic argument

22.5.1 What is an 'academic argument'?

It is putting forward a line of reasoning. An argument usually consists of claims (see 22.3.3 above) for which evidence is given (see 22.3.1), and which are put into the best order (organised, or structured) to persuade the reader or listener to agree.

22.5.2 Understanding an argument

This section consists of questions you could ask in relation to an argument you are considering now. Add your own questions and use them whenever you have to understand an argument.

When other people (eg *assessors*) look at **your** arguments in **your** work, they will ask similar questions about it, so also use the following to make sure your **own** arguments are strong.

Question	Your notes
What is the main point or claim being made?	
What subsidiary points/claims are being made?	
Do the subsidiary points/claims connect logically with the main one? Are all the points/claims linked together? Are they in an order which aids understanding?	
Is there appropriate evidence for each point/claim (see 21.3.1)?	
Have any steps/information/evidence been missed out of the argument?	
Has information/points/claims not relevant to the main point/claim been included?	
Do the conclusions follow from the points/evidence/claims? Have judgements been made about the topic or information?	
Your own questions (please add)	

22.6 Presenting your work

In presenting the results of your critical analysis you need to check:

- that you have given the sources for your information/evidence, correctly referenced (see Chapter 5 'Gathering and Using Information')
- that the reader/user/listener could find the information/evidence
- that the way you have presented your work will help the reader/user/listener understand it. This partly relates to how well you have presented your argument (see Section 22.5 above), but also to factors such as the layout and the appropriateness of the format (eg *presenting information visually or in text*). You may find Chapter 23 'Essay Writing' helpful here (even if you are not producing an essay).

22.7 IMPROVING YOUR SKILLS

22.7.1 Your current skills

Consider the following in relation to a current or recent piece of work:

What do you think you did well in critically analysing it?	What factors affected this (about you as a person or factors outside yourself)?
What do you think you did not do well?	What factors affected this (about you as a person or factors outside yourself)?

Do you find anything difficult about critical analysis? What?	Why?

22.7.2 Planning to improve

Use the following to help you plan to improve your skills of critical analysis

Aspect I need to improve	Action I need to take	By (deadline)

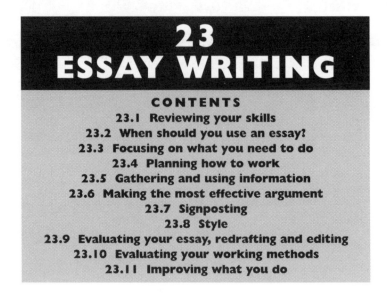

23
ESSAY WRITING

CONTENTS

Essays are often used in some subjects at university/college, occasionally in others, and often in exams across all subjects (eg *questions often require a reply in the form of a short essay*). In the final year/level of your course, you may be asked to produce a thesis or dissertation and this may be in the form of an extended essay (check with your tutor).

Essays are used because:

- the process of writing an essay helps you understand a topic – it is a valuable learning activity
- the freedom the essay format gives you also allows assessors to judge how far you have grasped a topic, and how well you can reason about it, in a way which more structured forms of writing (eg *reports*) do not do
- they help you develop your ability to express yourself in writing.

Your grade/mark will depend not only on how well you know your subject, but on how well you use the essay format.

We suggest you use this chapter:

- **when you need to produce a piece of written work, to identify if the essay format would be appropriate**
- **when you have an essay to write, to help you get the best possible mark/grade. You could look at it both before writing your first draft and once you have your first draft, to improve it**
- **to help you develop your essay writing skills in general.**

When you have completed it, you should be able to:

Develop a strategy
- identify when an essay is the appropriate format to use, including for complex topics
- identify the criteria against which to judge the standard or quality of the essay (eg *content, format, language*)
- identify and plan to use the most efficient and effective methods/ techniques (eg *use of time and resources*) to produce the essay.

Monitor progress
- use information which has been critically evaluated
- present information and argument in the most effective way
- signpost critical points, using language and layout
- appeal to and engage the reader, conveying particular effects and using relevant information and images
- edit/redraft to assure style, critical analysis and argument
- note choices made, judge their effectiveness and adapt strategies as needed (eg *to overcome difficulties*)
- seek and use feedback to improve process and outcomes.

Evaluate strategy and present outcomes
- evaluate the effectiveness of strategies used to produce the essay, identifying factors which had an effect
- identify ways of further developing your essay writing skills.

(Based on QCA Key Skill specifications, QCA 2000)

23.1 Reviewing your skills

The following aspects are covered by Chapter 6 on 'Essay Writing'. If you need to review or improve any items, refer back to it. Rate yourself on the following, where 1 = 'very good' and 4 = 'in need of considerable improvement'.

✔

	1	2	3	4
Identifying the features of essays in general				
Identifying what is required by your tutor from your essay (including what is the norm for essays in your subject area)				
Interpreting what the essay topic/question means, its purpose and what is needed to deal with/answer it				
Managing your time to meet a deadline				
Identifying the information you need to gather				
Using and recording information				
Referencing information in your essay				
Drafting				
Identifying opinion and bias in the information you use				

✔

	1	2	3	4
Structuring your essay				
Using standard English				
The style of your essay				
Editing your essay				
Evaluating your essay to improve what you do				

You could also look at Chapters 5 and 21 on 'Gathering and Using Information' and Chapter 4 on 'Note Taking'.

23.2 When should you use an essay?

You may have a choice of format to write in ('format' means how a piece of writing is arranged, eg *a report, an essay, a portfolio are all different formats*).

You may be told what format to use by your tutor/lecturer. If this is the case you **must** use that format. This section applies to those who have been given a choice of formats (and this may be unusual).

If you do have a choice, how will you know if the essay is the best format for your topic? The following table identifies some activities you may be asked to do, and suggests an appropriate format for each.

Do you need to...	Possible format
Present the findings of an investigation to somebody/an organisation, making recommendations for action they need to take?	Report (Beware, a thesis often reports the findings of an investigation, but it does not use the report format – see below)
Present actual evidence of what you have done, to demonstrate your abilities	Portfolio
Show the detail/amount of what you did in a particular situation, over a time period (eg *on placement*)	Log/diary
Write a paper for an academic journal	Academic paper. Very similar in format to an essay, but see the journal the paper is written for how a paper should be laid out, and for their requirements (usually on the back page)
Review a book or article	Usually very short and in a specific review format for that subject area

Do you need to...	Possible format
Explore a topic for its own sake, rather than presenting information to somebody to take action on. Write extensively about a topic. Explore it in ways which you decide are appropriate, rather than which somebody determines	Essay
Produce a major piece of work in the final year/level of a course. May be investigative, based on experiments or evidence collection	Likely to be a report
Review the literature on a topic	Likely to be an extended essay

If you have a choice, you could:

- discuss what format to use with your tutor
- discuss it with other students
- discuss it with somebody else who may benefit from your work (eg *an employer*)
- look at examples of work in the above formats to see what might best meet your needs.

Consider this in the light of the next section.

23.3 Focusing on what you need to do

23.3.1 Clarifying what is required

You may find it very helpful to work through this chapter thinking about an essay you are currently writing or are about to write.

Before you start any work for your essay you need to clarify your topic/question. At higher levels of courses you will be dealing with more complex topics, ie ones with more elements. The more complex your topic, the more important it is to be really clear about what you are doing, right from the start.

In particular you need to:

- identify if there are any requirements, such as word length
- look at the assessment criteria (what will get a good mark?)
- check what is the norm for essays in your subject area (eg *do you use the impersonal/third person or personal voice? Can you use sub-headings?*)
- look at the words in the topic/question and analyse what they mean, in particular: instruction words which tell you what to do; words which give you the focus; words which tell you what else to cover
- identify what is implied by the topic/question (ie not explicitly stated but which it implies you should consider).

See the Starter Level chapter (Chapter 6) on 'Essay Writing' for more guidance on the above.

23.3.2 Choosing your own essay topic/question

You may be able to choose your own essay topic or question. Making notes in the box below can help you identify a suitable one.

> **Would you prefer a topic you know a lot about, or one in which you are very interested, or would like to find out more about? What topic might this be?**

> **What are the implications of choosing this topic (eg *if you know a lot about it but are not interested in it, you may need to find less new information but it may be difficult to motivate yourself to work on it*)?**
> **What could you do about this (eg *choose another topic; find ways of helping you stay on track and to motivate yourself*)?**

> **Try to come up with the wording for a title here.**

Consider the following questions in relation to your possible title:

- is it too big a topic for one essay?
- is it too small or restricted a topic for a whole essay?
- could you find the information you need for it? How easily?
- would anybody else (eg *your tutor*) be interested in it (readers are more sympathetic towards something they find interesting)?
- what instruction word/s have you used and are they OK for this level of your course (eg *'describe' may be too simple for the higher levels of a course, you may need 'consider' or 'explore' or 'critique'; look at the learning outcomes for your course/unit/module at this level to check what is expected*)?

23.3.3 Identifying what you want to achieve

What do you want to get from this essay? It might be to get a certain mark or grade, or there may be other things (eg *to find out more about something, to practise certain skills such as IT*). In other words, what are your own aims?

How will you know if you have met your aims? If your aims are to get a certain mark or grade, do you know what you must do to get that grade and how your work will be judged (ie the assessment criteria)? If you are unclear about this, check it out (eg *in a course/unit handbook, assignment brief, or ask your tutor*). How will you know if your other aims have been met? For example, if you want to use IT skills in your essay, the criteria which will show you have done so might include that your work is easy to read, or looks attractive, or that the resources you found using IT were useful for your essay.

You can make notes here on your aims and the criteria you will use to see if you have met them. This will help you see what you need to do. They will help you keep focused as you work on your essay.

Your aims	Your criteria

23.4 Planning how to work

You may have to fit writing this essay in with other work, and other commitments. To help you meet your aims (see Section 23.3.3 above), you need to find ways of working which are efficient, so you can make effective use of your time.

It may help to identify:

- how you set about producing essays in the past – what worked well and what didn't
- how you carry out similar tasks (eg *how you usually gather and use information*), what works well and what doesn't
- the tasks you must do to meet your aims and the requirements for the essay (see Section 23.3 above) and then to identify the best ways of doing them.

Here are some suggestions:

- use electronic sources of information (eg *databases, the Web*)
- use IT to produce the essay (eg *word-processing*)
- ask specialists for help or advice (eg *library/learning centres, computer support staff, tutors*)
- be organised (eg *organise your notes and your working space*)
- plan your time (eg *can you combine several information seeking tasks and do them all in one visit to a library/learning centre?*)
- make a plan of what you have to do to produce the essay and monitor it regularly.

To help, you could look at:

- Chapters 3 and 20 on 'Organising Yourself and Your Time'
- Chapter 4 on 'Note Taking'
- Chapters 18 and 32 on 'Action Planning'.

You could complete this box now, or return to it when you have gone through the whole chapter.

Which of the tasks needed to produce your essay could you do better or more efficiently?	What/who would help you?

23.5 Gathering and using information

23.5.1 Review of what is needed

To help you gather information for your essay, see Chapter 6 on 'Essay Writing' and Chapters 5 and 21 on 'Gathering and Using Information'. This section will help you critique the information once you have gathered it.

At higher levels of courses you must also ensure that you:

- have critically evaluated any information you use
- make it clear in your essay that you have done so.

By 'information' we mean not only facts or data but also ideas, theories, visual images – anything you use as the basis for the information, ideas and arguments in your essay.

23.5.2 Criticising and evaluating information

Criticising information means not taking it at face value, not accepting it without question. The sort of questions you could ask about it include:

- is it accurate?
- is it based on evidence and where is that evidence?
- is it based on assumptions only (ie without evidence)?
- is it up to date?
- is it complete?
- what is the source, is it reliable and how do you know that?
- is it biased (does it emphasise certain aspects because of the views of the person producing it)?

Evaluating information means making judgements about how good you think it is (as a result of your criticising it). Do you agree with it or disagree with it and why? What other views might there be, or other ideas?

It may help to make notes on the following:

What information do you already have about your essay topic (summarise it with a few key words)?	What do you need to ask about this information?	What do you think of this information? Why?
What further information will you need about your essay topic (summarise it with a few key words)?	What will you need to ask about this information?	What will help you make judgements about this information?

For further help see Chapter 22 on 'Critical Analysis'.

23.5.3 Presenting your critical evaluation in your essay

How can you make it clear that you have critically evaluated any factual information, ideas or theories you refer to in your essay? Here are some suggestions:

- say if there are any inaccuracies (eg *'There are inaccuracies in these figures, for example...'*)
- say if you think something is biased and why (eg *'However, cigarette manufacturers may have a vested interest in underplaying the dangers of cigarette smoking, so this information may be biased.'*)
- identify assumptions ie ideas not backed up with evidence (eg 'This information seems to be based on the assumption that...')
- give alternative information and views (eg *'However, Drew and Bingham (1997) claim that...'*)
- challenge things (eg *'Is this really the case? Other possibilities are...'*)
- give your own evaluation (eg *'The evidence indicates that...'*).

Above all, make sure you provide evidence for your claims. If you say that somebody else's work is inaccurate or biased without giving evidence for your views, you will yourself be open to criticism. It is an essential feature of academic work that you make reasoned judgements based on evidence, which you can either show the reader or can direct them towards (eg *via a reference*).

23.6 Making the most effective argument

Chapter 6 on 'Essay Writing' explains how to structure your essay, to present 'an argument'. When used in an academic sense, this means to put forward a reasoned point of view (and does not refer to conflict).

One possible structure for an essay is:

- your introduction has a proposition or hypothesis, ie a statement of what you think to be the case (eg *'The world is round'*)
- you then, through a series of paragraphs, provide reasons (with evidence) for why you believe the proposition or hypothesis to be true (eg *in our example this might be mathematical or astronomical or physical reasons and evidence*)
- in your conclusion you summarise how you have proved that your proposition or hypothesis is true (eg *'So, x, y and z shows that the world is round'*).

You might then say that you have 'proved your argument'. The main point of your argument was that the world was round.

This is not the only possible structure for an essay. Some other possibilities are given below, but there are many, many more.

Possibility 1	Possibility 2	Possibility 3
Introduction: gives a question to be answered	**Introduction:** identifies a theory	**Introduction:** identifies a situation (eg *a historical event*)
Middle: – explores what the question means – looks at possible answers – evaluates them	**Middle:** – describes the theory – considers the research evidence for the theory – considers its implications, considers its applications	**Middle:** – describes it – explores it, gives different perspectives on it, identifies significant features of those perspectives – evaluates those perspectives
Conclusion: identifies the answer to the question which you think is the best answer	**Conclusion:** makes a judgement about the value of the theory	**Conclusion:** identifies the significance of the situation, or significant features
Main issue: the question	**Main issue:** the theory	**Main issue:** the situation
Main point: answer to question	**Main point:** your judgement about the theory	**Main point:** the significance of the situation

In the above, the items in 'the middle' show the steps or stages you might go through to get from your issue to your main point.

In the following box, you could identify the main issue in your topic and the main point you want to make. What steps or stages (ie line of argument) would best get you from the first to the second? The above 'possibilities' do not include actual examples of topics for fear of creating confusion, but in your notes we suggest you use your actual topic.

If you like to start work on your essay by brainstorming, you could do so, and then organise the items you come up with into the following boxes.

If you like to start by writing a draft straight off, do so and then read it through to identify your issue, your main point and your steps or stages. You can then start to move things around.

What is your main issue?

What is the main point you want to make?

How can you get from one to the other? You could make brief notes, using key words or phrases only, on the steps or stages you might have (see the 'possibilities' above for ideas).

You may then need to break this down further. Each step or stage may be made up of different aspects. You may have several paragraphs, each on a certain aspect, within one step or stage.

You will need to sequence your steps or stages in different ways for different topics. For example, your steps/stages may:

- need to be in a process order (you do this, then you do that)
- need to be in a chronological order (either working from the earliest date/time onwards, or 'reverse chronological' – backwards from the most recent date/time)
- may unfold (you can only see this, once you have seen that).

Whatever your sequence, it must be obviously logical to the reader. If you switch the basis for your sequence halfway through (eg *if you suddenly go into chronological order*) the reader may be very confused, unless you explain why.

23.7 Signposting

Have another look at the last sentence in the last section. In that case, if you were to change the logic of your sequence, the way to avoid confusing the reader is to tell them what you are doing and why. This would be an example of signposting - telling the readers where they are going eg *'It is most appropriate to explain the following aspects in chronological order, as there is a clear line of development from the earliest stages to the final stages'*.

In your essay, you can use signposting to tell the reader where you are heading, and to tell the reader your main points. If you want to make sure your reader really understands what you are trying to say, both of these are very important.

These are possible ways of signposting for direction:

- using words or phrases to link sentences or paragraphs (eg *'therefore', 'however', 'beforehand', 'as a result of', 'as a consequence of', 'because'*)
- having short summaries within your essay (eg *'We have seen up to now that...', 'so, briefly, the main points of the argument so far are that....'*)
- asking questions (eg *'What are the main issues to be considered at this point?'*)
- making statements which show a change in direction. (eg *'The essay will now consider....'*)
- using sub-headings – but check if this is acceptable in your subject area.

These are possible ways of signposting for emphasis:

- using emphasising words or phrases (eg *'The most important point is...', 'The critical features are....'*)
- the position of your points – points in the introduction and the conclusion are likely to have impact, as are points in the first or last sentence of a paragraph
- building up to a point (eg *'This shows.....This shows..... So, we can now see that...'*)
- using layout – but clarify what is acceptable for your subject (eg *sub-headings; using bold or underlining; bulleted lists*). If you use layout to emphasise be consistent. For example, in this chapter, all examples are given in italics.

Look at an essay you have written or, better still, a draft for one you are currently writing. How have you signposted things for your reader? If you've only used one or two ways this may become boring for them.

How have you signposted 'direction'?	How have you signposted your important points?

23.8 Style

23.8.1 Appealing to your reader

'Style' contributes to the overall impression the essay makes. It is made up of a mix of things, including: choice of words; the way you phrase things; whether or not you use visuals such as diagrams or tables or photos; the layout.

Perhaps the best way to capture the word 'style' is to think of all the things that go to make up a person's 'style' — it would include what they look like, the way they speak, their attitudes etc.

One of the main ways in which you will interest your reader is through your writing style. The more you appeal to the reader, the better their evaluation of your essay is likely to be. You need, therefore, to identify what will appeal to that reader.

To get your essay to stand out (in a positive way!) you also need to have your own personal style. You need a balance here. You need a style which does not conflict with the overall style the tutor expects to see. You also need one which is appropriate for your topic, your aims and your subject matter.

Have you considered the following in your essay?

✔

Using language which is acceptable in an academic context	
Avoiding words or phrases which are acceptable in speech but not in written language	
Avoiding slang	
Explaining jargon	
Using words the reader will understand	
Using words which are appropriate for your subject area	
The proportion of long and short sentences	
Length of paragraph	
The layout	
How you present the work (eg *hand-written, word-processed, type of paper*)	

23.8.2 Creating effects

You may want also to create certain effects. You may, for example, want to gain sympathy for a view. You may want to surprise or shock the reader. You may want to make an impact.

Be very careful of humour. You have to be very, very good at writing humour for it to work. Something which is verbally very funny may not work at all on paper. At the worst you may offend. It is probably best to play safe and avoid attempts at humour.

You can create effects by:

- **the words you use** – compare *'The soldiers attacked defenceless and vulnerable people'* with *'The soldiers attacked people'*. Beware – your words also have to be 'academic'. *'This is absolute rubbish'* has some powerful words in it and it certainly creates an effect, but it isn't 'academic' because it is too judgmental. *'This is highly inaccurate'* would be acceptable.
- **visual images** – check if you can use them in essays in your subject. For example, a graph or chart can show statistics in a very clear way.
- **the layout** – providing the layout features are acceptable in your subject area (again, check it out)
- **quotations** – a good one which clearly demonstrates a point can have a great impact
- **the evidence you use** – (eg *a surprising statistic*), and where you place it (eg *after something which led you to believe the opposite*).

What else have you or your friends tried?

Whatever you do, it must be relevant to your topic. 'Special effects' which are there for no good purpose other than to 'jazz it up' will not get you good marks. In fact, they may antagonise the tutor. If there is no good purpose for visual images in your essay, don't use any.

You can think about the following for an essay you are going to draft, or in relation to one you have drafted already.

What effect or impression do you want to create in your essay?

How can you do this?

23.9 Evaluating your essay, redrafting and editing

23.9.1 Evaluating your own work

One if the best ways to improve your work is to redraft it. Professional writers redraft their work several times. If the version you hand in is your first draft, it is unlikely to be as good as it could have been.

You need to allow time for redrafting. It may take you longer to redraft an essay than it did for you to write the first draft, so avoid leaving the actual writing until the last minute.

You need to evaluate how good your draft is. In doing so you could consider the following:

How far does your essay meet the assessment criteria?

How far does your essay meet any requirements given by the tutor?

How far does it meet the aims and criteria you identified in 23.3.3 above?

You could also consider the following in relation to your draft.

What choices did you make in terms of (eg *the information you included, the sort of language you used, your layout /presentation*) ?	Were these choices effective? Do they work well or not very well? In what way?	Might something else be better? If so, what?

Chapter 6 includes an editing checklist which you should find helpful. You could also use the following checklist which covers the areas addressed in this chapter. You need to consider them all when redrafting and editing your essay.

✔

Information used in the essay has been critically evaluated	
The main issue is clear	
The main point of the argument is clear	
The steps or stages in the argument are logical	
The steps or stages in the argument lead to the main point	

✔

There is signposting to make the direction of the argument clear to the reader	
There is signposting to emphasise the main points to the reader	
It is written and presented in a style which will appeal to the reader	
It creates a particular effect (which is...?)	

23.9.2 Using others' evaluations of your work to help you improve

Once you have handed the essay in and received your mark/grade and feedback, how will you use that information to help you improve future essays?

You could:

- check you have understood the feedback; look in detail at any notes the tutor has made on the work; read through your essay again to see if you understand what the feedback means
- look at the assessment criteria and read your essay again. Can you see why you got the mark/grade you did?
- see if the feedback is similar to feedback you have received on other written work. If you get similar comments on one aspect of your work, that may be a priority to improve.

If you don't understand the feedback or why you got the mark/grade you did you could:

- talk to other students about it, to see if that might make things clearer
- ask your tutor to explain.

You then need to identify what you need to do to improve and what might help you do so.

23.10 Evaluating your working methods

In the work you did to produce your essay, whether or not you did so consciously, you made choices about what to do. For example, you may have made choices about the sort of information to gather for your essay, how to gather it, when, how to record it etc. You may have made choices about how to interpret the essay topic/question, about the main point of your essay and how to structure your argument.

What choices do you think you made and what effect do you think they had? Were they good choices, or could you have done something which worked better? If so what? Making notes below may help you in thinking about what you may like to change in the future (see Section 23.11 below). The box is divided into main areas you might consider.

What choices did you make in your working methods?	What effect did these choices have? Did they work well or not?	What could you have done instead?
Getting started		
Gathering and using information		
Structuring your essay		
Drafting and editing		
Using IT to help you		
Planning time and being organised		

23.11 Improving what you do

Sections 23.9 and 23.10 should have helped you to identify what you could improve in the future, both in your actual essay and in how you go about producing it. You could now use the following to plan for what you need to improve.

See the references for this chapter for some published resources you can follow up, but other resources include library/learning centre, computing staff (for using IT in producing your essay), support staff and your tutor.

Actions I need to take to improve my essays	Sources of help/support	Deadline for action

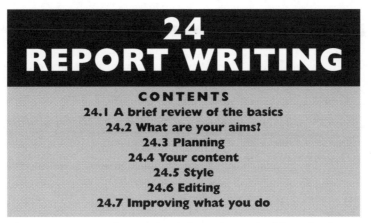

24
REPORT WRITING

A report is a common way of presenting information and advice related to a specific purpose. It is used by industry, business, commerce, professional areas, charities, and Government as a basis for decisions and policies. Courses wish to develop this skill in students because it will be applicable to all professional contexts. Employers want graduates and higher diplomates who can write effective reports.

We suggest you use this chapter:

- **in conjunction with a report you need to write**
- **before you begin any work**
- **while you are gathering information and writing your report.**

This chapter aims to help you turn an adequate report into a good one and produce more in-depth and professional reports, as you would at work.

When you have completed it, you should be able to:

Develop a strategy
- review your effectiveness in this area
- identify when a report is the most appropriate format to use, including for complex topics
- identify the criteria against which to judge the standard or quality of the report (eg *content, format, language*)
- identify and plan to use the most efficient and effective methods/ techniques (eg *use of time and resources*) to produce the report.

Monitor progress
- use information which has been critically evaluated
- present information and argument logically
- signpost critical points, using language and layout
- appeal to and engage the reader, conveying particular effects (eg *via attractive appearance*) and using relevant information and images
- note choices made, judge their effectiveness and adapt strategies as needed (eg *to overcome difficulties*)
- seek and use feedback to improve process and outcomes.

Evaluate strategy and present outcomes
- evaluate the effectiveness of strategies used to produce the report, identifying factors which had an effect
- identify ways of further developing your report writing skills.

(Based on QCA Key Skill specifications, QCA 2000)

24.1 A brief review of the basics

Chapter 7 on 'Report Writing' covers the basic requirements for producing a report. Can you meet these requirements?

✔

	Yes	Somewhat	No
Are you clear about the purpose of your report?			
Have you identified your readers' needs and characteristics?			
Do you know the correct structure of a report for your subject?			
Have you identified what needs to be done and planned your time?			
Have you allowed time to draft, write, edit and present your report?			
Do you know the information needed and how to gather it?			
Can you use information accurately?			
Can you identify the main points and order them?			
Can you present a report clearly and attractively?			
Do you know when to use images or visuals?			
Is your language appropriate for the subject, purpose, readers?			
Do you edit your draft?			

If you could improve on any of the above, the following can help:

- Chapter on 7 'Report Writing' in Part I
- Chapter on 22 'Critical Analysis' in Part II
- examples of reports from your subject area: a learning centre/library or your lecturer may have examples
- Chapters 5 and 21 on 'Gathering and Using Information'
- Chapters 3 and 20 on 'Organising Yourself and Your Time'.

24.2 What are your aims?

24.2.1 What do you want to achieve?

What outcomes do you want from your report? How will you know if you have achieved them? You could complete the following box in relation to a report you are writing.

Outcomes	Criteria which will tell me I've met them
eg *a well-evidenced report*	eg *all key points are accurately evidenced and referenced,*
eg *to present relevant information*	eg *key, up-to-date theories used, appropriate literature references, related to reader interests*

24.2.2 Deciding the format

You may be able to choose the format for your written assignment (eg *essay, report*). At higher levels in university, you may also be required to present complex material and ideas/concepts. Will your work:

	✔		✔
explore ideas? develop a complex argument? have a clear structure be for 'academic' use?		present information for a specific purpose? show the results of a project/investigation? be concise with a specific structure? be used by those outside university (eg *employer, charity, Government*)?	

If most of your answers are in the left-hand box, an essay is probably most appropriate. The right box illustrates a report.

To help you further, you could:

- decide which best suits your topic, focus, aims and audience (see Chapter 7 on 'Report Writing'on Part I)?
- look at the assessment criteria for your assignment
- consider producing a poster, or a portfolio instead (see Chapter 9 on 'Visual Communication' in Part I).

24.3 Planning

24.3.1 Getting inside your reader's head

Good reports meet the reader's needs. You may be asked to produce a report for other students, your lecturers, or perhaps for outside organisations or workplace supervisors. What will your reader need and why? It can help to put yourself in their position.

If I were the reader:
Why would I want the report?
What would I want it to tell me?
What sort of language would I understand?
What sort of language would impress me, or persuade me?
What aspects might I find difficult to understand?

24.3.2 Creating a plan

You could re-visit Chapter 7 on 'Report Writing' in Part I for basic information about planning. The box below gives a useful template.

What else would make the most efficient use of your time? Possibilities are:

- group tasks together and use resources/help for them once, rather than on several occasions
- regularly review your plan, amending it as needed. You may need to adapt your ideas as you progress
- identify methods to save time (eg *see other chapters, such as 'Organising Yourself and Your Time', 'Action Planning' and 'Note Taking'*)
- anticipate problems (see Chapter 26 on 'Solving Problems' in Part II)
- look after yourself (see Chapter 29 on 'Coping with Pressure' in Part II)

Tasks	Resources/ support needed	Time needed to complete	Deadline

Monitoring your progress helps you identify the choices you are making. Are they effective in helping you meet your goals?

Choices	Effectiveness

24.4 Your content

The information you use in the report must be critically evaluated – Chapter 22 on 'Critical Analysis' offers more detailed guidance on evaluating information.

Good reports make any criticisms clear for the reader. It helps to:

- be accurate, objective and evaluative (ie not accepting things at face value)
- back up claims or criticisms with evidence
- make your own biases, assumptions and stance clear
- make clear any biases, assumptions or stances of others
- include evidence and criticisms which are relevant (to your subject and aims) and meaningful to the reader
- be concise. Long-winded explanations are tedious.

Have you evaluated your information/evidence?

Information	Criticism	Evidence

You should present your information and criticisms/argument in a logical order. What will interest the readers? What angle is most likely to capture their interest? This can influence how you order your material. There is little point in having a fascinating conclusion if the reader stopped reading long ago. Your introduction can be used to gain interest.

A reader can very quickly extract the relevant information. Busy readers will want to scan the report to see what is relevant to them and then to read certain sections in more detail. What helps the reader do this is having:

- interest stimulated
- crucial points highlighted
- clear 'signposting'.

24.5 Style

24.5.1 Signposting, using language

Your reader should be able to get your meaning and find information quickly. Your use of language can help.

- Be concise – removing padding, repetition and too much detail

- Use linking words and phrases (eg *therefore, however, on the other hand*)
- Tell the reader what is coming next (eg *'as the following section indicates...'*, an *introduction which explains what is to follow, or an initial summary or synopsis of the main points*)
- Tell the reader what s/he has just read (eg *'to summarise...'*). The main summary should contain all your critical points. You could have very short summaries throughout.
- Tell the reader what is important (eg *'the main recommendation is...'*).

What sort of language will appeal to your reader? Consider whether or not to use:

- technical language/jargon
- formal/more informal language
- short/long sentences/a mix
- short/simple or long/unusual/complex words
- images, similes, metaphors (what sort would appeal to them?)
- examples.

24.5.2 Signposting, using presentation

Signposting means helping the reader find their way through your report. The following are possibilities:

- a contents page
- clear section numbering
- clear headings
- layout: use of bullets, short blocks of text
- use of images/visuals at appropriate points to make more impact, and help understanding.

    There may be particular effects you can create by using visuals (eg *to encourage charity donations, photos of maltreated animals carry an emotive message*).

Readers can be influenced by appearances. What would your reader like? You could consider:

- word processing your report
- typeface (don't use too many different one, use clear ones)
- have 'white space', not all text
- have margins for your reader to write notes
- present it in a binder
- graphics/images on the front cover (may not be acceptable for some reports – check first)
- the cost of whatever you do – money and time. Is it worth it?

24.6 Editing

You could use the checklists in Chapter 7 on 'Report Writing' in Part I. You could also ask yourself if you have:

- clarified what the reader wants
- put your content in an order to lead the reader to your main points
- criticised and evaluated your information
- used language to help the reader find their way through your report
- used language and visuals to appeal to the reader
- used layout to help the reader find their way
- used an attractive form of presentation.

24.7 Improving what you do

How effective is your report and what do you need to improve in the future? When completing the box below, you could:

- look at your report as the reader would. What is its overall impact?
- ask for feedback from your readers. This can give you useful evidence of your report writing skills and is essential if you are to accurately evaluate yourself. You could ask for feedback from different sources (eg *tutors, friends, other students, employers, work colleagues*).

  For more information on asking for and using feedback, see Chapters 17 and 31 on 'Reflecting on Your Experience'.

- look back at the criteria you identified in Section 24.2.1. Have you met them?
- think about the choices you made and what effect they had (eg *not to use visuals – would it be more effective to have done so?*).

	Notes on improvement needed	Actions to be taken	Resources/ support needed	By when?
Identifying aims				
Identifying readers' needs				
Planning (tasks, time, and resources)				
Structuring the report				
Gathering information				
Criticising/ evaluating				
Presenting the report				

✍

	Notes on improvement needed	Actions to be taken	Resources/ support needed	By when?
Using images/ visuals				
Signposting				
Editing				

✍

What have you learnt about how to produce a good report?

What do you most need to focus on?

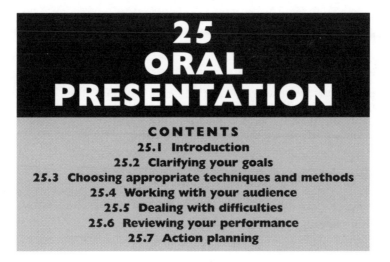

25
ORAL
PRESENTATION

CONTENTS

The verbal skills which are critical in oral presentations are much in demand by employers, who see communication skills as vital. In order to develop these skills many courses require students to give oral presentations – providing inputs for seminars or tutorials, or making individual or group presentations on projects.

Oral presentations can be useful in assessment as they demonstrate abilities in a way which does not require written skills, and they allow for dialogue (a viva is an example of an oral exam).

We suggest you use this chapter:

- **to help you prepare for an actual presentation**
- **to refer to before you begin any preparation.**

When you have completed it, you should be able to:

Develop a strategy
- Review your own effectiveness in this area
- identify hoped for outcomes and the criteria against which to judge the standard or quality of those outcomes
- select appropriate techniques and methods to suit the aim, purpose, audience, topic, context, and to create particular effects.

Monitor progress
- identify audience reaction and adapt the presentation appropriately to meet the outcomes (eg *to overcome difficulties*)
- respond appropriately to contributions from the audience
- monitor and critically reflect on the presentation, using feedback from others, noting choices made and judging their effectiveness.

Evaluate strategies and present outcomes
- evaluate the effectiveness of the presentation and identify factors affecting the outcomes
- identify ways of further developing your presentation skills.

(Based on QCA Key Skill specifications, QCA 2000)

25.1 Introduction

25.1.1 Your existing skills

Chapter 8 on 'Oral Presentation' in Part I covered the essentials. These are listed below and you can rate yourself against each item, where 1 is 'very good' and 4 is 'in need of considerable attention'. If your rating indicates that you need to give attention to any items you should refer to the chapter mentioned above.

✔

	1	2	3	4
Identifying aims and objectives for the presentation				
Identifying audience characteristics and needs				
Identifying the time available				
Checking out the room/location, its facilities and seating				
Selecting material to use				
Structuring material				
Having useful speaker's notes				
Preparing and using visual aids/handouts				
The delivery				
– being well organised				
– your voice and manner				
– relating to your audience				
– dealing with questions				
Combating nerves				

25.2 Clarifying your goals

Before planning your presentation, it is important to be clear about what are you trying to achieve. What results or outcomes do you want (eg *a good mark/grade, audience participation*)? This will help you keep a clear focus when selecting material, structuring your presentation and delivering it.

It is also important to identify how you will know if you have met your goals. How will you judge the outcomes of your presentation? Use the box below to list your goals, and the criteria you will use to decide whether you have achieved the right standard/quality.

Goals/outcomes	Criteria
eg *audience participation*	• *people feel comfortable enough to ask questions* • *people ask relevant questions* • *sufficient time allowed for responses*

25.3 Choosing appropriate techniques and methods

You need to tailor your presentation to meet your goals and suit your aims, the audience, the topic and the context. You can also use your personal style, and the skills of others, if relevant. This section helps you think about what will be most appropriate.

25.3.1 Using your personal style

Effective presentations often make use of the presenter's personal style and characteristics. It is important to identify and build on your strengths, and to recognise and allow for your weaknesses (eg *if you are a terrible joke teller it may be better to avoid jokes; if you are very good at visuals, you could emphasise visual aids*).

The first stage is to identify your strengths and weaknesses. The second is to identify what to do about them. You could refer back to Section 25.1.1 in thinking about possible strengths/weaknesses. If you have difficulty in thinking of ideas and solutions you could ask friends or tutors.

Strengths	Actions I could take to build on them
eg *funny, strong voice, open manner, sense of timing, concise/pithy, relaxed, provocative, non-aggressive*	eg *humour – use a short witticism to help get over a difficult concept* *strong voice – use pitch and tone to emphasise points*

Weaknesses	Actions I could take to allow for them
eg *fidgeting, nervous, too quiet, rambling/over verbose, unfocused, aggressive, defensive, poor timekeeping*	eg *fidgeting –find something constructive to do with hands – hold prompt cards.* *quiet voice – use lots of visual aids, rearrange the seating, use a microphone*

25.3.2 Using group members in group presentations

How can you use all the group members in the presentation, and how can you use their particular skills and reduce their weaknesses? See also Chapters 11 and 27 on 'Group Work'.

What will make the most impact and help structure the presentation (eg *different presenters for different sections*)?

Who would be best at something? For example:

- *who knows more about/has a special interest in a topic?*
- *who could attract the audience's attention at the start?*
- *who is good at explaining detail?*
- *who is good at using projectors, videos, models?*
- *who is good at fielding questions?*
- *who can put a point of view forward strongly?*
- *who can appear sympathetic or open and encourage the audience to speak?*

Who would like to develop their expertise in a particular area (eg *trying something they are not very good at (if you don't try you never will be)*)?

Levels of confidence. How could the group help each other? Group members may want to try something they are not very good at (eg *a nervous person needs the opportunity to speak to build their confidence*). The group can offer ideas, help and support.

Group member	Task/role in the presentation

25.3.3 Which strategies?

Which techniques and methods will most help you to meet your goals? Which will suit your audience and purpose? You could consider the following.

	Possible strategies/methods
Your goals (see Section 25.2) (eg *good grade*)	(eg *check my presentation against the assessment criteria*)
*Your aims (eg *raise awareness of an issue*)	(eg *give information, then generate discussion*)
*Audience characteristics (eg *peers and tutor*)	(eg *explain technical language/concepts, use straightforward examples*)
*Time (eg *15 mins*)	(eg *total of 7 minutes audience activity, split into short tasks*)
*Room (eg *large, many tables*)	(eg *seating in small groups around a table*)
*Topic/material (eg *includes two main theories*)	(eg *present both sides equally*)
*Structure	(eg *introduction sets expectations, main body gives information, conclusions draws ideas together, questions*)

	Possible strategies/methods
*Visual aids (eg OHPs)	(eg bullet points of key information – clear and short)
*Handouts	(eg reminder of key points, include instructions for activities, keep to two sides)
*Your dress, voice and manner	(eg casual but smart, use non-emotive language)
Relating to your audience (see Section 25.4)	(eg verbal and non-verbal language to encourage responses and engagement)
Your personal style (see Section 25.3.1)	(eg use open manner by welcoming all contributions, non-judgemental)

*This area is covered more fully in Chapter 8 on 'Oral Presentation' in Part I.

Are there any particular effects you want to create (eg a sympathetic response, a challenging debate)? What would help you achieve this?

Effect you want	What do you need to do?

25.4 Working with your audience

25.4.1 Relating to your audience

Good presenters engage with the audience and build up a rapport with them. How do they do this?

You could use the following checklist and also add items you can think of. Which do you use now or could you try to use more?

✔

	Use now	Could use more
Maintain eye contact (not with one person, but scanning the audience)		
Ask if they can hear you or see the visual aids		
Check they are comfortable. Do windows need opening/shutting?		
Make references to them and their interests or needs		
Use examples and stories which are relevant to them		
Ask if they have understood (but not too often), especially if you are explaining complex ideas/information		
Ask for questions		
Ask if anybody has different or additional views or information		
Others, please list		

15.4.2 Judging audience reaction

You need to be aware of your audience's reaction, so that you can adjust your responses accordingly.

Look for positive signs that your audience is interested and responding to you:

- sitting forward
- looking alert
- concentrating on you and your visual aids
- facial expressions and non-verbal communication (eg *smiles, nods*)
- wanting to ask questions.

Signs of difficulty in your audience might be:

- straining to see your visual aids
- looking uncomfortable (eg *hot/cold*)
- looking puzzled
- unexpected facial expressions (eg *smiling when you didn't intend it to be funny*).

Signs of a bored audience:

- slumping
- fidgeting
- reading (other than your handouts)
- looking at watches, putting on coats
- gazing out of the window
- chatting.

25.4.3 Responding to your audience

Appropriate responses to your audience's reactions can make your presentation more effective. If you sense a positive response, continue to use your personal style and the strategies you selected; it's clearly working.

If you have identified any difficulties, try to do something about them:

- ask a puzzled-looking audience if they understand and if not, explain again
- open windows for a hot audience
- if they can't see, move your visual aids or the audience
- invite questions to help clarify understanding
- if people look irritated, ask for their opinions and deal with the irritation.

For a bored audience you could:

- move onto another section
- leave out some sections
- finish quickly
- cover your material more quickly (but don't gabble)
- use a visual aid
- change your position (eg *stand instead of sit*)
- change your voice (eg *speak louder, pitch the tone at differing levels*)
- ask them a question or for an opinion.

When you do your presentation you could ask yourself afterwards how you responded, what worked and what you would do differently in future. You could ask your audience for their comments on how you responded to them (eg *via an evaluation sheet*).

Audience reaction	My response	What I'd do in the future

25.4.4 Responding to questions/comments

If you encourage audience participation you are likely to generate questions or comments. How can you deal with them? Part of the answer to this depends on your personal style – you need to respond as you feel comfortable but also you need to be able to handle the consequences (eg *putting somebody down will discourage others from speaking*). What are other possible responses and their consequences?

Response	Possible effect
A straight reply	welcomed, creates trust, openness
'I'm afraid I don't know, does anybody else?'	welcomed, opens up a debate (so you want this?)
Waffle	irritation, lack of respect
'What do you think?', 'Could you give me an example?' (back to the questioner)	either flattered or put on the spot. May create discussion, but could lead to an argument
'I wonder if Jane can answer that?'	OK if Jane knows the answer. If not she may be annoyed
Answer a different question	irritation
With humour	releases tension, but questioner may feel put down
Calming response	reduces tension

What are your concerns in dealing with questions? What could you do about it?

✎

Concerns	Actions

25.4.5 Timing

It is much easier to keep to time with no audience questions – you just practise in advance how long it will take to say it. But good presentations involve the audience.

How many questions do you want? Allowing 10 minutes for questions or discussion at the end is easy to plan for, although it is helpful to build in some flexibility, to cope with a talkative/non-talkative audience. You could:

- vary the pace, adjusting timing as you go
- have extra material available in case the audience keeps quiet
- be tough on timing. Allow a specific time for each question and move on (*'I'm afraid we need to move on if we are going to cover everything', 'Can we stop at that point and move on?'*).

Do not run over! Your audience may have other things to do, the room may be needed, and if you run over it may cut down the time others have.

25.5 Dealing with difficulties

25.5.1 Combating nerves

Chapter 8 on 'Oral Presentation' in Part I will have helped you to get the essentials right. Being prepared, well organised and having good visual aids are very important in dealing with nerves. You could also look at Chapters 14 and 29 on 'Coping with Pressure'.

What might make you nervous? What happens when you are nervous? What could you do about this? It might help to look back over this chapter and ask which of the ideas:

a)   you could feel comfortable with
b)   would stretch you a bit
c)   would scare you.

Why not include in your presentation a lot of a), some of b) and little of c)? Practice is a great help with nerves. Next time you will find some of the things you thought would stretch you are now OK, and some of those which seemed scary fall into the 'stretching' category.

You could watch other presentations or videos to become more familiar with techniques. Ask others how they deal with nerves. You may be surprised at how those who appear confident also feel nervous.

25.5.2 Practical problems

You may find some unexpected practical difficulties (eg *accommodation: room too small; resources: equipment not working*). You could check some things in advance:

* the room:
     Is it large enough? What can you do?
     How do you want the seating?
* the resources:
     Is everything you want there? (If not, where can you get it?)

On the day, it helps to take:

* spare OHP pens, whiteboard markers etc
* photocopies of your OHPs (in case the projector is not working). You can hand these out for your audience to refer to as you speak.
* OHPs of your computer-based presentation (in case electronic equipment is faulty).

What difficulties can you anticipate, and how will you plan for them?

How will you cope with an unexpected problem (eg *heating not on, another class is in the room*)? You need to keep calm and retain your sense of humour.

25.6 Reviewing your performance

25.6.1 Reviewing goals and plans

Improving your skills is helped by thinking through what you did afterwards. What choices did you make when planning your presentation? Were they effective in helping you meet your goals? What would you do differently?

You could ask for feedback from your audience – verbally, one to one, or hand out an evaluation form. Some courses use peer feedback or peer assessment to help you develop your skills in this area – see the section on feedback in Chapter 17 on 'Reflecting on Your Experience'.

The following could help in identifying actions needed for the next presentation.

	Strengths to build on	Areas to improve
Clarifying goals and criteria to judge them		
Choice of strategies (techniques and methods)		
Using your personal style		
Relating to your audience		
Judging audience reaction		
Responding to audience reaction		
Responding to questions		

	Strengths to build on	Areas to improve
Timing		
Combating nerves		
Others (eg *working in a group*)		

What affected the outcomes of your presentation? What was within your control? What could you have done about the things outside your control?

25.7 Action planning

Are there aspects of your presentation skills that you'd like to improve? You could consider sources of help, such as:

- other chapters in this book (see contents page)
- books on giving presentations (see references; libraries may have many more including videos)
- friends, other students (they may help you monitor what you are doing), and tutors
- using this or the equivalent chapter in Part I again when you next need to work on a presentation.

What do you need to improve? What further help do you need? By when?

Actions needed to improve	Resources or people I need to help	By when

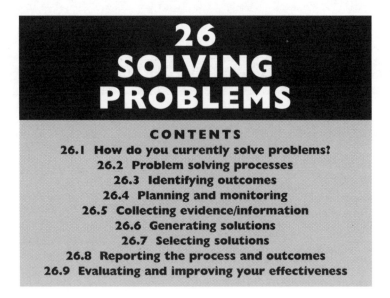

26
SOLVING
PROBLEMS

CONTENTS

Many of the assignments or activities you have to do on a course are concerned with solving problems (eg *projects, case studies, essays, seminar discussions, examinations*). This is because employers rate being able to solve problems very highly and lecturers want students to develop their skills in this area.

Graduates and higher diplomates are expected to solve unexpected problems at work, and to be able to do more than only carry out routine procedures.

We suggest you use this chapter:

- **when you have an assignment, course or placement activity which involves solving problems**
- **before you begin work on the assignment or task**
- **then whilst you are working on it.**

Develop a strategy
- review your own effectiveness in this area
- identify hoped for outcomes and the criteria against which to judge the standard or quality of those outcomes
- explore a problem (eg *looking at it in different ways, simplifying it, making comparisons*)
- research information and consult people to establish critical features
- choose and use methods to tackle the problem likely to achieve the outcomes
- plan and use problem solving skills, taking into account factors that may affect plans
- record information in useful ways.

Monitor progress
- identify a variety of ways to tackle the problem, identify and use those most likely to be effective
- obtain the resources needed
- monitor progress and critically reflect on your problem solving (eg *using feedback, checking results, noting choices made and judging effectiveness*)
- adapt strategies if needed.

Evaluate strategy and present outcomes
- select and use ways of presenting the problem solving process and any results, clearly, accurately, with evidence
- assess the effectiveness of your strategy and identify factors which had an impact on it
- identify ways of further developing your problem solving skills.

(Based on QCA Key Skill specifications, QCA 2000)

26.1 How do you currently solve problems?

Which of the following do you use?

If you are unsure about any of them refer to 'Solving Problems' in Chapter 10.

✔

A logical step by step process determined by yourself	
Follow a hunch/your instincts	
Follow procedures set by somebody else (eg *in a lab*)	
Discuss with others	
Trial and error	
Creative idea generation (eg *brainstorming*)	
Identify advantages, disadvantages, interesting aspects	
Others (please add)	

How would you rate your ability in the following, using a rating scale where 1 = 'very good' and 4 = 'in need of considerable improvement'? This chapter focuses on these areas.

✔

	1	2	3	4
Identifying the essential elements of a problem				
Collecting and selecting information to help solve the problem				
Identifying and using procedures to solve the problem				
Identifying solutions				
Deciding on solutions				
Evaluating solutions				

How effective are you in solving problems? Add your own items.

✔

I could solve problems in less time (be more efficient).	
I could find better solutions (be more effective).	
I could feel less anxious or enjoy solving problems more.	
Others (please add)	

26.2 Problem solving processes

There is no right or wrong way to solve a problem – only a way which is best for the situation and you.

You could start:

- by generating possible solutions
- or by identifying what procedures you will use
- or by identifying the essential elements of a problem.

Wherever you begin, at some stage you need to give attention to the following aspects. These are presented in circular, rather than linear form, as it is important to acknowledge that there is no one place to start.

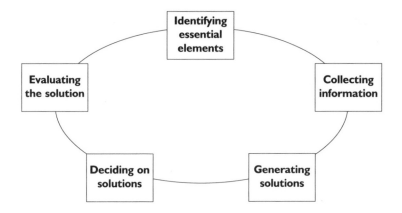

You might find it helpful to refer back to Chapter 10 on 'Solving Problems' in Part I, which has more detailed information/ideas about the process involved.

26.3 Identifying outcomes

26.3.1 What does your *solution* need to achieve?

Your desired outcomes will vary from problem to problem and may include those which are given to you (eg *a piece of coursework requiring a solution by a specific deadline*) and other, more personal ones (eg *getting a high mark/grade; reducing anxiety*).

What criteria will you use to judge your possible solutions? How will you know the

Your problem	
eg *your student loan is not lasting the semester/term*	
Your solution	
eg *taking a part-time job*	
Desired outcomes of the solution	**Criteria to judge**
eg *enough money to live on, allow time to do well on the course*	• *pays £x per week* • *no more than 12 hours per week* • *fits in with academic timetable*

You could complete a similar box for a problem you are currently dealing with.

Your problem

Your solution

Desired outcomes of the solution	Criteria to judge

26.3.2 How can you judge the *process* you use?

As well as outcomes you want from the solution to your problem, it will be helpful to make judgements about the effectiveness of the process you use to solve the problem (the criteria).

What will help your problem solving process to be efficient and effective? Your criteria might cover aspects such as:

- time
- effort
- stress
- use of resources.

Criteria to judge the process
eg *relevant information gathered; range of solutions identified, all possible options covered*

26.4 Planning and monitoring

26.4.1 Planning

It is helpful to draw up a plan – Chapter 10 on 'Solving Problems' in Part I includes an action plan with further guidance on possible methods. You might also find it helpful to look at the chapters on 'Action Planning' (see contents page).

You need to select methods which are most likely to help you achieve the outcomes you identified in 26.3.1 and 26.3.2. You could assess their likely effectiveness by grading the on a scale of 1–4, where 1 is 'very effective' and 4 is 'highly ineffective'.

Which methods will you use to solve the problem?	How effective will they be? (on a scale 1–4)

What factors might affect your plans? You could consider:

- time
- other commitments and pressures
- other people
- changing priorities
- problem solving techniques you selected not being as effective/efficient as you hoped
- access to resources (could there be problems with finding the resources you've identified?). How will you obtain those you need?

26.4.2 Monitoring and amending your strategies

You are expected to take responsibility for your own learning, so you will need to review your plan regularly:

- as your skills develop
- as situations/priorities change.

As you carry out your plan, keep a note of what you do and critically reflect on your progress by:

- using feedback from others (eg *tutors, friends, employers, other students, learning centre/library staff*)
- looking at the choices you make. How effective are they?

Reviewing your strategies will help you identify any amendments/improvements/ adaptations as needed. What could you do differently? Are resources/facilities needed sufficient/adequate?

26.5 Collecting evidence/information

What information/evidence do you need to help you with the problem? Once you have gathered information about your problem your ideas may be clearer (eg *about its essential elements, and the criteria for judging your solutions*).

26.5.1 Reviewing your information

You may need to find information to solve your problem. What questions and sub-questions are there? One piece of information may lead to a new question or angle.

eg Project about energy. Can coal emissions from power stations be reduced? What will it cost? What is the cost in relation to nuclear power?

eg Part-time job. What hours must you work? Will they clash with study time? How do you spend the rest of your time?

The following suggests three stages, but there could be more or fewer.

Initial questions	Information/answers

Secondary questions	Information/answers

Final questions	Information/answers

Once you have done some work on your problem, you could keep a note of new questions which arise and/or new information you need.

26.5.2 Confusing or contradictory information

The information relating to your problem may be ambiguous. There may be opposing or different views, or conflicting information from different sources. It can help to identify what information is confusing or contradictory, eg:

- **a seminar discussion** (eg *one person is entertaining and interesting* **but** *talks too much and prevents others from talking*)
- **project about energy** (eg *the cheapest fuel is also the most environmentally damaging*)
- **work** (eg *you need a part-time job to earn money* **but** *it will take time from studying*).

How can you weigh up confusing or contradictory information in an effective and efficient way? There are several possible strategies:

- Identify the reasons for the information being confusing or contradictory.
- Identify the critical features you need to consider. Is one aspect of the information more important for your solution than another? Does one aspect have a higher priority? (eg *project about energy: is it more important for the fuel to be cheap or for it not to be environmentally damaging*)?
- Sort the information (eg *by advantages/disadvantages, by identifying the costs and benefits of each, by level of importance*).
- Consult others who have an interest in the issue. Discuss it with friends?
- Identify your immediate gut reaction/feelings and then question the reaction (eg *if somebody told you to take the part-time job, regardless of the course, would you be relieved or worried?*).
- Gather more information. It might swing the weight of evidence in one direction.

What other strategies have you or your friends tried?

Contradictory/confusing elements	Reasons for this

You might also find it helpful to look at the chapters on 'Gathering and Using Information' and 'Critical Analysis' (see contents page).

26.5.3 How do you know that you have enough information?

✔   ✔

Is it repeating itself		Will more information make your solution better?	
Is it really relevant?		Others? Please specify.	
Is it worth the time taken to gather it?			
Is it adding anything?			

26.5.4 Recording information

You may need to record information for a variety of reasons, eg:

* on the processes or strategies used to solve the problem
* to show your method of working to tutors
* so that you do not lose/forget ideas or suggestions
* to help others who are working on a problem (eg *for a group project*)
* to create a list of references of the sources of information you have used.

Before you decide on the sort of records to keep, it helps to identify their purpose. Are these to provide evidence about your solutions and results, and/or about your methods? For further guidance, look at Chapter 4 on 'Note Taking' in Part 1.

26.6 Generating solutions

Chapter 10 on 'Solving Problems' in Part I identifies a range of techniques to help in thinking about a problem and some strategies for generating solutions. You could refer back to it. They include:

* brainstorming
* trial and error
* creative thinking
* following set procedures.

It helps to generate as many ideas for solutions as possible, then to narrow down those to investigate more seriously, and to do detailed work on the most likely solution.

You could:

* identify how this problem is similar or different from those you have faced before. What has worked/not worked for similar problems in the past?
* consider how complicated the problem is. What are all the aspects to consider? Would a diagram or map of these aspects help? Can you simplify the problem by identifying the crucial aspects?

- look at the problem in a new way (eg *as someone else might see it, from a different angle, as an opportunity rather than a problem, describe it using different media such as writing or drawing*).
- talk to others about the problem. How do they see it? What do they think are the essential features? (**Warning**. It is important to make use of other views, but you need to make your own judgements).

What methods will you use to tackle the problem? Which will help you achieve the outcomes?

✍

Methods/techniques to generate solutions

You could now highlight those methods you think will be most effective.

26.7 Selecting solutions

26.7.1 What might influence your decision?

You have already identified the criteria to judge the solution (see 26.3.2). However, there may be other factors which will influence your decision. It is important to recognise them, and to consider how important they are and why.

Factors	Why are they important for your problem?
Other people? (Who?)	
What the course/tutor wants?	
What will get high marks?	
Your own feelings?	
Your own values?	
Ethical considerations?	
Your personal goals/criteria?	
Your state of health (eg *stress level*)?	
Obtaining the resources needed	
The consequences of your choice	
Others?	

26.7.2 Selecting the solution

You will need to evaluate each possible solution before making a final decision. You could consider:

- which solution(s) is/are most likely to achieve the desired outcomes? (Check the criteria you identified (26.3.1))
- the likely consequences of each option. What might happen as a result of the solution(s) you have chosen?
- how risky each solution is.

Accepting your solution
Decisions are not always clear-cut. You may feel uncomfortable about rejecting some options, even if your decision/solution was well informed and considered. You may have to come to terms with it.

26.8 Reporting the process and outcomes

You may be expected to report back on the methods you used to solve problems and the solutions you chose (eg *course-related: for part of an assignment; work-related: for an interview*). You need to select the best way to present your information, clearly and accurately. Ideas include:

- describing and reflecting on the process you used (eg *if you used problem solving strategies which involved drawing, modelling or visualisation techniques, use them in your reporting back. How well did they work?*). See the chapters on 'Reflecting on Your Experience' (see contents page).
- providing clear reasons for decisions, justifying and evaluating both the process and the solution
- describing and evaluating other techniques you considered, but did not use
- identifying appropriate evidence (eg *for activities in this chapter, logs/diaries, written evidence from others, own self-evaluations*)
- depending on the way in which you present your information, using the chapters on 'Oral Presentation', 'Essay Writing' or 'Report Writing'
- using the chapters on 'Gathering and Using Information' and 'Critical Analysis'.

26.9 Evaluating and improving your effectiveness

How effective were your strategies? What influenced the decisions you made (eg *techniques/resources you selected*)? Feedback from others could help you complete the following box.

Strategies which were effective	Factors which had an influence
Strategies which were less effective	**Factors which had an influence**

What are your strengths in solving problems? Where do you need to improve?

You could adopt a problem solving approach to your own skill development in this area:

- What are the essential elements of your problem solving skills? Which need improving?
- What evidence (information) do you have for your ability to solve problems?
- How could you improve your skills (what are the possible methods you could use to improve your skills – what are the possible solutions)?
- What will you do to improve your skills (which solution will you select)?
- How will you monitor your improvement (evaluate your solution)?

You could complete the following:

Areas I need to build on or improve	Action to take	By when?

You might also find it helpful to look at the chapters on 'Action Planning' (see contents page).

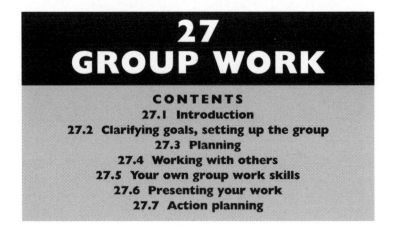

27
GROUP WORK

Courses include group work:

- because in employment most work is carried out by people working together to share resources, perspectives, ideas and abilities. When recruiting, employers place great store on evidence that you can work well with others
- to help you develop and practise your own individual skills in working with others. Group work can be exciting and enjoyable, but a group that is not working well can be frustrating. Improving how you work in groups should improve the end result. Your course may assesses such skills
- so that students can learn from and help each other.

Group work can include discussions (eg *seminars or tutorials*), workshops (eg *laboratory work*), and project work.

Groups are effective not just because of luck, or because of the particular mix of members, but because of individuals working together to make them effective.

There is no one 'correct' way to behave in a group. This chapter aims to help you think about what is happening and to identify strategies which will work for you.

We suggest you use this chapter:

- **right at the start of a group activity**
- **and then throughout that activity.**

When you have completed it, you should be able to:

Develop a strategy
- review your effectiveness in this area
- identify hoped for outcomes and the criteria against which to judge the standard or quality of those outcomes
- agree responsibilities based on an identification of expertise/ experience needed.

Monitor progress
- accept your responsibility for effectiveness and efficiency
- contribute to group processes to meet group responsibilities
- exchange feedback and use it to improve performance
- monitor and critically evaluate your skills in working with others
- contribute to the group's evaluation of the group's effectiveness
- note choices made by you and your group and judge their effectiveness
- monitor and adapt strategies and plans as needed.

Evaluate strategy and present outcomes
- agree effective ways of presenting the process and outcomes of work using the skills of those involved
- evaluate the effectiveness of your strategy, identifying factors which had an impact on it
- identify ways of further developing your skills in working with others.

(Based on QCA Key Skill specifications, QCA 2000)

27.1 Introduction

27.1.1 A review of the basics

The following aspects are covered by Chapter 11 'Group Work'. You could rate yourself on them on a scale where 1= 'very well' and 4 = 'needs considerable improvement'.

✔

	1	2	3	4
Agreeing ground rules				
Agreeing goals				
Planning actions and allocating tasks				
Meeting own agreed responsibilities				
Checking on progress				
Co-operating with others				
Dealing with problems				
Your own behaviour in groups				

27.1.2 Your issues

How do you feel about group work? What issues do you want to consider about working in groups? After working through this chapter you can return here to check if your needs have been met.

27.2 Clarifying goals, setting up the group

27.2.1 Your goals

Chapter 11 'Group Work' suggests you begin by clarifying your goals as a group. What are you trying to achieve (what results or outcomes do you want)? Do you all have the same understanding of this? Your instructions for your group task may be vague and you may need to agree what you are aiming for. To remind you about this see Chapter 11.

This section and Section 27.3 below help you consider your goals in more detail.

How will you, as a group, judge if the results of your work are good? Identifying this before you start helps keep you on track. Use the box below to note the goals (results or outcomes) your group wants/needs to achieve, and the criteria you will use to know if they are the right quality or standard.

Goal(s)	Criteria
Example: *give a group oral presentation about a topic*	Example: *complete/accurate information on the topic; presentation clear/understandable to the audience, clear/relevant visual aids/ handouts; all group members participate in the presentation/deliver their part competently.*

27.2.2 Setting up the group

Chapter 11 'Group Work' suggests you begin by agreeing ground rules for how you operate as a group. This sets a positive tone and can avoid future problems. You could also consider whether or not you need formal roles.

In small co-operative groups, formal roles may not be needed. In larger groups or where more structure is needed, it can help to have a chairperson and a secretary for meetings, or perhaps a co-ordinator for a project. These roles could be fixed or you could rotate them, so everybody practises them.

A chairperson
- agrees an agenda (asks for items from the group), either in advance or at the start of a meeting
- helps the group work through the agenda and keeps an eye on time
- encourages contributions, involves quiet people, asks talkative people to let others speak
- makes people feel comfortable.

A secretary
- takes accurate notes (minutes) of meetings (it can be helpful to use the last 5 minutes to check what was said and to clarify the actions to be taken). See Chapter 4 'Note Taking'
- arranges meetings, venues.

A project group co-ordinator
- is similar to a secretary, but may also keep track of who is doing what.

Does the group need a leader and if so what sort of leadership would be appropriate for the situation? If vital decisions need to be made quickly you may need a leader. In other situations (eg *where it is important for everybody to agree and share responsibility*) it may be better to operate collectively.

27.3 Planning

Consider Sections 27.3.1, 27.3.2 and 27.3.3 then complete Section 27.3.4.

27.3.1 Dividing up tasks

To plan, break your group's task down into sub-tasks with deadlines, which are then allocated to group members (see Chapter 11 'Group Work').

In dividing up work, you could consider what might be the best way to group tasks to make chunks of work, eg: tasks: all requiring the same resources/the same skills or techniques; needing to be done at a certain time; related to a certain topic or aspect of the topic. What would make the best use of time and resources and give the best results? In agreeing who will do what, you could consider:

- fair and equal workloads
- personal interests
- group members' expertise (eg *skills, knowledge, experience*). Members might want to use existing expertise or develop new expertise by doing tasks which are new to them. Group members are a resource and it is important to use them well.
- what might be the most efficient way to share work (eg *who could do things quickly; who has access to resources needed; can any members meet up more easily than others?*).

What if you can't agree who will do what? Drawing lots may result in a lack of commitment by members and a failure to do the work. Negotiating is a better method and is an important skill in working with others. The whole group can work together to:

- identify everybody's preferences
- identify conflicts of preferences
- identify any solutions (eg *re-divide or redefine the sub-tasks, work together on a sub-task*).

To help you agree matters, see Chapters 13 and 28 'Negotiating and Assertiveness'.

27.3.2 Reviewing goals and plans

Circumstances change. New information comes to light and new angles emerge. You may need to do more work than you originally thought. You may have unexpected issues and have to decide as a group how to respond to these. You may need to rethink your goals, the division of sub-tasks and who will do them.

You may need to return to, review and agree the basics you are operating from. These might be: your criteria for judging the results or outcomes of your work (see 27.2.1 above); how you operate as a group (see 27.2.2 above and Chapter 11 on 'groundrules'); concepts, theories or techniques from the subject area (eg *scientific, engineering or sociological principles*). The following should help you carry out regular reviews (eg *at every group meeting*).

27.3.3 Making sure all do the work agreed

It is essential that you and everybody in the group meets their responsibilities. Not to do so is likely to damage the group's results or outcomes and cause conflict or resentment. How will the group ensure everybody does what they agree? Possibilities include:

- write down what you agree
- review progress regularly as a group
- regularly exchange information with each other about progress (see 27.4.1 below)
- help each other see how to sort out difficulties and problems (see 27.4.1 below). For help, see Chapters 10 and 26 'Solving Problems'
- to find ways of asking others to do their share, use Chapters 13 and 28 'Negotiating and Assertiveness'.

You may need to seek help from your tutor.

27.3.4 The plan of work

Initial goals	Amended goals

You could use the layout below to make a group plan.

Initial sub-task	Amended sub-tasks	Resources/ support needed	By (group member)	Deadline

27.4 Working with others

27.4.1 Co-operating, and using group members

If you work mainly on your own on your sub-task, you will miss a major benefit of group work – getting ideas, new perspectives and information from others to improve your work. Have you:

✔

discussed how you'll go about your sub-task with other group members?	
discussed how your sub-task relates to theirs?	
discussed progress with them (yours and theirs)?	
asked them for feedback on your work, and for information/ideas to help you?	
accepted their views openly and non-defensively?	
helped them by giving them feedback, discussing their sub-task and reviewing their work?	

For help on giving and receiving feedback, see Chapter 17 'Reflecting on Your Experience'.

27.4.2 Group process

The following may help you think about what is happening in your group. It has a scale of 1–4, where 1 is 'very helpful' and 4 is 'very unhelpful'.

✔

Group process list – in your group do the group members:					
	1	2	3	4	
express feelings openly?					grumble afterwards?
ask others for views/ideas?					not ask others for views/ideas?
listen/respond to others?					ignore others/their ideas?
share work evenly?					fail to share work evenly?
participate equally in discussion?					dominate, or keep quiet?
use group members' abilities well?					fail to use group members' abilities well?
help each other?					form cliques/pairs/act uncooperatively?
trust each other?					feel suspicious of each other?
show enthusiasm?					show apathy?
understand group goals?					not understand group goals?
accept group goals?					not accept group goals?
achieve group goals?					not achieve group goals?
use resources well?					not use resources well?
all agree decisions?					not make decisions, or fail to involve all?
use time effectively?					not use time effectively?

What are the reasons for any problems you have identified by using the above list? For example, if you feel you are wasting time, why does this happen? What could the group do differently (eg *set deadlines, appoint a 'time keeper' for meetings, have formal roles*)?

What is your part in any problems? What could you do personally to improve things? You could return to the Group process list at intervals to see if things are improving.

The group's main problems	Group action to be taken	Actions to be taken by me

27.4.3 Problems between people

If there are problems between group members (eg *somebody not pulling their weight, being domineering*), it is important to deal with them, or you may end up with too much work, be resentful, or get a lower mark or grade. It can help to:

- identify the cause (eg *does someone have a good reason for not contributing?*)
- focus on the group, not the person (eg *'We've got a problem, what can we do about it'*)
- focus on the problem, not the person (eg *not 'You are lazy' but 'If it isn't done we won't meet the deadline'*)
- express your feelings before they get out of hand (eg *'I am worried about ...', 'I am getting angry about...'*)
- acknowledge and apologise for your mistakes.

See also Chapters 13 and 28 'Negotiating and Assertiveness'.

27.5 Your own group work skills

27.5.1 How do you behave in groups?

You could ask for feedback from other group members or from others who may have seen you in groups (eg *a friend, tutor or workplace supervisor*) – look at the section on feedback in Chapter 17 'Reflecting on Your Experience'.

You could think about the following on your own (to help you use Chapter 17 'Reflecting on Your Experience').

How well did you...	Why did you do what you did (what choices did you make)?	Was it effective and why?
do your own work for the group?		
act in a flexible way (able to take on different roles or tasks)?		
contribute to meetings?		

27.5.2 How can you help others in the group?

How can you encourage others in meetings and in the work they do outside meetings? Tick those items you feel you need to try harder with.

✔

Asking for the views of others	
Listening carefully to what they say	
Being positive about and commenting on good things they say and do	
Checking with them that you have understood what they mean	
Making sure they are included in group activities or discussions	
Giving feedback which is helpful (not destructive)	

For help with giving feedback to others see Chapter 17 'Reflecting on Your Experience'. For help with taking part in discussions see Chapter 12 'Seminars, Group Tutorials and Meetings'.

27.6 Presenting your work

In your group you will probably have to present the results of your work to others (eg *a tutor, workplace supervisor*). There may be two aspects:

• products from your group work (eg *report, poster, oral presentation, model*)
• evidence of the process you undertook to carry out your group work.

26.7.1 A product

The same criteria will probably be used to judge the quality of the product, whether a group has produced it or an individual. Other chapters which can help include those on 'Report Writing' and 'Oral Presentation'. There are chapters to help you produce work, such as 'Solving Problems' and 'Gathering and Using Information'.

27.6.2 Evidence of your process

You may need to provide evidence of how you worked together as a group, or to evaluate how well you did so. What is the person asking for this (eg *a tutor*) looking for? What criteria will s/he use to decide how well you worked as a group and how well you contributed? What will give them evidence of that?

Possible sorts of evidence include:

• plans, including amended plans and the dates you amended them
• notes on progress on plans
• agendas and minutes of meetings
• logs or diaries showing the work you did (including how much, when)
• evidence that you met deadlines
• notes from an observer (eg *one group member could observe each meeting in turn*)
• notes/letters/emails/references/letters from others you were in contact with saying what you did and how good it was (eg *from a workplace supervisor or client*)
• evaluations (group or individual). This chapter and Chapter 11 have exercises to help you evaluate how you have worked together (eg *see 27.4.2 and 27.5.1 above*).

27.7 Action planning

Are there aspects of your own group work skills that you'd like to change? You might wish to try out new behaviours. You could seek feedback or suggestions from group members, tutors, or workplace supervisors where relevant.

In completing the following box you could consider sources of help, such as:

• other chapters
• books on group work (see the references for this chapter at the end of the book; libraries/learning centre will have more)
• friends (they may help you monitor what you are doing) and tutors
• a diary (you could keep a record of what you do)
• using this or Chapter 11 again when you next need to work in a group.

Return to Sections 27.1 and 27.4 above. Has this chapter met your needs? If not what else do you need to do? What do you need to improve? What further help do you need? From where or whom? You can now complete the following box.

What I do in groups that is helpful

What I do in groups that is unhelpful

What I would like to do differently

Complete the following to help you plan how to do things differently.

Actions I need to take to improve	Resources or people I need to help me	Date when I will do this by

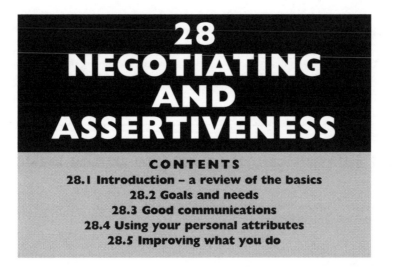

28
NEGOTIATING
AND
ASSERTIVENESS

CONTENTS
28.1 Introduction – a review of the basics
28.2 Goals and needs
28.3 Good communications
28.4 Using your personal attributes
28.5 Improving what you do

Our effectiveness in most situations depends at least partly on how well we deal with others. What we and others want from a situation is rarely identical and this usually means having to negotiate. This applies:

- to day to day situations (eg *who does domestic jobs*)
- to courses (eg: *agreeing things in group projects; sometimes students agree work to do and a grade/mark with a tutor; getting help from busy tutors/technicians*)
- to placement or to work when you graduate or gain your diploma (eg: *in all jobs you agree work activities with other people; in many jobs negotiation is crucial – surveying, social work, contract management, buying, selling etc*).

We suggest you use this chapter:

- **when you face a situation when you need to negotiate or be assertive**
- **on an ongoing basis to help you review and monitor what you do.**

In this chapter we use an example: *asking a lecturer/workplace supervisor for advice or help.*

When you have completed it, you should be able to:

Develop a strategy
- review your effectiveness in this area
- clarify goals of all involved
- identify how to use own strengths and allow for your weaknesses in agreeing matters with others
- plan how to approach the issue or person.

Monitor progress
- check mutual understanding
- monitor and critically reflect on your skills
- note methods used and choices made and judge effectiveness
- make ongoing improvements/adaptations.

Evaluate strategy and present outcomes
- ensure that all involved share an understanding of what has been agreed
- evaluate the effectiveness of your strategy, identifying factors that affected it
- identify how to develop skills further.

(Based on QCA Key Skill specifications, QCA 2000)

28.1 Introduction – a review of the basics

The following aspects are covered by Chapter 13 'Negotiating and Assertiveness'. We suggest you rate yourself against them on a scale where 1 = 'very well' and 4 = 'in need of considerable improvement'.

✔

Possible ways of learning	1	2	3	4
I'm aware of how I currently try to agree matters with others				
I am familiar with negotiating strategies				
- separate the people from the problem				
- focus on interests not positions				
- generate options before deciding				
- agree criteria against which to judge solutions				
I know what assertiveness is				
I'm aware of when I am assertive, passive, manipulative or aggressive				
I know why I don't behave assertively				
I can identify my own needs and goals				
I can identify other people's needs and goals				
I am familiar with assertiveness techniques				
- 'broken record'				
- acknowledging criticism				
- accepting compliments				
- asking for clarification				
- avoiding preambles				
- recognising my own feelings				
- 'going up the gears'				
- saying no without excuses				
- awareness of personal appearance				

If in doubt about any of these, before reading on refer to Chapter 13 'Negotiating and Assertiveness'.

28.2 Goals and needs

28.2.1 Know what you want

Identifying what you want or need in advance helps you be clearer when discussing it. You could consider the following questions about a situation currently facing you.

What is the basic issue or problem?

What are my feelings about this situation?

Do my feelings about the situation relate to the other person(s) involved – or are they really about other things (eg *general high stress level*)?

What do I want to happen?

What is my responsibility?

What is their responsibility?

What is somebody else's responsibility?

What rights have I got in this situation?

28.2.2 What do they want?

What are 'the others' likely to want or need? What is good or difficult about their situation (eg: *a lecturer/workplace supervisor may: want to help but be unsure what you need; be very busy; have personal problems you can't know about*)?

You cannot accurately know what another person thinks, but what is your best guess? Can you put yourself in their position? You can make notes on the following about a situation currently facing you.

What is likely to be their basic issue or problem?

What are their feelings likely to be about this?

What information do they need in order to deal with the issue or problem?

What is rightly their responsibility?

What rights have they got in this situation?

28.2.3 How will you approach the issue?

It might help you to think about using the following suggestions in a situation currently facing you or which recently faced you.

Suggestion	What effect might this have?
Begin by stating exactly what you want, right at the start of a discussion	
Begin by asking the other person what they want or how they see things	
Being by asking yourself in whose advantage it is to begin	
Lay out the issue so both parties know the 'agenda' (eg *I need to talk to you about my workload*'), then ask for their views before saying what you want (eg *'What do you think my priorities should be?'*)	

The best approach depends on the situation and the person. You could look back at your above notes and consider how they would be different for other situations you are/have been in. What would work best for you and when (in what sort of situations)?

28.3 Good communications

Effective communication helps you meet your goals (and allows the other person to meet theirs). What is effective depends on the situation and what you and the others want.

28.3.1 Checking understanding

Difficulties in finding solutions acceptable to all parties often come from misunderstanding. Are others clear about what you want or are you clear about what they want? Whatever your approach check:

- if others have understood you (eg *Do you need any more information?*)
- that you have understood them (eg *Did I understand you correctly that…?*).

Once you have reached agreement, check that everybody has the same understanding of this. Unless the situation is very informal, it helps to write down what was agreed and to make sure that everybody has a copy. This clarifies things at the time and can be useful later if anybody disputes what was agreed. In formal situations it may be useful for those involved to sign a common piece of paper saying they agree – in very formal situations this may be 'witnessed'.

27.3.2 Choosing approaches to use

Being **assertive** is about saying what you need in a way which respects what the other person needs. It is different from being **passive** (eg *I'm sorry I troubled you*) **manipulative** (eg *If you don't see me now I know I'll fail*), or **aggressive** (eg *It's your job to see me now*).

To get what you want, you may need to be flexible and to pick up clues about the situation (eg *if your tutor is very busy when you call to see her/him, s/he may be less sympathetic than at another time. If you want help it may be counter productive to insist on it there and then, and better to ask to discuss it at a more convenient time*).

It might help to think of what approaches you could use in a situation facing you now. Think about the following questions. For more ideas on possible approaches, look at Chapter 13 for this topic (particularly Sections 13.1.2 and 13.2.4).

- What approaches will you use when you talk to the person?
- Have you used similar approaches in the past?
- What effect would it have on you if you were on the receiving end?
- What short-term effect might it have on the other person?
- What long-term effect might it have on your relationship with the other person?
- Will it lead to a solution which is acceptable to both of you?

Approach/strategy	Comments

28.4 Using your personal attributes

28.4.1 Strengths

What attributes do you have which help when trying to agree things with others? Identifying them can make you feel more confident. Beware, however, of using your strengths manipulatively (eg *charm used to manipulate others can seem 'smarmy'*).

✔

Possible strengths	
Humour	
Relaxed manner	
Trustworthy, reliable	
Good listener	
Able to explain clearly	
Patient	
Others – please add your own	

28.4.2 'Weaknesses'

What attributes do you have which may cause problems in agreeing things with others (eg *'weaknesses' may include impatience, not listening, interrupting, being pushy)*? What could you do about it? For example, *If you are irritable...*

- avoid it (eg *communicate by letter or email and ask a friend to check them before you send them*)
- change it (eg *identify what makes you irritable and try to deal with it, do relaxation exercises before meeting, write thoughts down before you say them, count to 10 before replying, look at Chapter 14 'Coping with Pressure'*).
- allow for it (eg *ask the others for feedback – 'Let me know if I sound irritable'*).

In relation to your weaknesses, what could you do to:

- avoid them? How?
- change them? How?
- allow for them? How?

'Weakness'	Actions to take

28.5 Improving what you do

28.5.1 Monitoring on going improvements

You will constantly have situations where you need to agree matters with others – sometimes what you do will work and sometimes not. You can build on your experiences to become more and more effective. You could:

• keep a diary to record and review progress
• or return to this chapter at regular intervals to do so.

You could make notes in the following. There may be other questions you could add to help you.

What works for me?

What doesn't work for me?

Why did I choose to use the approaches I used?

What are the effects of the approaches I've used?

Do I feel any better about my dealings with others?

Are others reacting more positively to me?

Are my needs/goals being met?

Add your own questions here.

28.5.2 Actions to take to improve

Having answered the questions in 28.5.1, what do you need to improve?

Areas for improvement	Actions to take (including resources and support you need to help you)	By (deadline)

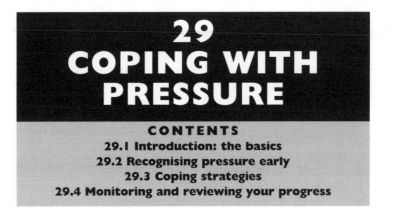

29
COPING WITH PRESSURE

CONTENTS
29.1 Introduction: the basics
29.2 Recognising pressure early
29.3 Coping strategies
29.4 Monitoring and reviewing your progress

This chapter aims to help you cope more effectively with pressures which you can anticipate and those you can't.

Developing the ability to cope with pressure means you are more likely to succeed on your course. Inevitably there will be pressures – heavy course workload, applying for jobs and studying for exams, lots of things going on.

After you have graduated or gained your diploma, work may have its pressures, as may other areas of your life. Coping well means being more effective, healthier and able to enjoy what you do.

We suggest you use this chapter:

- **when you anticipate a pressurised time ahead (eg *exams*)**
- **if you currently feel under pressure**
- **to handle ongoing pressures.**

When you have completed it, you should be able to:

Develop a strategy
- review your current reactions to, and abilities in dealing with, pressure
- identify what you want to achieve in the future
- select personally relevant strategies to cope with pressure
- produce realistic plans to cope with pressure, with deadlines and resources/support needed.

Monitor progress
- take responsibility for your own reactions to pressure and for action taken
- critically reflect on your own coping skills, seeking and using feedback and support
- note choices made in your coping with pressure and their effectiveness
- adapt coping strategies as needed.

Evaluate strategies and present outcomes
- evaluate the effectiveness of your personal coping strategies
- identify ways of further developing your own coping skills.

(Based on QCA Key Skill specifications, QCA 2000)

29.1 Introduction: the basics

Can you put into practice the basics of coping with pressure? You could score yourself on the following on a scale of 1–4, where 1 is 'very well' and 4 is 'needs considerable attention'. You could use the margin for notes (eg *on how you respond effectively or ineffectively to pressure*).

✔

	1	2	3	4
I'm aware of what I tend to find pressurising				
I'm able to identify current sources of pressure				
I'm aware of how I respond to pressure in an effective/positive way				
I'm aware of how I respond to pressure in a negative way.				
I'm aware of the advantages and disadvantages of how I respond to pressure				
I'm able to use the following strategies to deal with pressure:				
- removing the cause of the pressure				
- trying new approaches				
- changing my way of thinking				
- keeping healthy/fit				
- using relaxation techniques				
- seeking and using feedback from others				
- seeking and using support				

Chapter 14 on 'Coping with Pressure' in Part I covers all the above items. Do your ratings suggest you would find it useful to refer to it?

29.2 Recognising pressure early

Spotting pressure early, or even before it starts at all, is very helpful. Pressure can creep up on you. Once you get to the point of feeling overwhelmed it is harder (though not impossible) to cope.

29.2.1 What causes you to feel stressed?

What one person considers pressurising, another might not. What sort of things do you usually tend to find pressurising?

✍

Areas which I tend to find pressurising

29.2.2 Your early warning signs

How can you spot pressure early or anticipate it?

- Although exactly the same situation may not recur, you could look out for situations similar to those you have found pressuring in the past (eg *being required to meet several deadlines close together; having to deal with certain sorts of people*).
- Become more sensitive to your own reactions to pressure. Chapter 14 on 'Coping with Pressure' helps you identify both your positive and negative reactions to pressure.
- Stress can occur if you find it difficult to react positively or to use up the tension caused by pressure. What are your early warning signs (eg *positives may include excitement, exhilaration; negatives may include not sleeping, irritability*)?

✍

Early warning signs of stress in me

29.2.3 Your current and future pressures

Do you have any pressures? Can you spot any pressures which are building up now or may occur in the near future? You need to maintain a balance between being prepared in a positive way, and negatively expecting the worse.

Current pressures	Pressures just beginning (short term)	Possible future pressures (medium/long term)

29.3 Coping strategies

29.3.1 Set realistic targets

Setting yourself unrealistic targets which you cannot achieve can cause pressure or stress. When you set targets (eg *things you want to achieve/do on your course, in social or domestic situations*), ask yourself if they are SMART:

- **Specific** (eg *'coping better with pressure'* is not specific enough. *'Setting aside half an hour each day to relax'* is specific)

- **Measurable** (ie how will you know when you've achieved it?)

- **Achievable** (eg *you may not be able to improve how you cope with stress all in one go, but you may be able to relax for half an hour a day*)

- **Realistic** (eg *setting aside half an hour a day is realistic, 3 hours may not be*)

- **Time-bound,** ie you need to identify when you will have done it (eg *to set aside half an hour a day for the next month, and then review it*).

See the chapters on 'Action Planning' (see contents page).

29.3.2 Self-awareness

You have already identified your early warning signs of stress (in Section 29.2.2). You could also look at your strengths and weaknesses in dealing with stress.

Strengths in dealing with stress	How can I make good use of these?
Weaknesses in dealing with stress	**How can I allow for or improve these?**

It may help to look at the chapters on 'Reflecting on Your Experience' and 'Improving Your Learning' (see contents page).

You need to choose strategies for coping with pressure which are relevant to you. What suits your nature, needs and situation?

29.3.3 Dealing with the unexpected

In the past have you had pressures you hadn't anticipated? A sudden rush of work? An increase in demands placed on you? A crisis? What did you do? Was it effective or not?

What might have made things better? Here the focus should not be on factors outside yourself, which you may not have control over, but within yourself. You might like to think about:

* your goals (what were you trying to achieve?)
* your attitudes (were they helpful?)
* your feelings (were they justified?)
* your behaviour (did it meet your goals?)
* what you could have done to see it coming.

What I did	Effectiveness

Possible strategies for dealing with the unexpected include:

- don't plan your time so tightly that an unanticipated pressure will be the straw that broke the camel's back. Build in leeway (see the chapters on 'Organising Yourself and Your Time')
- be clear about what you want out of life at the moment. Is the unexpected pressure worth your concern?
- say no to unreasonable sudden demands (see the chapters on 'Negotiating and Assertiveness')
- prioritise. What else can be put aside or abandoned?
- stop, stand back, think it through, talk it over with somebody.

What else have you done in the past that worked (or didn't)? What would you now do differently.

29.3.4 Looking after yourself

This is essential when you are facing pressure.

✔

Are you:	
doing things you enjoy as well as things you have to do?	
giving yourself treats?	
letting yourself off the hook, giving yourself a break?	
resting, relaxing, sleeping?	
having fun, pursuing interests?	
keeping fit?	
eating properly?	
not over-drinking alcohol?	
not over-smoking?	

29.3.5 Seeking and using support

Are you identifying at what point you need support and where you could get such support? The 'point' will vary from individual to individual. What is important is knowing what your 'point' is and not being concerned about whether other people's 'points' are sooner or later.

Think about your current, short, middle and long-term pressures (see Section 29.2.3). Where do you need support? How will you know **when** you need it?

For example:

Short-term target: *to complete an assignment*		
Pressures	**Possible point at which support is needed**	**Possible support source**
eg *gathering information for an assignment*	eg *have looked in library catalogues, CD-ROM but can't find material*	eg *library information desk*
eg *several coinciding deadlines*	eg *can't see how to meet them all*	eg *lecturers*
eg *health problem*	eg *recurring, persistent, interfering with effectiveness*	eg *medical centre/doctor*

You might find if helpful to fill in the same table in relation to your own circumstances.

Target:		
Pressure	**Possible point at which support is needed**	**Possible support source**

(You may find it helpful to take copies of this box, to use with other targets).

Possible sources of support include:

- lecturers, tutors
- friends, other students, family members
- services at your university or college:
    - Learning centre/library
    - Computer Support Services
    - Students Union
    - Careers Service
    - Counselling Service
    - Chaplaincy

- – Recreation Services
- – hall wardens
- – International Office
- Citizens' Advice Bureau*
- Social Services*
- Relate*
- your doctor.

* The local telephone directory will have contact numbers.

This is only a short list to act as an idea starter. Any of the agencies listed above would themselves know of other individuals or groups who may be more relevant.

29.3.6 Plan ahead

It might help to draw up a plan now for the short term (eg *this week*), the middle term (eg *this month*), the longer term (eg *this term/semester, this year*). It is important to build into each stage an allowance for the unexpected (even at a simple level like longer queues than you thought).

Things nearly always take longer than you think. If the unexpected doesn't materialise you'll have a bonus in terms of extra time and energy.

What actions do you need to take, and when, for the pressures you identified in Section 29.2.3?

Short-term pressure	Middle-term pressure	Long-term-pressure

Short-term plans	Action needed	By when?

Medium-term plans	Action needed	By when?

Long-term plans	Action needed	By when?

If you find planning difficult refer to the chapters on 'Organising Yourself and Your Time' (see contents page).

29.4 Monitoring and reviewing your progress

You are responsible for your own reactions to pressure, and for how you cope with stressful events/situations. You need to monitor your plans, to see if you progressing as well as you can.

29.4.1 Reviewing plans and actions

It helps to regularly review your action plan as your coping skills develop and as situations/events change or arise.

When monitoring your progress you could:

- ask others for feedback on your performance (eg *tutors, friends, other students, employers*). They may have suggestions to help you further.
- keep notes on the strategies you tried
- monitor changes in situations/priorities
- amend your plans accordingly.

Are your strategies working? If you are not coping as well as you hoped, you could ask:

- what is stopping me?
- what is any feedback telling me?
- do I need a different approach?
- do I need more support?
- was I being realistic in my plans?

After each review, you may need to adapt your plan for coping. Which other strategies would suit you?

In the middle of a stressful situation, it helps to stop and think about what you are doing. Is it working? What needs to change? When we're under stress, we tend to stick to what we're doing, even if it isn't working.

29.4.2 Evaluating your effectiveness

You could keep notes on the actions you take and on how effective they are.

Actions tried/choices made	How effective were they?

What could you do to further develop your skills of coping with pressure? What can you do differently?

What could you do to improve?	What resources/support are needed?	By when?

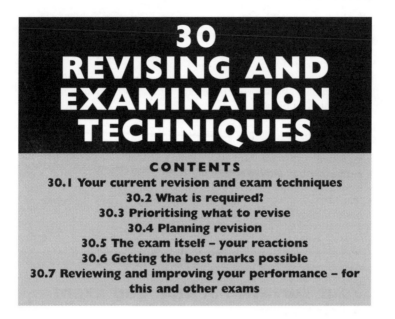

30
REVISING AND
EXAMINATION
TECHNIQUES

CONTENTS

This chapter aims to help you give your best performance, and to cope effectively with the increasing demands of exams as you progress through your course. Many courses use exams as a major way of assessing students. Skills in this area may be vital to academic success.

As you progress through your course, exams are likely to test more advanced abilities and draw on a wider range of material. You can improve your performance by identifying techniques which could work well for you.

Practising these revision and examination techniques throughout your course should improve your performance in final exams and help you with any professional exams in the future.

We suggest you use this chapter:

- **in relation to an exam or set of exams you have to take**
- **well in advance of those exams, to help you plan your revision. We suggest you read in advance through both the sections on revision (Sections 30.2, 30.3, 30.4) and exam techniques (Sections 30.5, 30.6), as your response to the exam technique section may cause you to change your revision.**

When you have completed it, you should be able to:

Develop a strategy
- review your current skills in this area
- identify aims for the future and how the exam affects them
- set realistic targets, with action plans and deadlines
- allow for your own weaknesses and strengths in planning revision and exam techniques
- choose revision and exam techniques likely to get the best possible results, and overcome difficulties.

Monitor progress
- monitor and critically reflect on your progress
- note choices made and their effectiveness
- adapt strategies as needed (eg *to cope with unexpected demands*)
- take responsibility for your own learning and performance in revising and exam techniques.

Evaluate strategies and present outcomes
- select the best way of demonstrating your own knowledge/abilities in the exam
- evaluate the effectiveness of your own revising and exam strategy/techniques
- identify ways of further developing your own learning and performance in revising and exam techniques.

(Based on QCA Key Skill specifications, QCA 2000)

30.1 Your current revision and exam techniques

Do you use the following techniques in revising?

✔

Identifying in advance the format of the exam and what it is for. What do the examiners want?	
Identifying which revision techniques seem appropriate for the subject, the exam and yourself, eg *sorting your material out, checking you understand it* *identifying likely questions* *relating topics to each other* *making summaries and 'flash cards'* *making lists* *making and listening to tape recordings of material* *testing yourself, or a friend* *allowing for your own capacity for concentration* *working in a pleasant environment*	
Making a revision plan	
Monitoring your revision progress and amending your plan	
Identifying what you need to improve next time round	

Do you use the following techniques in exams?   ✔

Spending the first 10 minutes:
     clarifying the instructions
     identifying what the questions mean and what is required
     deciding which questions to answer in what order
     planning how much time to allocate to the questions	

Planning answers	
Using appropriate evidence for your statements	
Presenting your information neatly	
Doing a final check on your work	
Identifying what you need to improve next time round	

If you are unable to tick many of these revision and examination techniques, it may help to refer to Chapter 15 on 'Revising and Examination Techniques' in Part I, which considers all the above basics. This chapter considers how you can improve on these.

30.2 What is required?

30.2.1 What you want – your aims

It is important to identify what you want to achieve from your exam(s). How crucial is it to your short-term and long-term aims?

What are your main short/long-term aims for the future? (eg *relating to the course, your career*)
What effect will your exam(s) have on these aims?
What does this mean for how well you do in the exam(s)? Do you need to do better in some exams than others?

30.2.2 What examiners want

To perform well in exams it is important to know what is expected. Misunderstanding about this can lead to poor results (eg *a student may think an exam answer needs a lot of detailed factual information without any evaluation of it. If the examiner is actually looking for an evaluation, the student will receive a low mark and be puzzled about why this was*).

As you progress through your course you should find that what examiners look for changes. They are more likely to want you to:

- show a deeper knowledge and understanding about a subject
- analyse and criticise information (eg *look at 'why', explore opposing views and arguments, identify inaccuracies*)
- pull together a variety of information or elements of a problem/theory to identify essential points
- show an understanding of the whole field and how a topic fits into it. They are likely to want you to show 'deep learning' (ie an understanding of concepts and principles), as well as 'surface learning' (ie memorising facts).
- show what you know – they are less likely to want to find out what you don't know
- apply knowledge, rather than reproducing it. (You might find that in first year exams the question gives you hints about how to answer it, but that by the final year questions are worded with fewer hints.) See Chapter 22 on 'Critical Analysis'.

In order to find out what is needed you could:

- look at past exam papers
- look at the aims of the units/modules you are taking
- look at the assessment criteria (to see what is required to pass/get a good mark)
- ask your lecturers
- read the exam regulations. They cover: what you need to do to pass; what happens if you fail; what evidence you need if you are ill before or during the exam or have serious personal problems likely to affect your performance.

Having identified what you think will be wanted in your exam(s), it may be helpful to summarise this and to check it out with your lecturers. You can keep referring back to this as you prepare for the exam.

> What will the examiner(s) be looking for in the exams you will be sitting?

If you have a disability which may influence your exam performance discuss alternative arrangements with your lecturer well in advance.

30.3 Prioritising what to revise

This chapter assumes you have identified what you need to revise (if in doubt – refer to Chapter 15 on 'Revising and Examination Techniques' in Part I). It is then important to prioritise the topics/items. This may help maximise your marks by focusing your attention on your important areas.

In prioritising, what do you need to consider?

✔

How much time is available for revision?	
How much material is there to cover?	
Breaking down a subject into smaller, manageable topics	
What the examiner is looking for (see Section 30.2.2)	
What topics are those you may do best at (does this mean you should spend more/less time on them)?	
What topics are those you may do worst at (does this mean you should spend more/less time on them)?	
What topics are the crucial ones for the subject?	
What do you like/dislike doing?	
What other demands on your time will there be?	
Others. Please list	

Which of the above will help you get the best mark you can?

What can you do if you have problems? For example, what if a crucial area which is very likely to crop up is the one you find most difficult?

What if you have other demands on your time or other personal difficulties?

What are your problems?

What are your options (think of as many ideas as possible)?

Who can help?

30.4 Planning revision

Think about your revision in the past and your current revision. Which of the following do you feel confident about?

✔

Motivation and self-discipline	
Time management	
Coping with difficulties	
Handling stress and pressure	
Being aware of how you learn best	
Being aware of a range of revision techniques	
Judging which revision techniques work best	

30.4.1 What revision techniques work for you?

This chapter assumes that you are familiar with basic revision techniques such as those listed in Section 30.I. If this is not the case, refer to Chapter 15 on 'Revising and Examination Techniques' in Part I.

Which techniques suit you best? What are your strengths and weaknesses in revising? How can you make use of your strengths?

✍

My strengths in revising. What I do well	How can I make use of these?	Resources/support needed

My weaknesses in revising. What I do less well	How can I allow for these, or improve them?	Resources/support needed

Are there other factors in your personal circumstances you need to take account of when planning your revision?

30.4.2 Revision plan

Before you draw up a revision plan, we suggest you read Sections 30.5 and 30.6, which may give more ideas for what to include. We also suggest you make a few photocopies of this blank plan.

When deciding on which revising techniques to use, consider those which will:

- best suit your strengths (see 30.4.1)
- help you over come your weaknesses (see 30.4.1)
- best suit the subject and the type of exam (see 30.6.2)
- help you get the best possible result (see 30.6.1).

You need to make sure your revision plan is realistic. Can you actually do it (eg *do you have enough time, access to resources*)?

As you are expected to take responsibility for your own learning and performance, you will need to review your plan at regular intervals. To help you amend it, ask yourself the following questions:

- are your priorities still the same?
- is your timescale realistic? Have any unforeseen demands arisen?
- are your revision techniques working?
- do your plans still help you meet your aims (see 30.2.1)?

You may find it helpful to get feedback from others on how well you are progressing.

Subject/topic to revise (in priority order)	What techniques will you use to revise?	By when?	Progress review & notes of further actions needed

30.5 The exam itself – your reactions

30.5.1 What do you usually do in exams?

By now you should have experience of taking exams at university/college. What do you usually do? Does it work? How do you feel in exams? What do they do to you? What do you need to do differently?

Positives	How can I build on these?	Resources/ support needed

Negatives	How can I allow for these, or improve them?	Resources/ support needed

In considering how to improve, you could identify sources of help.

- Chapter 15 on 'Revising and Examination Techniques'

- The chapters on:
  - 'Critical Analysis'
  - 'Organising Yourself and Your Time'
  - 'Coping With Pressure'
  - 'Reflecting on Your Experience'
- Share ideas with friends
- Seek lecturers' advice
- Look in a learning centre/library for materials on this area
- Consider for yourself what would help you. Sometimes identifying a problem makes the solution obvious.

30.5.2 Coping with nerves

If you feel your nervousness may hamper rather than improve your performance, you could consider past situations. What effect did nervousness have? What might have made it better? Possibilities include (though solutions will vary from person to person):

- **good preparation** eg *learning your topic well in advance, practising answering similar exam papers*
- **find out in advance what the exam conditions will be** (eg *date, time, room, the 'rules' about going to the toilet/leaving early, what equipment you can take in*)
- **identify what to do in the first 10 minutes in what order and try to stick to it** (eg *check instructions, write name, read through paper etc*). Doing simple things in the first place will steady you down. Jumping straight into a question without this planning/settling phase may mean you misunderstand what has to be done and panic.
- **make yourself as comfortable as possible for the exam** – have enough handkerchiefs, wear comfortable clothes (how hot/cold will it be?)
- **avoid alcohol** (exams and hangovers don't mix), or **being overtired** (is it really worth staying up late to cram in extras?), **have some exercise** (walk to the exam)
- **avoid last minute revision.** Anxiety created by last minute 'surface learning' (ie memorising facts) may block out 'deep learning' (ie understanding of principles and concepts), which is likely to be very important, particularly in final year exams.
- **Work out in advance what you will do if you panic.** Options include:
  - stop, close your eyes, breathe in to a count of six and out to a count of six, 10 times
  - stop, re-read the question and jot down any ideas you have, then sort them into some sort of order
  - stop and move on to another question, returning to the question you are having difficulty with later
  - stop and do a question you **can** answer to get a 'success" under your belt.

Whichever option you try, all involve stopping what you are doing, and then deciding what to do next.

30.6 Getting the best marks possible

Basic techniques in dealing with exams are:

- spend the first 10 minutes clarifying the instructions, what the questions mean, which you will answer, how long you will allocate to each, and in what order you will answer them
- watch the time and try to stick to your plan
- spend 10 minutes at the end checking your work.

30.6.1 Identifying what gets good marks

What will get good marks in this sort of exam in your subject? How can you improve your marks? If in doubt, check with your lecturer. The following are possibilities

✔

accuracy (eg *dates, calculations, names*)	
writing style (eg *spelling, grammar, how you express yourself*)	
presentation of data/visuals (and handwriting)	
steps in an argument/calculation/process?	
analysing information (eg *what are the implications, underlying issues, correlations*)	
being critical (eg *considering questions like why, for whom, when, what are the alternatives, what are the shortcomings or inaccuracies*)	
backing up your views, opinions, ideas with referenced evidence	
arguing your case	
organising the information	
Others. Please list.	

The following offer suggestions for improving on the basic exam techniques.

30.6.2 Dealing with different types of exams

Do not assume that exams at each level/year will be the same format as before. You may find that as you progress you will encounter fewer multiple choice or short answer exams, and more 'seen exams'.

Unseen exams

An unseen exam is one where you do not know in advance what the questions will be and you cannot take material in with you (eg *essay or problem based papers; multiple choice; short questions requiring short answer*).

Seen exams

In seen exams you see part or all of the exam in advance, for example:

- **a case/data seen in advance.** You will need to:
  - make yourself very familiar with the material
  - look at it from all angles to see what issues might arise in the exam.

- **open book.** You need to:
  - decide in advance whether to use the original material during the exam or to use notes summarising it
  - choose a method of finding the correct sections in the material during the exam. You might feel flustered, so you will need a simple system.
  - avoid over-quoting from material. The examiner wants your ideas / views / arguments, not rewritten extracts from the original.

- **take away.** You need to:
  - keep to any word limits
  - allow enough time to write up.

If you can take notes into the exam:

- what sort of notes would be most helpful (eg *of critical aspects, relevant theories; issues you think will crop up in the exam question*)?
- are they easy to follow? Use headings, underlining, marker pens, lists, diagrams.

Plagiarism

You need to avoid plagiarism. Plagiarism is where you copy somebody else's work without acknowledging it by giving a reference. It will be seen as cheating and may have serious consequences.

30.6.3 Practising in advance

You could identify a question you think will arise in your exam and draft a reply. Now look back at the items you ticked on the checklist on the previous page. Has your reply catered for those items?

You could do this with a friend. Exchange questions and replies and look at each other's reply in the light of the ticked items. This should reveal where you need to improve. You may find that you need to be more critical, or need to select more carefully the main points to cover, or to be more accurate.

30.6.4 Planning

Would it be best to answer those questions where you feel you will get high marks first, or to get the more difficult ones over with? If the latter it will be important to leave enough time to do yourself justice on your best topics.

Do you operate best if you draft a brief outline answer before writing, or if you write an answer straight off? If the latter you will need to allow time for checking.

Are there any personal aspects you need to take into account (eg *nervousness*)? How can you plan to deal with it?

30.6.5 Organising material/ordering your answer

For exams taken under normal exam conditions, how much can you cover in the time allowed for the question? How much can you physically write in, for example, the 30 – 45 minutes you have – 500 words? If a paragraph is 100 words, and you make one main point per paragraph, you can make five main points. Which of the points you could make are the most important?

As your course progresses exams are more likely to require you to organise information in a more effective way. Possibilities include:

- a clear opening paragraph (eg *explaining what you intend to cover in a clear order*) and writing a final paragraph drawing conclusions, summarising
- step by step, where a sequence or stages are important
- a main initial point to make impact which you then develop
- a series of points leading to a conclusion which has impact
- putting different sides of an argument
- grouping theories or concepts together through a theme
- introduction, presentation of information, critique or evaluation, conclusions.

30.6.6 Presentation of material

Headings, sub-headings and good layout make it easier to read and follow what you have written.

Any tables or graphs need to be clear with the correct labelling.

30.6.7 The final check

If you leave 10 minutes at the end of the exam to check your work, how can you best use that time? You might:

- check something which is a weak spot, either a particular answer or something running through all answers (eg *poor spelling*)
- check on layout, (eg *have you underlined headings, sub-headings*)
- finish off a question
- check details, such as figures, references, names, dates.

What will most improve your marks?

30.6.8 Getting the best marks – ideas to try

Which of the ideas in Section 30.6 will you try?

30.7 Reviewing and improving your performance - for this and other exams

To help you improve, you need to evaluate your effectiveness at the time, and afterwards. This will help you amend your revision plans. It may also help in the exam if you stop half way through to check on how you are doing, and what you could do differently.

You may have further exams on your current course, or you may have exams in the future – for example for professional qualifications.

	Revising	In the exam
What choices have/did you make?		
How effective are/were they?		
What is influencing/ influenced what you did? What can/could you have done about it?		

How could you improve your performance, now or in the future?

Action needed	What will help? (resources/people)	By when?

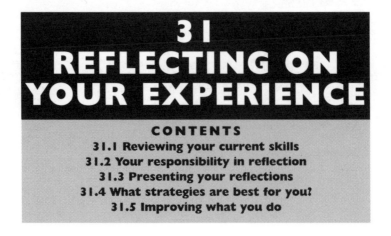

31
REFLECTING ON
YOUR EXPERIENCE

CONTENTS
31.1 Reviewing your current skills
31.2 Your responsibility in reflection
31.3 Presenting your reflections
31.4 What strategies are best for you?
31.5 Improving what you do

Being able to reflect effectively is essential to improve your learning. At the later levels of courses your learning will be more complex, covering many different elements. The way you reflect must be able to handle this, if you are to perform well on your course.

At work, in professional areas, you continually need to check that what you are doing is appropriate for the situation. Many professional bodies build reflection into their accreditation and Continuing Professional Development schemes, and most organisations have yearly appraisal interviews where you review your performance and plan to improve it.

This chapter aims to:

- help you get better grades or marks for assessed work requiring reflection
- help you improve how you reflect on your experiences, therefore helping you improve your learning and performance across the whole course
- begin to prepare for the reflection you need to do at work.

We suggest you use this chapter:

- **when a tutor asks you to reflect on something, evaluate something, or self-assess**
- **to reflect on something personally important to you on the course or in a course-related activity (eg *a work placement*)**
- **to generally improve your reflection skills.**

The chapter is concerned with your reflection on the course, but you could also use it, if you wish, to think about how you reflect on personal matters.

When you have completed it, you should be able to:

Develop a strategy
- review your current effectiveness in reflecting, and identify needs for developing this skill
- select and use personally relevant strategies

Monitor progress
- take responsibility for reflecting on your performance
- critically review your reflection skills, seeking and using feedback and support
- note choices made in how and when to reflect, and their effectiveness
- adapt reflection strategies as needed.

Evaluate strategies and present outcomes
- evaluate the effectiveness of your reflection strategies
- identify ways of further developing your reflection skills
- where required, select and use appropriate ways of showing the results of reflection, with appropriate evidence.

(Based on QCA Key Skill specification, QCA 2000)

31.1 Reviewing your current skills

How good are you at reflecting, particularly on your course? What do you need to improve?

The following can help you identify areas of strength, to build on, and areas to improve. Rate yourself on a scale, where 1 = 'very good' and 4= 'in need of considerable improvement'.

✔

	1	2	3	4
I know what reflection is, why courses want it, what its main features are				
I am aware of what I do when I reflect				
I know of ways of reflecting (strategies) and can use them				
I can use strategies which work well for me				
I can seek and use feedback				
I can identify appropriate evidence for my claims about my own performance				
I can produce a summary of the results of my reflection				
I can see what worked or didn't in how I reflected				
I can plan how to improve my reflection				

If you would like to review the above items, see Chapter 17 'Reflecting on Your Experience'.

31.2 Your responsibility in reflection

31.2.1 Your attitude

Reflection is a very personal thing. In your personal life you can choose not to do it – to go on doing things the same way. However, if you want to learn anything new or to change how you do things, you need to reflect – if only to identify what works when!

Reflection is seen as so important on courses that lecturers/tutors often set up situations where you 'have to' do it. You may see this as a hurdle to get over, or as an opportunity to improve your learning.

All lecturers and tutors can do is to encourage you, by setting up situations which ask you to reflect. They cannot determine how genuinely you take part in the process. That is up to you. If you want to learn, to improve what you do, to become a 'professional', you need to accept responsibility for your own reflection.

31.2.2 Academic reflection

Reflection in an academic context is not necessarily the same as personal reflection. If you are asked to produce reflective work for your course it must meet academic standards.

- The language you might use in personal reflection may not be appropriate (eg *slang, jargon, swearing*) – you need to use language acceptable in an academic context.
- If you refer to other people's work (eg *linking your practice to theory*) you must correctly reference it.
- The content of any reflective work should be relevant to or appropriate for the academic context.
- You may wish to consider your privacy. If work is to be handed in there may be aspects you prefer the tutor not to know, or if it is discussed in class, aspects you prefer other students not to know. Check in advance what will happen to the work – you can then decide what to include.

Chapter 17 'Reflecting on Your Experience' looks at what tutors expect from reflective work.

31.3 Presenting your reflections

You may need to present the results of your reflection. This might include:

- telling somebody how something they have done has affected you
- giving somebody else feedback (formal or informal)
- explaining a problem or difficulty to a tutor
- producing a piece of work which is not explicitly reflective, but which requires you to pull your thoughts together (eg *a poster, a report*)
- producing a Curriculum Vitae or job application form
- telling an interviewer what you are good at
- producing a formal piece of reflective work for assessment (eg *log/diary, portfolio, evaluation, self-assessment*).

When else might you need to present the results of your reflection and to whom?

To decide how to present your reflection to others, it helps to identify what you want from the situation, eg:

- *if you want to 'punish' somebody for upsetting you then it may be OK to 'let rip' with your feelings. If, however, you want to avoid them doing it again that won't be very helpful. You will just antagonise them. You need to tell them in a way which encourages them to do things differently*
- *if you want to get a job you need to present the best aspects of yourself, and to relate them to what the job needs*
- *if the work is to be assessed, what will get a good grade (what are the assessment criteria)?*

You may want to consider:

- the evidence needed to prove what you say – how much, what sort (eg *if telling somebody they upset you, too much detail may distract from your main point; employers may want your evidence in summary form; an assessor may want to see the actual evidence*)?
- how long it needs to be (eg *how long the conversation will be/how long you have in class; the amount of space on an application form; how long assessed work should be*). This may determine what to include and help you focus on what is important.
- what sort of language the other person will understand (eg *jargon*).

For a situation facing you at the moment:

🖎

How will you present the results of your reflection and to whom?

What do you want to achieve or get out of the situation?

What will work best in presenting the results of your reflection?

What evidence (and how much) should you include?

For help look at:

- Chapters 13 and 28 'Negotiating and Assertiveness'
- the other chapters in this book on presentation formats (ie 'Essay Writing', 'Report Writing', 'Note Taking', 'Oral Presentation', 'Visual Communication').

31.4 What strategies are best for you?

Ways of reflecting work differently for different people and different situations (eg *drawing may help visual people to reflect but may not help more verbal people; you may need to reflect on technical matters differently from those involving people*).

31.4.1 Types of experiences

On your course, what situations or experiences do you have (eg *seminars, labs, lectures*), what sort of work must you do (eg *reports, posters, experiments*), what sort of subjects do you study (eg *technical, professional/work related, theoretical, creative*)?

31.4.2 Your preferred ways of reflecting

From your experience of reflecting on course work, what ways of reflecting do you like or find easy, and what do you dislike or find difficult?

What do others think of your reflection skills? You could ask for feedback from tutors (on assessed reflective work; comments made in class or 1:1), from other students (eg *in class discussion*), employers, or friends or family.

These strategies are from Chapter 17 'Reflecting on Your Experience'. Tick the appropriate column.

✔

	Like/find easy/can do	Dislike/find difficult/ can't do
Talk to somebody about it		
Write about it		
Draw something about it		
Think about it on your own		
Look at it in new ways		
• replay it as it happened		
• for new insights read (eg *books*), watch (eg *TV*)		
• think about what might have been		
• think what you could have done		
• think about it in the opposite way from how you normally would		
• describe it as somebody else might		
• identify your feelings about it		
• ask yourself questions		
• identify the main/crucial aspects		
Ask for feedback from others		
Use feedback from others		
Use a logical process (ie identify what happened, how you felt, how others reacted/felt, positives, negatives, choices you made and their effects, what you learnt for the future)		
Other ways you use (please list)		

Look again at the ways you dislike/find difficult/can't do. Are you limiting yourself, or can you genuinely not get on with them? You could ask 'is it more that...':

- I need more practise at using them
- I need help or support or guidance in how to use them
- I haven't really tried them, I've just stuck to my tried and tested ways.

31.4.3 Appropriate strategies

Do you have to produce any reflective work for your course? If so what?

✔

Reflective log or diary	
Evaluation of your work	
Self-assessment	
A reflective portfolio	
Critical incident analysis	
Stories/fictional writing (which are reflective)	
A report (eg a *placement report*)	
Others (please list)	

Look again at the list of strategies in 31.4.2 above. For the moment, try to ignore your likes and dislikes. Highlight the strategies you think will be particularly effective:

- for the type of assessed reflective work you must do (if it is assessed)
- for the types of experiences you may meet (see 31.4.1 above).

If your highlighting coincides with the strategies you like, fine – if not you may need to return to Chapter 17 to see if you can get to grips with those strategies.

31.5 Improving what you do

31.5.1 Choices

Think of a recent situation when you reflected on something. This does not have to be a piece of reflection required by the course (although it could be) – you could just be thinking about something after it has ended (eg *a project, a class, something good, a problem/difficulty/upsetting experience*).

For that situation – what did you reflect on and how?

Although it may not have felt like it, you chose what to reflect on and how. What choices did you make and what effect did they have? What other choices could you have made and what effect might they have had (eg *if you focused on negatives, what if you had focused on positives, or visa versa?*)

31.5.2 What might stop you reflecting effectively?

Could you be doing any of the following?　　　　　　　　　　　　　✔

Being defensive	
Needing to justifying everything you did or thought	
Going along with what others think	
Trying to please others	
Basing your views on an outdated situation (eg *what worked at school, in former jobs*)	
Operating from a set of values/attitudes without questioning them	
Seeing things as black/white, right/wrong	
Looking at the issue while not feeling very well, or feeling a bit down	
Stereotyping	
Using language which encourages stereotyping (eg *race or gender*)	

31.5.3 What would you like to change?

What do you want to continue to do in reflection? What seems to work well for you? What would you like to do differently? Could you adapt any strategies to make them work better for you? How?

31.5.4 Action plan

Use the following to help you plan to improve. You could think about the support you need to help you. This might be:

* written guidance (eg *in the chapters in this book, other publications*)
* help from other people (eg *tutors, other students, friends*)
* feedback from others (who could best give you this feedback?)
* class sessions (eg *on how to produce work in a certain format*).

What else might help you?

Areas for improvement	Actions to take	By (deadline)

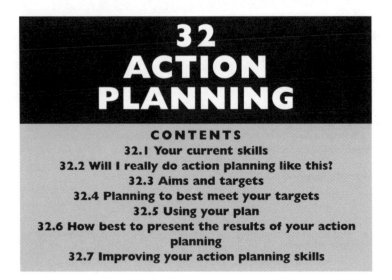

32
ACTION
PLANNING

CONTENTS
32.1 Your current skills
32.2 Will I really do action planning like this?
32.3 Aims and targets
32.4 Planning to best meet your targets
32.5 Using your plan
32.6 How best to present the results of your action planning
32.7 Improving your action planning skills

Action planning helps you make the most of your time, your abilities, your resources; to focus on what you want or need and then to achieve it. It will help you to:

• achieve the best possible results for you on your course
• develop or change skills or other aspects of yourself (ways you do things, attitudes, values, qualities)
• identify what you currently want from life and then to achieve it
• monitor how well you are achieving what you'd like to achieve.

This is a skill needed in employment. Action planning is important for the staff appraisal schemes which most organisations have, the Continuing Professional Development schemes of professional bodies, and generally for efficient working. For some jobs or tasks it is essential (eg *project management*). You can also use it to develop career plans.

We suggest you use this chapter:

• **when you have course work to do or exams to prepare for, to help you plan**
• **to help you plan how to develop your skills.**

This chapter focuses on action planning related to your course, but you could also use it to think about other areas of your life (eg *work, social, domestic, family*).

When you have completed it, you should be able to:

Develop a strategy
• review current action planning skills
• identify the outcomes desired and the criteria by which to judge them
• set realistic targets (eg *SMART – specific, measurable, achievable, realistic, time-bound*) taking into account personal preference, motivation, needs and circumstances
• select methods to best meet the outcomes.

Monitor progress
- keep to timescales
- deal with unexpected demands
- take advantage of new opportunities
- monitor and critically reflect on action planning
- adapt strategy to produce best possible outcomes.

Evaluate strategy and present outcomes
- select most effective way to present achievements with evidence
- evaluate effectiveness of action planning and factors influencing it
- identify ways of further improving your action planning.

(Based on QCA Key Skill specifications, QCA 2000)

32.1 Your current skills

Do you: ✔

do action planning in a formal way, writing down your plans?	
do action planning in your head?	
do action planning for some things but not for others?	
do action planning when somebody (eg *course tutor*) requires you to do it, but not otherwise?	
do some bits of action planning (eg *make lists of things to do*)?	
not do action planning, just take things as they come?	
not know what action planning is?	

If you ticked the last item, see Chapter 18 'Action Planning'.

How would you rate your current skills on the following scale, where 1 = 'very good' and 4 = 'in need of considerable improvement'?

✔

	1	2	3	4
Identifying your overall aims (eg *what you currently want out of life*)				
Identifying your more immediate targets				
Identifying the action/tasks needed to meet those targets				
Identifying the methods you will use for those actions/tasks				
Identifying what might affect your plans and allowing for this				
Identifying deadlines for those actions/tasks (to meet your overall deadline)				
Using a format to put the above into a plan				
Reviewing your plans and amending them if need be				
Dealing with difficulties				
Reviewing your skills in action planning				

Chapter 18 'Action Planning' covers all the above. If you have rated yourself low on any items, have a look at the section dealing with it in that chapter.

32.2 Will I <u>really</u> do action planning like this?

This chapter will help you produce a well thought through action plan (eg *if one is required for course work*). If you have a major piece of work to do (eg *a final year project or dissertation*) then such a plan is essential. It will be invaluable in planning your career and job seeking. If there is a skill which you must improve in order to achieve something, this chapter will help.

You may not want to go though such a formal process for everything (you may spend more time planning than doing!). However, if you follow the processes suggested here for something you want or need to achieve, you may find yourself thinking about aspects of the planning process whenever you do things more informally – this will generally help what you do.

It is therefore well worth trying this process out on something you need to do now.

32.3 Aims and targets

32.3.1 Long-term, medium and immediate aims

An aim is what you are heading towards, eg Aim. *Improve my skills in dealing with people.*

The starting point for action planning is to identify your aims. These might be long term, medium term and immediate (short term). Your long-term aims will influence the others (eg *if you need to get a good degree for the career you are interested in*).

What are your long-term aims (eg *for the next 5 years*)?	What are your medium term aims (eg *for this year*)?	What are your immediate aims (eg *for this month*)?

You could now consider the following questions.

Will my medium and immediate aims help my long-term aims? What would best help my long-term aims?
Which medium-term/immediate aims are irrelevant to my long-term aims?
Do I want to reconsider or re-prioritise my medium-term/immediate aims?

Feeling committed to your aims is important if you are to make the effort to meet them. Working out why they are important can help you feel more committed to them.

32.3.2 Clarifying your aims and targets

A target is a specific end point – you can clearly see when you have got there. An outcome is the results of your efforts, eg:

Aim. *Improve my skills in dealing with people.*
Target. *Listen to people.*
Outcome. *Can listen to people.*

You need to be clear how you will know when you have achieved your target to the standard you want. What are the criteria against which you will judge your outcomes? For example:

Target. *Listen to others.*
Criteria for judging the outcome

- *how often I interrupt others*
- *clarity of my descriptions of what others have said*
- *accuracy of my interpretation of what others mean.*

At this moment, what are your aims and your targets and how will you judge your outcomes (ie what are your criteria for judging effectiveness)?

Aims	Targets	Criteria to judge outcomes

32.3.3 Setting useful targets

It helps to identify targets which are SMART (QCA 2000).

- **Specific**, eg *'to improve my IT skills'* is not specific *(it is an aim rather than a target)*, *'to make a table using a computer'* is specific

- **Measurable** (ie you must know when you have achieved it). It must be possible to identify criteria against which to judge the outcome (see 32.2.1 above), eg *'to improve my IT skills'* is too vague to measure; *'to make a table using a computer'* can be measured *(you can see you have made one, if it is accurate and well laid out etc)*

- **Achievable** (eg *if you have no access to a computer you will not be able to learn how to make a table on one*)

- **Realistic** (eg *if you have never touched a computer before, you may need to develop more basic skills before you can make a table*)

- **Time-bound**, ie you need to identify when you will have done it (eg *'to make a table on a computer by next week'*).

Look back at the targets you noted in 32.3.2 above. Are they:

- Specific?
- Measurable?
- Achievable?
- Realistic?
- Time-bound?

If not, how do you need to amend them?

Appendix 1 gives a blank form you could use as an action plan. It helps to check if targets you put in your action plan are SMART.

32.3.4 Setting appropriate targets

Your targets also need to be appropriate for

- **your own preferences, motivations and needs.** The literature suggests that what is critical is your acceptance of responsibility for your plans and your ability to carry them out (using help, but not being reliant on others) (Neath 1998). You are more likely to do this if you want or need to do what you are doing.

- **your circumstances.** What is appropriate for you now, in your situation? This relates to the 'Realistic' in 'SMART' (see 32.3.3 above) - if your circumstances make your targets unrealistic it will be hard to reach them (and stressful).

However, your circumstances may change soon, as may your preferences and needs. This is why you need to keep revising your plans. You could think now about how these things might change, so you can build some flexibility in your plans.

You could note any aspects of relevance to the aims and targets identified in 32.3.2 above.

What are your current preferences, motivations and needs?	What is/are your current situation/circumstances?	How will this affect your targets?

32.4 Planning to best meet your targets

Chapter 18 'Action Planning' looked at identifying methods to meet your targets. What would be the best methods, to get you the best results, to help you meet your criteria for success (see 32.3.2 above)?

You may first need to identify all the possible methods – at this stage it might be best not to worry about whether you can actually use that method yourself (eg *whether you have the skills to do so*). You could then ask which methods would best:

- fit the subject/area/topic/issue
- fit your preferences and needs
- fit your situation or circumstances
- help you meet your criteria
- if you can actually do them. If not, do you need help, training, or guidance from another chapter?

For example:

Target and criteria to judge outcomes	Possible methods	Considerations	Methods I will actually use
Target. *Listen to others.* **Criteria for judging the outcome.** *Accuracy of my interpretation of what others mean*	• *work out myself what a person means* • *ask others what they mean* • *ask them what they mean*	• *I might be wrong* • *their views may support mine, though they may also be wrong* • *most likely to get it right, but don't like doing it, can't always do it easily, eg ask lecturer in lecture*	• *only do this if sure of my interpretation* • *do this to check others interpret it like I do* • *Chapters 13 & 28 'Negotiating and Assertiveness'; if can't ask at the time ask later*

Consider which methods would get you the best results when you complete your action plan (see Appendix 1)

32.5 Using your plan

32.5.1 Monitoring and critically reflecting on your plan

You need to look at your plan often, to check how you are getting on. Ticking items off can make you feel good!

The checklist below can help you think about how well your plan is working.

Feedback from others can help you complete the checklist (for guidance on seeking and using feedback see Chapter 17 'Reflecting on Your Experience'), eg:

- *if you need to find information, check if you have found all the possible sources with library/learning centre staff*
- *check with computing support staff that you are using computer applications well*
- *ask for feedback from tutors or friends on drafts, or on your behaviour (eg 'Am I improving how I listen to you?').*

✔

Did you omit any targets you should have included?	
Do you still think your targets are SMART?	
Do the criteria against which to judge your outcomes still look appropriate?	
Are there any actions/tasks you need to do which need adding to your plan?	
Are any actions or tasks unnecessary?	
Are your methods appropriate for your topic/area/issue, yourself, your situation?	
Are your methods working?	
Are the methods getting the results you want (ie meeting your criteria)?	
Are things taking less time to do than you thought?	
Are things taking longer to do than you thought?	
Are you keeping to your deadlines and timescale?	
Do you feel committed to what you are doing?	

32.5.2 Dealing with unexpected demands or problems

You may well come across things you didn't expect. Did you build time into your plan to allow for this? Did you anticipate them in your plan and allow for them? Chapter 3 'Organising Yourself and Your Time' also looks at this issue.

The other chapters can help you think about how to deal with problems or issues, eg:

- feeling stressed – look at Chapters 14 and 29 'Coping with Pressure'
- difficult people – look at Chapters 13 and 28 'Negotiating and Assertiveness'
- problems in a group – look at Chapters 11 and 27 'Group Work'
- problems in general – look at Chapters 10 and 26 'Solving Problems'.

Keep referring to your aims and targets to keep on track.

You also need to identify resources or people who could help. If you find it hard to ask for help, look at Chapters 13 and 28 'Negotiating and Assertiveness'. Resources might include, eg:

- books or other information sources; computers; equipment; space/accommodation etc
- people – tutors; specialists (eg *library/learning centre staff; computing support staff, careers advisers or counsellors*); friends.

32.5.3 Take advantage of new opportunities

If you are flexible, you can take advantage of unexpected opportunities – another good reason for building extra time into your plans! You need to avoid having such tight plans that there is no time to explore other things.

Do you: ✔

like to stick to plans and find it hard to do anything not in the plan?	
dislike sticking to plans and like exploring whatever new turns up?	
generally stick to plans but keep an eye out for new ideas or opportunities which might help?	

Rigidly sticking to your plans may mean you miss good ideas and opportunities, but following every new idea or opportunity will mean you won't achieve your plans.

A middle path may be best. Using the 'listening' example – *a new book on listening skills may come out; there may be a TV programme on it; somebody may run a workshop on it.*

32.5.4 Adapting your plans

Changing plans involves costs. It may mean work you have done has to be abandoned; take more time; have repercussions which mean you have to change everything; cost money. Before you change something you could think about:

* how much it will help you get the best possible outcomes
* what effect it will have on everything else (will you have to change everything, a few things, only one thing?)
* how much it will 'cost' (eg *in terms of time or money)*
* if it is worth it.

Sections 32.5.1–32.5.3 contain suggestions about changing your plans.

If you change your action plan, it helps to give the new plan a number and to date it, and to keep your old plan to keep track of your progress, particularly if you need to provide evidence of your action planning (eg *for an assignment or an interview).*

32.6 How best to present the results of your action planning

Chapter 18 'Action Planning' looked at presenting the results of action planning and other chapters cover methods of presenting achievements and work (eg *the chapters on 'Report Writing', 'Essay Writing', 'Oral Presentation' etc).*

Chapters 17 and 31 'Reflecting on Your Experience' help you identify your achievements, your learning from a situation, how well something went, what you will do again.

To identify how best to present the results of your action planning, you could consider:

- who will see the results of your action planning and why? What will they want to know?
- if it is for assessment, what will get the best grade/mark (the assessment criteria)?
- if it is to present to an employer or admissions tutor for another course, what will persuade them to accept you?

It is important to identify what is needed. Should you present the **outcomes** of your planning in the best possible light, or show how you went through the **process** of action planning? This might affect how much emphasis you give to positives or to the more negative aspects of what happened.

The 'other person' will want to know not just what happened or the results, but an evaluation of what happened, identifying what you learnt and what you would do differently in future (eg *employers will not just want to hear that everything went well, but that you have faced difficulties and handled them; tutors will want to know what you learned and that you can evaluate and criticise*). For help see Chapter 22 'Critical Analysis'.

When presenting the results of action planning, you should give evidence. For an employer in an interview or on an application form, this might be examples of what you did. For tutors it might be notes or pieces of work. Whatever evidence you use it should be:

- current and up to date
- relevant to the claim you are making
- sufficient to demonstrate what you claim.

32.7 Improving your action planning skills

How effective is your action planning? You can make notes below.

What do you do well in action planning?	What do you find difficult or need to improve?	What factors have affected your action planning?	What could you have done about those factors?

What do you do well in action planning?	What do you find difficult or need to improve?	What factors have affected your action planning?	What could you have done about those factors?

You could now use the blank action plan in Appendix 1 to create an action plan to improve your action planning! You can take copies to use for how ever many targets you have.

Appendix I
Action Plan

Target			Deadline to meet it	
Tasks	Methods	Resources, support, help	Start date	End date

REFERENCES AND BIBLIOGRAPHY

Chapter 1: How to Use this Book

Drew, S. and Thorpe, L. (eds) (2000), *Key Skills Online: Intranet Support for Students*, Gower

QCA (2000) *Key Skills Units*, QCA

Pettigrew, M. and Elliott, D. (1999), *Student IT Skills*, Gower

Chapters 2 and 19: Identifying Strengths and Improving Skills

AGCAS (1992), *Discovering Yourself. A Self-Assessment Guide for Older Students*, AGCAS

Bingham, R. and Drew, S. (1999), *Key Work Skills*, Gower

Hawkins, P. (1999), *The Art of Building Windmills: Career Tactics for the 21st Century*, Graduate Into Employee Unit

Maxhall, P. (1998), *Unlocking Your Potential*, How to Books

Chapters 3 and 20: Organising Yourself and Your Time

Buzan, T. (1973), *Use your Head*, BBC Publications

Bingham, R. and Drew, S. (1999), *Key Work Skills*, Gower

Gibbs, G. (1993) *Learning to Study: The Secret of Success*, National Extension College

Hopson, B. and Scally, M. (1989), *Time Management: Conquer the Clock*, Lifeskills

Lewis, R. (1994), *How to Manage Your Study Time*, Collins Educational

Maitland, I. (1995), *Managing Your Time*, Institute of Personnel and Development

Northedge, A. (1990), *The Good Study Guide*, Open University Press

Pettigrew, M. and Elliot, D. (1999), *Student IT Skills*, Gower

Stuart, R. R. (1989), *Managing Time*, The Pegasus Programme Understanding Industry Inst.

Chapter 4: Note Taking

Bingham, R. and Drew, S. (1999), *Key Work Skills*, Gower

Longman, D. G. and Holt Atkinson, R. (1999), *Study Methods and Reading Techniques*, 2nd edn, Wadsworth

Northedge, A. (1990), *The Good Study Guide*, Open University Press

Payne, E. and Whittaker, L. (2000), *Developing Essential Study Skills*, Pearson

Chapters 5 and 21: Gathering and Using Information

Bell, J. (1987), *Doing Your Own Research Project: A Guide for First-time Researchers in Education and Social Science*, Open University Press

Carroll, J. (2000), 'Academic Dishonesty and the Internet', in *Reaching Out, SEDA Spring Conference 2000*, SEDA

Cohen, L. and Manion, L. (eds) (1985), *Research Methods in Education*, Croom Helm

Cooke, A. (1999), *A Guide to Finding Quality Information on the Internet: Selection and Evaluation Strategies*, Library Association

Deer Richardson, L. (1992), *Techniques of Investigation: An Introduction to Research Methods*, National Extension College

Gash, S. (2000), *Effective Literature Searching for Research*, 2nd edn, Gower

Huff, D. (1973), *How to Lie with Statistics*, Penguin

Northedge, A. (1990), *The Good Study Guide*, Open University Press

Pettigrew, M. and Elliott, D. (1999), *Student IT Skills*, Gower

Chapters 6 and 23: Essay Writing

Cederblom, J. and Paulsen, P. W. (1990), *Critical Reasoning*, 3rd edn, Wadsworth

Clanchy, J. and Ballard, B. (1998), *How to Write Essays: A Practical Guide For Students*, 3rd edn, Longman

Fairbairn, G. J. and Winch, C. (1991), *Reading, Writing and Reasoning: A Guide for Students*, Society for Research into Higher Education and Oxford University Press

Hamp-Lyons, L. and Heasley, B. (1987), *Study Writing: A Course in Written English for Academic and Professional Purposes*, Cambridge University Press

Hounsell, D. and Murray, R. (1992), *Essay Writing for Active Learning, Effective Learning and Teaching in Higher Education*, CVCP Universities Staff Development and Training Unit

Newby, M. (1989), *Writing. A Guide for Students*, Cambridge University Press

Parrott, M. (2000), *Grammar for English Language Teachers: With Exercises and a Key*, Cambridge University Press

Raimes, A. (1998), *Grammar Troublespots: An Editing Guide for Students*, 2nd edn, Cambridge University Press

Roberts, D. (1997), *The Student's Guide to Writing Essays*, Kogan Page

Chapters 7 and 24: Report Writing

Barass, R. (1978), *Scientists Must Write*, Spon

Bartram, P. (1994), *The Perfect Report*, Arrow

Bell, J. (1987), *Doing your Research Project: A Guide for First-time Researchers in Education and Social Science*, Open University Press

Bingham, R. and Drew, S. (1999), *Key Work Skills*, Gower

Bowden, J. (2000), *Writing a Report: How to Prepare, Write and Present Powerful Reports*, How To Books

Cooper, B. M. (1964), *Writing Technical Reports*, Penguin

Gowers, E. (1986), *The Complete Plain Words*, HMSO

Huff, D. (1973), *How to Lie with Statistics*, Penguin

Peel, M. (1990), *Improving Your Communication Skills*, Kogan Page

Stanton, N. (1990), *Communication*, Macmillan Education

Van Emden, J. and Eastel, J. (1993), *Report Writing*, McGraw-Hill

Chapters 8 and 25: Oral Presentation

Bernstein, D. (1988), *Put it Together. Put it Across. The Craft of Business Presentation*, Cassell.

Bingham, R. and Drew, S. (1999), *Key Work Skills*, Gower

Peel, M. (1990), *Improving Your Communication Skills*, Kogan Page

Stanton, N. (1990), *Communication*, Macmillan Education.

Videos

The Floor is Yours Now – A Guide to Successful Presentations, Gower (24 minutes)

We Can't Hear You at the Back (1992) (part of a series – *Work is a Four Letter Word*), BBC

Discovering Presentations (1991), British Telecom Interactive Video, Longmans Training

Chapter 9: Visual Communication

Drew, S. and Gibson R. (1999), *The Student Guide to Making an Oral Presentation*, CD ROM, Gower

Ellington, H. and Race P. (1993), *Producing Teaching Materials. A Handbook for Teachers*, 2nd Edn, Kogan Page

Microsoft (1997), *Quick Course in Microsoft PowerPoint 97*, Microsoft/Online Press Inc.

Pettigrew, M. and Elliot, D. (1997), *Student IT Skills*, Gower

Stanton, N. (1990), *Communication*, Macmillan Educational

Chapters 10 and 26: Solving Problems

Bingham, R. and Drew, S. (1999), *Key Work Skills*, Gower

Bransford, J. D. and Stein, B. S. (1993), *The Ideal Problem Solver: A Guide for Improving Thinking*, W. H. Freeman

Centre for Science Education (1990), *Problem Solving with Industry*, Sheffield Hallam University

Comino Foundation (1990), *GRASP – Getting Results and Solving Problems*, Comino Foundation

Cowan, J. (undated) *Individual Approaches to Problem Solving*, Department of Civil Engineering, Heriot Watt University

de Bono, E. (1982), *De Bono's Thinking Course*, Ariel Books, BBC

Whetten, D. Cameron, K. and Woods, M. (1996), *Effective Problem Solving*, HarperCollins

Wilson, G. (2000), *Problem Solving*, 2nd edn, Kogan Page

Chapters 11 and 27: Group Work

Belbin, R. M. (1981), *Management Teams. Why They Succeed or Fail*, Butterworth

Belbin, R. M. (1993), *Team Roles at Work*, Butterworth-Heinemann

Bingham, R. and Drew, S. (1999), *Key Work Skills*, Gower

Hardingham, A. (1995), *Working in Teams*, Institute of Personnel Managment

Hartley, P. (1997), *Group Communication*, Routledge

Johnson, D. W. and Johnson, F. P. (1991), *Joining Together: Group Theory and Group Skills*, Prentice-Hall

Rackham, N. and Morgan, T. (1977), *Behaviour Analysis in Training*, McGraw-Hill

Turner, C. (1983), *Developing Interpersonal Skills*, The Further Education Staff College

Chapter 12: Seminars, Group Tutorials and Meetings

Bingham, R. and Drew, S. (1999), *Key Work Skills*, Gower

Hodgson, P. and Hodgson J. (1992), *Effective Meetings*, Century Business

Fry, R. (1997), *How to Study*, Kogan Page

Northedge, A. (1990), *The Good Study Guide*, Open University Press

Hargie, O., Saunders, C. and Dickson, D. (1994), *Social Skills in Interpersonal Communications*, 3rd edn Routledge

Chapters 13 and 28: Negotiating and Assertivness

Back, K., Back, K. and Bates, T. (1991), *Assertiveness at Work*, McGraw-Hill

Bingham, R. and Drew, S. (1999), *Key Work Skills*, Gower

Dickson, A. (1982), *A Woman in Your Own Right*, Quartet Books

Fisher, R. and Ury, W. (1987), *Getting to Yes. How to Negotiate to Agreement Without Giving In*, Arrow

Gillen, Y. (1997), *Assertiveness*, Institute of Personnel Management

Harris, Thomas A. (1973), *I'm OK you're OK*, Pan

Steele, P., Murphy, J. and Russill, R. (1989). *Its a Deal: A Practical Negotiation Handbook*, McGraw-Hill

Townend, A. (1991), *Developing Assertiveness*, Routledge

Chapters 14 and 29: Coping with Pressure

Atkinson, J. M. (1988), *Coping With Stress At Work*, Thorsons Publishers

Bingham, R. and Drew, S. (1999), *Key Work Skills*, Gower

Cooper, C., Cooper, R. and Eaker, L. (1988), *Living with Stress*, Penguin

Farmer, R., Monahan, L. and Hekeler, R. (1984), *Stress Management for Human Services*, Sage Publications

Looker, T. and Gregson, O. (1989), *Stresswise*, Hodder & Stoughton

Patel, C. (1989) *The Complete Guide to Stress Management*, Optima

Chapters 15 and 30: Revising and Examination Techniques

Acres, D. (1987), *How to Pass Exams*, Hamlyn

Bingham, R. and Drew, S. (1999), *Key Work Skills*, Gower

Buzan, T. (1973), *Use Your Head*, BBC Publications

Gibb, G. (1981), *Teaching Students to Learn*, Open University Press

Habeshaw, S., Habeshaw, J. and Gibbs, G. (1987), *53 Interesting Ways of Helping Your Students to Study*, Technical and Educational Services Limited

Hills, C. M. (1989), *How to Pass Exams*, Hamlyn

Jacques, D. (1990), *Studying at the Polytechnic*, Education Methods Unit, Oxford Polytechnic

National Extension College (1994), *Learning Skills*, Units 42–50 National Extension College

Northedge, A. (1990), *The Good Study Guide*, Open University Press

Secrets of Study (1989), Interactive Video, Mast Learning Systems

Chapter 16: Improving Your Learning

Gibbs, G. (1992), *Improving the Quality of Student Learning*, Technical and Education Services Ltd

Kolb, D. A. (1984), *Experiential Learning*, Prentice-Hall

Marton, F. and Saljo, R. (1984), 'Approaches to Learning' in Marton, F., Hounsell, D. and Entwistle, N., *The Experience of Learning*, Scottish Academic Press

Pettigrew, M. and Elliott, D. (1999), *Student IT Skills*, Gower

Chapters 17 and 31: Reflecting on Your Experience

Bannister, D. and Fransella, F. (1971), *Inquiring Man*, Penguin

Bingham, R. and Drew, S. (1999), *Key Work Skills*, Gower

Gibbs, G. (1992), *Improving the Quality of Student Learning*, Technical and Educational Services Limited

Kolb, D.A. (1984), *Experiential Learning*, Prentice-Hall

Moon, J.A. (1999), *Reflection in Learning and Profesional Development: Theory and Practice*, Kogan Page

Pettigrew, M. and Elliott, D. (1997), *Student IT Skills*, Gower

Schon, D. A. (1987), *Educating the Reflective Practitioner*, Jossey Bass

Chapters 18 and 32: Action Planning

Bingham, R. and Drew, S. (1999), *Key Work Skills*, Gower

Neath, M. (1998), 'The Development and Transfer of Undergraduate Group Work Skills' (PhD thesis), Sheffield Hallam University

Pettigrew, M. and Elliott, D. (1999), *Student IT Skills*, Gower

QCA (2000), *Key Skill Units. Improving Own Learning and Performance*, QCA

Chapter 22: Critical Analysis

Bloom, B. S. (1979), *Taxonomy of Educational Objectives*, Longman

Huff, D. (1973), *How to Lie with Statistics*, Penguin

Perry, W. G. (1970), *Forms of Intellectual and Ethical Development in the College Years*, Rinehart and Winston

Ruggiero, V. R. (1996), *Becoming a Critical Thinker*, Houghton Mifflin

STUDENT SKILLS PRODUCT LIST

Student Skills Tutor's Handbook

This provides supplementary material designed specifically for tutors who use *The Student Skills Guide* with their students. It contains an introductory section on how and when to use the *Guide* to best effect as well as details of the learning outcomes for each of the sections in the book. From Spring 2002 this will be available online from www.studentskills.org

Student IT Skills

Mark Pettigrew and David Elliott

This book presents a completely new approach to learning and developing IT skills. It is based on experience of how people really learn, has been tested with real students and then rewritten to take their observations into account. It has been written in the same interactive style as *The Student Skills Guide*.

Paperback   208pp   0 566 08053 2

The Student Guide to Making an Oral Presentation

Sue Drew and Richard Gibson

This CD-ROM takes students carefully and rigorously through every step necessary for them to deliver a successful presentation. The package is extremely interactive and is divided into clear, manageable sections. Details of the one-off single-user, department and site licences are available on application to the publisher.

Minimum requirements: Windows 95 with speakers or headphones.

CD-ROM   0 566 08246 2

Key Skills Online

Edited by Sue Drew and Louise Thorpe

This CD provides content for the Key to Key Skills project system, which is designed to be networked across an entire institution. (To obtain the system itself see the project website at www.shu.ac.uk/keytokey/) It delivers guidance for the major skill themes as well as self evaluation skill checks, on-screen guidance and resource details. Details of licences are available on application to the publisher.

CD-ROM   0 566 08396 5

Student Skills SkillPack Masters

Lecturers purchasing a SkillPack Masters pack receive a set of photocopiable masters for both the Starter Level and Development Level in the chosen subject (where available). Also included is a licence – valid for one year – to make unlimited copies of each SkillPack within the Department purchasing the Masters. Site licences are also available. Each pack also comes with information on how to use the material to best effect, including details of the learning outcomes for all of the SkillPacks and a consolidated bibliography.

These SkillPack Masters cannot be supplied on approval although sample material is available.

ISBN	Title
0 566 08471 6	Identifying Strengths and Improving Skills
0 566 08472 4	Organising Yourself and Your Time
0 566 08473 2	Note Taking*
0 566 08474 0	Gathering and Using Information
0 566 08475 9	Essay Writing
0 566 08476 7	Report Writing
0 566 08477 5	Oral Presentation
0 566 08478 3	Visual Communication*
0 566 08479 1	Solving Problems
0 566 08480 5	Group Work
0 566 08481 3	Seminars, Group Tutorials and Meetings*
0 566 08482 1	Negotiating and Assertiveness
0 566 08483 X	Coping with Pressure
0 566 08484 8	Revising and Examination Techniques
0 566 08485 6	Improving Your Learning*
0 566 08486 4	Reflecting on Your Experience
0 566 08487 2	Action Planning
0 566 08488 0	Critical Analysis**

* = Starter Level only   ** = Development Level only

A licence is available for the entire set of Masters (0 566 08489 9) at a reduced price.